1798

University of London

Travelling Libraries

The "Teaching of English" Series

General Editor—SIR HENRY NEWBOLT

A SHORTER BOSWELL

No. 39

JAMES BOSWELL

From a pen-drawing by
E. Heber Thompson

A
SHORTER BOSWELL

Edited with an Introduction by

JOHN BAILEY

Author of " Dr. Johnson and His Circle"

THOMAS NELSON & SONS, LTD.

LONDON, EDINBURGH, AND NEW YORK

First Edition published May 1925.
Reprinted November 1925 ; May, October 1927 ; February,
June, September 1928 ; January 1929 ; May 1930.

PREFATORY NOTE

This book consists of 195 extracts, short and long, from James Boswell's *Life of Dr. Samuel Johnson*. No attempt has been made to connect one extract with another by adding explanatory matter : each extract stands by itself, and is left exactly as Boswell wrote it. The divisions between these extracts or sections point to the conclusions of the quotations from Boswell ; each new section beginning after an omission, sometimes of a few lines, sometimes of many pages, from the text of the *Life*.

INTRODUCTION

THIS book is a selection of passages from what all Englishmen consider by far the greatest biography in the world. We have in this generation very decidedly rebelled against many of the judgments, once so universally accepted, of Macaulay. The insults he heaped on Boswell now recoil upon himself. But his judgment of Boswell's great work stands even firmer than when he first pronounced it. The lapse of something like a century since he wrote only leaves us surer than ever that, as a biographer, Boswell is first and has no second. " He has distanced all his competitors so decidedly that it is not worth while to place them. *Eclipse* is first and the rest nowhere."

The judgment is of course an English judgment, as indeed its illustration shows. No one but an Englishman would use the language of the racecourse to enforce a literary verdict. And no doubt the full appreciation of the great *Life* is only possible to an Englishman. Johnson was as essentially and entirely English as Racine was French. Many Englishmen have fallen into, and even published, hasty judgments about Racine because they had not given themselves time to become French enough to understand him. Few foreigners have got inside England and the English enough to perceive the greatness of Johnson. Like Racine in this, if in nothing else, he must be content with the delighted admiration of his countrymen and of those few foreigners who can fully enter into the art, mind, and character of a nation not their own.

What, after all, is it that makes the greatness of Johnson ? Why is it that a hundred and forty years after his death he is still quoted and talked about, produced on the stage, and even used as an advertisement, as no other writer except Shakespeare is ? He has obviously no kind of claim to the superlative genius which compels the universal worship of Shakespeare. He wrote almost entirely in prose, which is never so quotable and very rarely so well worth quoting as verse. And his prose works, though they have great qualities of which no competent critic ever thinks he has said enough, are yet little read except by professed students of literature. Why, then, is he a familiar name, as scarcely any other writer is, to blacksmiths and cabmen ? Why are his sayings for ever in the mouths, and he himself continually in the memory and affections, of all Englishmen who give much time to English letters ?

The answer is twofold. It is because he was incomparably the best talker of whom the world knows anything, and because he had the luck to have Boswell for his friend and biographer. Possibly there may have somewhere been other talkers as good : a better there can hardly have been. But the rivals, if they ever existed, are lost in the waste of oblivion : they had no Boswell to keep their talk eternally alive for their own fame and our unending delight. I have elsewhere related that I once overheard some London cabmen at a shelter quoting Johnson over their dinner. The fact which that incident illustrates, the fact that his name is friendly and familiar on the lips of all Englishmen, the least lettered as well as the most scholarly, is due not to what Johnson wrote, but to what he said, and to that most happy of all accidents which committed what he said to the admiring love, the industry, and the biographical genius, of James Boswell.

Johnson and Boswell were men strangely unlike each other. Johnson came of comparatively humble origin, and had known the struggles of the extremest poverty. Boswell was the eldest son of a Judge, and the descendant of a line of lairds who had enjoyed their estate for centuries. Johnson, much as he liked idleness, had worked as few men have worked, and had made his extraordinary memory a storehouse of such wide and varied learning as is possessed by only one or two men in a century. Boswell was full of intellectual curiosity, but was without either the moral or the intellectual persistence required for serious study. Boswell sincerely praised and loved virtue, Johnson practised it. Johnson was generally liked and universally respected. Boswell was universally liked and universally laughed at. Johnson was physically grotesque. Boswell was intellectually and socially a little ridiculous. Johnson had something of the ruggedness of the poor scholar, Boswell much of the weakness of the elegant gentleman. Johnson was a wit who often became an executioner, Boswell a disciple who often became a butt.

Yet they were wonderfully made for each other; and, what is even more surprising, as they go down the centuries together it is even more Boswell who carries Johnson than Johnson who carries Boswell. It is true that without Johnson Boswell would have been nothing, while Johnson without Boswell is still a very considerable figure. But when each has been given his proper material to handle, it is Boswell, not Johnson, who produces a work of genius. With his chosen subjects, with Shakespeare and the English Poets, with the English language and the English character, Johnson did very great things. We can never read the Preface to Shakespeare or the Life of Pope too often. But with Johnson Boswell did something more. He produced a new creation, unique then and unique still; a book which imitated no one, and which, after a hundred and thirty years, no one has yet succeeded in imitating. It is not a question of reading Boswell's book too often. We all know that we cannot read it often enough. It is at once one of the wisest and one of the most amusing of all books : and no imaginary creation in all the range of fiction is more alive than the Johnson of Boswell.

The book could not be what it is if, in spite of their unlikenesses, the two men had not been so admirably suited for its making. Genius always demands its proper subject. Boswell could not have made such a book out of Gibbon or even out of Burke. Discipleship is of its essence, and the inspiration of discipleship could never have grown on such a soil as that of the learned and agreeable worldliness of Gibbon. Nor could Burke, a much greater man than Gibbon, a greater perhaps than Johnson, have given Boswell what he wanted. His genius and wisdom would have satisfied the hero-worshipper. But there was more than hero-worship in Boswell. What attracted him in Johnson, what he so wonderfully seized and reproduced for us, was not merely the scholar and the saint. It was the humorist, the " oddity," as the innkeeper at Edensor called him; above all, the human being. Boswell and Johnson were both amateurs of life; they were interested, as neither Gibbon nor Burke were, in all kinds of life and all sorts and conditions of men. A great part of the interest of the *Life* lies in Johnson's odd experiences and surprising acquaintances. On one page we find him dining at Inveraray, or visiting at Chatsworth and Alnwick ; at another he is in the company of Bishops and Heads of Houses, or at " The Club " with Burke and Goldsmith, Reynolds and Fox. But we turn over a few pages and find we have said good-bye to Dukes and Bishops, poets and statesmen, and our sage is running about Covent Garden at three o'clock in the morning, making bowls "of that liquor called Bishop," and singing songs of defiance to sleep in company with Topham Beauclerk, whose immoralities were the talk of the town. And yet the strict and serious Johnson, who often rebuked and never condoned the sins, could love the sinner : so that he could say when Beauclerk lay dying, " I would walk to the extent of the earth to save Beauclerk," and when he was dead could write of him to Boswell with tender affection, " Poor dear Beauclerk !—*nec, ut soles, dabis joca.*" He could not resist the intellectual gifts and social charms of that true descendant of Charles II. ; of whom, again, and for the same reasons, he was a great admirer. But there were much stranger people about Johnson than Beauclerk. He had in his house as its permanent inmates a curious collection of poor people whom Mrs. Thrale described as "the lame, the blind, the sad, and the sorrowful." They were neither interesting nor amiable : their perpetual quarrels made him afraid to go home. But he replied to all expostulations, " If I did not assist them, no one else would " ; and he has immortalized two of them, a poor surgeon named Levett, by the well-known verses, and a certain Miss Carmichael by the account he gave of her to Mrs. Thrale. " Poll is a stupid slut. I had some hopes of her at first ; but when I talked to her tightly and closely, I could make nothing of her; she was wiggle-waggle, and I could never persuade her to be categorical." A still more singular personage to find in the company of the grave and learned Johnson was one Bet Flint, a woman of all or most of the vices, slut, drunkard, thief, and worse. Yet Johnson could boast to Mrs. Thrale that he had known "all the wits from Mrs. Montagu to Bet Flint," and could coolly exclaim to a respectable company, "Oh, I loved Bet Flint!" The creature was a character and that was enough for him : she had written her own life in verse and asked him to correct it, which he refused, but gave her half a crown, which, he said, she " liked as well."

Of course this personage is an extreme instance of the variety to be found in the world of Johnson. But she has plenty of companions whom one would scarcely have expected to find in the company of the author of *Rasselas*. There is the beautiful Duchess of Devonshire who would hang on the sentences that fell from his lips, and Kitty Clive, the actress, whom he used to go and see in the green-room, and Foote, the comedian, who talked of taking him off on the stage, and for whose chastisement he was ready to pay double the price of " a common oak stick," and Wilkes, the disreputable member for Middlesex, to whom the virtuous voter whom he was canvassing said, " Vote for you, Sir ! I would rather vote for the devil," and received the reply, " But—in case your friend does not stand ? " They are all there, they and fifty others, men and women of all sorts, all alive still for us as they once were in the flesh for Boswell and Johnson, who loved all life and all the livers of it.

That is a great part of the triumph of the book. It is at once so grave and so gay. People are apt to picture a scholar as a censorious and pontifical prig, or a timid valetudinarian afraid to leave his study. Nothing could be less like Johnson, who hated a prig as much as he hated a Whig, and for all his bad health was as active as an athlete and as brave as a lion. His schoolfellows worshipped him : and boys don't worship muffs. Johnson was no muff either as a boy or man. He rode fifty miles after hounds, ran a race in the rain at Paris when he was past sixty, and when he was past seventy threw away his coat and wig in order to jump a railing which he had jumped when a boy. He faced four ruffians who attacked him on the street and proved more than a match for the four ;

and when a man took his chair at the theatre he simply tossed man and chair together into the pit. He would eat seven or eight peaches in the garden before breakfast, and he would make Fleet Street echo with his laughter at midnight. And yet this perpetual schoolboy was one of the most serious, he himself would have said one of the saddest, men who ever lived. The most awful issues of life and death were never long out of his mind. Not only his private prayers, which we can now read, but his published writings and his daily talk exhibit a man whose conscience was always on the watch, an earnest Christian as very few are earnest, a man who lived all his life in the presence of God.

Perhaps it was that more than anything else that was his original attraction for Boswell. No doubt Boswell loved celebrities of all sorts, cultivated the rascally Wilkes, and went to visit Voltaire and Rousseau whom Johnson would gladly have sent to "work in the plantations." But he did not feel for them as he felt for Johnson. They could not give him what he most wanted, what weakness always flies to, character and strength. He had in him, as few men have, the primary element of religion, which is reverence. Voltaire and Rousseau were men whom no one could reverence. Boswell reverenced Johnson even before he knew him, loved him from the first day of their acquaintance, and leaned upon him all his life. Except for the great book and his happiness in the friendship of some of the best and wisest men then alive, his life must be counted a failure, so far as human eyes can see. In the end he did not conquer his vices : on the contrary, after his wife's death and Johnson's, they conquered him. His life was a long series of repentances : but it is the sins and not the repentances which seem to have had the last word. Still the repentances and the good resolutions were certainly sincere, even though they were not maintained ; and can we be sure, with the Gospel before us, that he who sins and repents and sins again is not in as hopeful a case as the common run of men who have no notion of their sins and no thought of repentance ? Weakness is weakness, and not to be palliated or confused with strength. Boswell's life ended in shame. He is not to be compared with those who see their enemy and conquer him. But he may be nearer the kingdom of heaven than those who have never discovered that there is an enemy to conquer. And we who are grateful to him, and love him, and yet cannot but think gravely in the grave atmosphere of his book, may well make that our last thought of the benefactor to whom we owe so much. For indeed the gratitude which we owe him is partly of the most serious sort of all. What we have to thank him for is not only a quantity and quality of intellectual pleasure in which he has few rivals. There is another thing too. The *Life of Johnson* is a book which no one has ever read without being the better for it.

Still the last word about a great work of art can never be edification. A great book or a great piece of sculpture may edify : in fact it generally does. But that is not its proper or primary business, which is to give us a certain kind of pleasure, that belonging to the perception of a work of art, one of the best and purest pleasures of which our nature is capable. No one has ever denied or doubted that Boswell's book does that. We see in it, as we see in all great art, life made more alive, men and women made more vivid and human, more arresting and amusing, than we have ever been able to find them in actual experience. Art has delivered them from the confused irrelevances and insignificances of experience and set them free to be themselves. Truth has emerged from a chaos of facts. Only a great artist can produce that result, and the longer Boswell's book is known, the more every competent judge recognizes the greatness of his art. Great art is never accessible to every-body at first acquaintance. More particularly is that the case when it is more than a century old. The majority of readers read nothing that is older than yesterday or the day before. They have never given their imaginations a chance. They have never tried to make the great escape from time or tried to dis-cover the books which never grow old. To do so requires a little effort, but only a little, and that soon over and richly rewarded. For those who will not make it neither Boswell nor any one else who has been dead a century can compete with the illus-trated papers. But it is worth while remembering that the newspaper which is alive to-day will be very dead to-morrow, while Boswell will be alive a hundred years hence. That must mean something worth get-ting at. It cannot be got at without a little of the spirit of adventure. Few things that are worth any-thing can. But for those who will make the ad-venturous excursion into great literature, few of its regions are so easy of access as the *Life of Johnson*. It is so full not only of wisdom, which we do not all care about, but of wit and laughter and life, which we all do. And when we have got there we find that it is no long journey that we have made. Indeed, we find ourselves at home and we wish to stay there ; like Stevenson who said, " I am taking a little Bos-well daily : I mean to read him now until the day I die." That is because the figure Boswell sets before us is so very human, made of the same stuff of which we ourselves are made : not an angel like Shelley, nor a seer and mystic like Blake, but the sort of man we might imagine ourselves to have been if we had had more brains and more character. And Johnson comes still nearer to us. He is not merely human as we are. He is English as we are, English of the English ; with the frankness and sanity, the honesty, good sense, and good humour which we believe to be characteristic of our race. Neither Blake nor Shelley would ever do for the typical Englishman. Johnson will and does. The genius of Boswell is one reason why we know him so well. The other is that there is none of our men of letters whom Englishmen find it so easy, natural, and pleasant to know.

A SHORTER BOSWELL.

A SHORTER BOSWELL

THE LIFE OF SAMUEL JOHNSON, LL.D.

§ 1

To write the Life of him who excelled all mankind in writing the lives of others, and who, whether we consider his extraordinary endowments, or his various works, has been equalled by few in any age, is an arduous, and may be reckoned in me a presumptuous task.

Had Dr. Johnson written his own Life, in conformity with the opinion which he has given, that every man's life may be best written by himself ; had he employed in the preservation of his own history, that clearness of narration and elegance of language in which he has embalmed so many eminent persons, the world would probably have had the most perfect example of biography that was ever exhibited. But although he at different times, in a desultory manner, committed to writing many particulars of the progress of his mind and fortunes, he never had persevering diligence enough to form them into a regular composition. Of these memorials a few have been preserved ; but the greater part was consigned by him to the flames, a few days before his death.

As I had the honour and happiness of enjoying his friendship for upwards of twenty years ; as I had the scheme of writing his life constantly in view ; as he was well apprised of this circumstance, and from time to time obligingly satisfied my inquiries, by communicating to me the incidents of his early years ; as I acquired a facility in recollecting, and was very assiduous in recording, his conversation, of which the extraordinary vigour and vivacity constituted one of the first features of his character ; and as I have spared no pains in obtaining materials concerning him, from every quarter where I could discover that they were to be found, and have been favoured with the most liberal communications by his friends ; I flatter myself that few biographers have entered upon such a work as this with more advantages ; independent of literary abilities, in which I am not vain enough to compare myself with some great names who have gone before me in this kind of writing.

§ 2

SAMUEL JOHNSON was born at Lichfield, in Staffordshire, on the 18th of September, N. S. 1709 ; and his initiation into the Christian church was not delayed ; for his baptism is recorded, in the register of St. Mary's parish in that city, to have been performed on the day of his birth : his father is there styled *Gentleman*, a circumstance of which an ignorant panegyrist has praised him for not being proud ; when the truth is, that the appellation of Gentleman, though now lost in the indiscriminate assumption of *Esquire*, was commonly taken by those who could not boast of gentility. His father was Michael Johnson, a native of Derbyshire, of obscure extraction, who settled in Lichfield as a bookseller and stationer. His mother was Sarah Ford, descended from an ancient race of substantial yeomanry in Warwickshire. They were well advanced in years when they married, and never had more than two children, both sons ; Samuel, their first-born, who lived to be the illustrious character whose various excellence I am to endeavour to record, and Nathaniel, who died in his twenty-fifth year.

§ 3

Of the power of his memory, for which he was all his life eminent to a degree almost incredible, the following early instance was told me in his presence at Lichfield, in 1776, by his step-daughter, Mrs. Lucy Porter, as related to her by his mother. When he was a child in petticoats, and had learnt to read, Mrs. Johnson one morning put the Common Prayer Book into his hands, pointed to the collect for the day, and said, " Sam, you must get this by heart." She went upstairs, leaving him to study it : but by the time she had reached the second floor, she heard him following her. " What's the matter ? " said she. " I can say it," he replied ; and repeated it distinctly, though he could not have read it more than twice.

§ 4

He was first taught to read English by Dame Oliver, a widow, who kept a school for young children in Lichfield. He told me she could read the black letter, and asked him to borrow for her, from his father, a Bible in that character. When he was going to Oxford, she came to take leave of him, brought him, in the simplicity of her kindness, a present of ginger-bread, and said he was the best scholar she ever had. He delighted in mentioning this early compliment : adding, with a smile, that " this was as high a proof of his merit as he could conceive." His next instructor in English was a master, whom, when he spoke of him to me, he familiarly called Tom Brown, who, said he, " published a spelling-book, and dedicated it to the UNIVERSE ; but I fear no copy of it can now be had."

§ 5

He used to mention one curious instance of his casual reading, when but a boy. Having imagined that his brother had hid some apples behind a large folio upon an upper shelf in his father's shop, he climbed up to search for them. There were no apples ; but the large folio proved to be Petrarch, whom he had seen mentioned, in some preface, as one of the restorers of learning. His curiosity having been thus excited, he sat down with avidity, and read a great part of the book. What he read during these two years, he told me, was not works of mere amusement, " Not voyages and travels, but all literature, Sir, all ancient writers, all manly : though but little Greek, only some of Anacreon and Hesiod : but in this irregular manner," added he, " I had looked into a great many books, which were not commonly known at the Universities, where they seldom read any books but what are put into their hands by their tutors ; so that when I came to Oxford, Dr. Adams, now master of Pembroke College, told me I was the best qualified for the University that he had ever known come there."

§ 6

He, however, went to Oxford, and was entered a commoner of Pembroke College, on the 31st of October, 1728, being then in his nineteenth year.

The Reverend Dr. Adams, who afterward presided over Pembroke College with universal esteem, told me he was present, and gave me some account of what passed, on the night of Johnson's arrival at Oxford. On that evening, his father, who had anxiously accompanied him, found means to have him introduced to Mr. Jorden, who was to be his tutor. His being put under any tutor, reminds us of what Wood says of Robert Burton, author of the *Anatomy of Melan-*

choly, when elected student of Christ Church ; " For form's sake, *though he wanted not a tutor*, he was put under the tuition of Dr. John Bancroft, afterward Bishop of Oxon."

His father seemed very full of the merits of his son, and told the company he was a good scholar, and a poet, and wrote Latin verses. His figure and manner appeared strange to them ; but he behaved modestly, and sat silent, till upon something which occurred in the course of conversation, he suddenly struck in and quoted Macrobius ; and thus he gave the first impression of that more extensive reading in which he had indulged himself.

His tutor, Mr. Jorden, fellow of Pembroke, was not, it seems, a man of such abilities as we should conceive requisite for the instructor of Samuel Johnson, who gave me the following account of him. " He was a very worthy man, but a heavy man, and I did not profit much by his instructions. Indeed, I did not attend him much. The first day after I came to college, I waited upon him, and then stayed away four. On the sixth, Mr. Jorden asked me why I had not attended. I answered, I had been sliding in Christ Church meadow : and this I said with as much *nonchalance* as I am now talking to you. I had no notion that I was wrong or irreverent to my tutor." BOSWELL : That, Sir, was great fortitude of mind. JOHNSON : No, Sir ; stark insensibility.

§ 7

How seriously Johnson was impressed with a sense of religion, even in the vigour of his youth, appears from the following passage in his minutes, kept by way of diary : " Sept. 7, 1736. I have this day entered upon my 28th year. Mayest thou, O God, enable me, for Jesus Christ's sake, to spend this in such a manner, that I may receive comfort from it

at the hour of death, and in the day of judgment!
Amen."

§ 8

Johnson was peculiarly happy in mentioning how
many of the sons of Pembroke were poets ; adding,
with a smile of sportive triumph, " Sir, we are a nest
of singing birds."

He was not, however, blind to what he thought the
defects of his own College : and I have, from the information of Dr. Taylor, a very strong instance of that
rigid honesty which he ever inflexibly preserved.
Taylor had obtained his father's consent to be entered
of Pembroke, that he might be with his schoolfellow
Johnson, with whom, though some years older than
himself, he was very intimate. This would have been
a great comfort to Johnson, But he fairly told Taylor
that he could not, in conscience, suffer him to enter
where he knew he could not have an able tutor. He
then made inquiry all round the University, and having found that Mr. Bateman, of Christ Church, was the
tutor of highest reputation, Taylor was entered of that
College. Mr. Bateman's lectures were so excellent,
that Johnson used to come and get them at second-
hand from Taylor, till his poverty being so extreme,
that his shoes were worn out, and his feet appeared
through them, he saw that this humiliating circumstance was perceived by the Christ Church men, and
he came no more. He was too proud to accept of
money, and somebody having set a pair of new shoes
at his door, he threw them away with indignation.
How must we feel when we read such an anecdote of
Samuel Johnson !

§ 9

The *res angusta domi* prevented him from having
the advantage of a complete academical education.
The friend to whom he had trusted for support had
deceived him. His debts in College, though not great.

were increasing ; and his scanty remittances from Lichfield, which had all along been made with great difficulty, could be supplied no longer, his father having fallen into a state of insolvency. Compelled, therefore, by irresistible necessity, he left the College in autumn, 1731, without a degree, having been a member of it little more than three years.

§ 10

And now (I had almost said *poor*) Samuel Johnson returned to his native city, destitute, and not knowing how he should gain even a decent livelihood. His father's misfortunes in trade rendered him unable to support his son : and for some time there appeared no means by which he could maintain himself. In the December of this year his father died.

§ 11

In the forlorn state of his circumstances, he accepted of an offer to be employed as usher in the school of Market-Bosworth, in Leicestershire, to which it appears, from one of his little fragments of a diary, that he went on foot, on the 16th of July.—" *Julii* 16, *Bosvortiam pedes petii.*" But it is not true, as has been erroneously related, that he was assistant to the famous Anthony Blackwall, whose merit has been honoured by the testimony of Bishop Hurd, who was his scholar ; for Mr. Blackwall died on the 8th of April, 1730, more than a year before Johnson left the University.

This employment was very irksome to him in every respect, and he complained grievously of it in his letters to his friend, Mr. Hector, who was now settled as a surgeon at Birmingham. The letters are lost ; but Mr. Hector recollects his writing " That the poet had described the dull sameness of his existence in these words ' *Vitam continet una dies* ' (one day contains the whole of my life) ; that it was unvaried as the note of the cuckoo ; and that he did not know whether it was more disagreeable for him to teach, or the boys to learn, the grammar rules.'' His general aversion to this painful drudgery was greatly enhanced by a disagreement between him and Sir Wolstan Dixie, the patron of the school, in whose house, I have been told, he officiated as a kind of domestic chaplain, so far, at least, as to say grace at table, but was treated with what he represented as intolerable harshness ; and, after suffering for a few months such complicated misery, he relinquished a situation which all his life afterward he recollected with the strongest aversion, and even a degree of horror. But it is probable that at this period, whatever uneasiness he may have endured, he laid the foundation of much future eminence by application to his studies.

Being now again totally unoccupied, he was invited by Mr. Hector to pass some time with him at Birmingham, as his guest, at the house of Mr. Warren, with whom Mr. Hector lodged and boarded. Mr. Warren was the first established bookseller in Birmingham, and was very attentive to Johnson, whom he soon found could be of much service to him in his trade, by his knowledge of literature ; and he even obtained the assistance of his pen in furnishing some numbers of a periodical Essay printed in the newspaper, of which Warren was proprietor. After very diligent inquiry, I have not been able to recover those early specimens of that particular mode of writing by which Johnson afterward so greatly distinguished himself.

He continued to live as Mr. Hector's guest for about six months, and then hired lodgings in another part of the town, finding himself as well situated at Birmingham as he supposed he could be anywhere, while he had no settled plan of life, and very scanty means of subsistence. He made some valuable acquaintances there, amongst whom were Mr. Porter, a mercer, whose widow he afterward married, and Mr. Taylor, who, by his ingenuity in mechanical inventions, and his success in trade, acquired an immense fortune. But the comfort of being near Mr. Hector, his old schoolfellow and intimate friend, was Johnson's chief inducement to continue here.

§ 12

In a man whom religious education has secured from licentious indulgences, the passion of love, when once it has seized him, is exceedingly strong ; being unimpaired by dissipation, and totally concentrated in one object. This was experienced by Johnson, when he became the fervent admirer of Mrs. Porter, after her first husband's death. Miss Porter told me, that when he was first introduced to her mother, his appearance was very forbidding : he was then lean and lank, so that his immense structure of bones was hideously striking to the eye, and the scars of the scrofula were deeply visible. He also wore his hair, which was straight and stiff, and separated behind : and he often had, seemingly, convulsive starts and odd gesticulations, which tended to excite at once surprise and ridicule. Mrs. Porter was so much engaged by his conversation that she overlooked all these external disadvantages, and said to her daughter, " This is the most sensible man that I ever saw in my life."

Though Mrs. Porter was double the age of Johnson, and her person and manner, as described to me by the late Mr. Garrick, were by no means pleasing to others, she must have had a superiority of understanding and talents, as she certainly inspired him with a more than ordinary passion ; and she having signified her willingness to accept of his hand, he went to Lichfield to ask his mother's consent to the marriage, which he could not but be conscious was a very imprudent scheme, both on account of their disparity of years, and her want of fortune. But Mrs. Johnson knew too well the ardour of her son's temper, and was too tender a parent to oppose his inclinations.

I know not for what reason the marriage ceremony was not performed at Birmingham; but a resolution was taken that it should be at Derby, for which place the bride and bridegroom set out on horseback, I suppose in very good humour. But though Mr. Topham Beauclerk used archly to mention Johnson's having told him, with much gravity, "Sir, it was a love marriage on both sides," I have had from my illustrious friend the following curious account of their journey to church upon the nuptial morn, (9th July):—" Sir, she had read the old romances, and had got into her head the fantastical notion that a woman of spirit should use her lover like a dog. So, Sir, at first she told me that I rode too fast, and she could not keep up with me; and, when I rode a little slower she passed me, and complained that I lagged behind. I was not to be made the slave of caprice; and I resolved to begin as I meant to end. I therefore pushed on briskly, till I was fairly out of her sight. The road lay between two hedges, so I was sure she could not miss it; and I contrived that she should soon come up with me. When she did, I observed her to be in tears."

This, it must be allowed, was a singular beginning of connubial felicity; but there is no doubt that Johnson, though he thus showed a manly firmness, proved a most affectionate and indulgent husband to the last moment of Mrs. Johnson's life: and in his " Prayers and Meditations," we find very remarkable evidence that his regard and fondness for her never ceased, even after her death.

He now set up a private academy, for which purpose he hired a large house, well situated, near his native city. In the Gentleman's Magazine for 1736, there is the following advertisement; " At Edial, near Lichfield, in Staffordshire, young gentlemen are boarded and taught the Latin and Greek languages, by SAMUEL JOHNSON." But the only pupils who were put under his care were the celebrated David Garrick and his brother George, and a Mr. Offely, a young gentleman of good fortune, who died early.

§ 13

Johnson was not more satisfied with his situation as the master of an academy, than with that of the usher of a school ; we need not wonder, therefore, that he did not keep his academy above a year and a half. From Mr. Garrick's account he did not appear to have been profoundly reverenced by his pupils. His oddities of manner, and uncouth gesticulations, could not but be the subject of merriment to them ; and in particular, the young rogues used to listen at the door of his bed-chamber, and peep through the key-hole, that they might turn into ridicule his tumultuous and awkward fondness for Mrs. Johnson, whom he used to name by the familiar appellation of *Tetty* or *Tetsey;* which, like *Betty* or *Betsey*, is provincially used as a contraction for *Elizabeth*, her Christian name, but which to us seems ludicrous, when applied to a woman of her age and appearance. Mr. Garrick described her to me as very fat, with a bosom of more than ordinary protuberance, with swelled cheeks, of a florid red, produced by thick painting, and increased by the liberal use of cordials ; flaring and fantastic in her dress, and affected both in her speech and her general behaviour. I have seen Garrick exhibit her, by his exquisite talent of mimicry, so as to excite the heartiest bursts of laughter ; but he, probably, as is the case in all such representations, considerably aggravated the picture.

§ 14

Johnson now thought of trying his fortune in London, the great field of genius and exertion, where talents of every kind have the fullest scope and the highest encouragement. It is a memorable circumstance that his pupil David Garrick went thither at the same time, with intent to complete his education, and follow the profession of the law, from which he was soon diverted by his decided preference for the stage.*

§ 15

He had a little money when he came to town, and he knew how he could live in the cheapest manner. His first lodgings were at the house of Mr. Norris, a staymaker, in Exeter-street, adjoining Catherine-street, in the Strand. " I dined," said he, " very well for eightpence, with very good company, at the Pine-Apple in New-street, just by. Several of them had travelled. They expected to meet every day ; but did not know one another's names. It used to cost the rest a shilling, for they drank wine ; but I had a cut of meat for sixpence, and bread for a penny, and gave the waiter a penny ; so that I was quite well served, nay, better than the rest, for they gave the waiter nothing."

§ 16

Johnson's residence at Lichfield, on his return to it at this time, was only for three months ; and as he had as yet seen but a small part of the wonders of the

* Both of them used to talk pleasantly of this their first journey to London. Garrick, evidently meaning to embellish a little, said one day in my hearing, " We rode and tied." And the Bishop of Killaloe, [Dr. Barnard,] informed me, that at another time, when Johnson and Garrick were dining together in a pretty large company, Johnson humorously ascertaining the chronology of something, expressed himself thus : " That was the year when I came to London with twopence halfpenny in my pocket." Garrick overhearing him, exclaimed, " Eh ? what do you say ? with twopence halfpenny in your pocket ? " JOHNSON : " Why, yes ; when I came with twopence halfpenny in *my* pocket, and thou, Davy, with three halfpence in thine."

metropolis, he had little to tell his townsmen. He related to me the following minute anecdote of this period : " In the last age, when my mother lived in London, there were two sets of people, those who gave the wall, and those who took it ; the peaceable and the quarrelsome. When I returned to Lichfield, after having been in London, my mother asked me, whether I was one of those who gave the wall, or those who took it. *Now* it is fixed that every man keeps to the right ; or, if one is taking the wall, another yields it ; and it is never a dispute."

He now removed to London with Mrs. Johnson ; but her daughter, who had lived with them at Edial, was left with her relations in the country.

§ 17

Thus was Johnson employed during some of the best years of his life, as a mere literary labourer " for gain not glory," solely to obtain an honest support. He, however, indulged himself in occasional little sallies, which the French so happily express by the term *jeux d'esprit,* and which will be noticed in their order, in the progress of this work.

But what first displayed his transcendent powers, and " gave the world assurance of the MAN," was his " London, a poem in Imitation of the Third Satire of Juvenal " ; which came out in May this year (1738), and burst forth with splendour, the rays of which will for ever encircle his name.

§ 18

He this year, and the two following, wrote the Parliamentary Debates. He told me himself, that he was the sole composer of them for those three years only. He was not, however, precisely exact in his statement, which he mentioned from hasty recollection; for it is sufficiently evident, that his composition of them began November 19, 1740, and ended February 23, 1742–3.

§ 19

Johnson told me, that as soon as he found that the speeches were thought genuine, he determined that he would write no more of them; "For he would not be accessory to the propagation of falsehood." And such was the tenderness of his conscience, that a short time before his death, he expressed his regret for his having been the author of fictions, which had passed for realities.

He nevertheless agreed with me in thinking that the Debates which he had framed were to be valued as orations upon questions of public importance. They have accordingly been collected in volumes, properly arranged, and recommended to the notice of parliamentary speakers by a preface, written by no inferior hand. I must, however, observe, that although there is in those Debates a wonderful store of political information, and very powerful eloquence, I cannot agree that they exhibit the manner of each particular speaker, as Sir John Hawkins seems to think. But, indeed, what opinion can we have of his judgment, and taste in public speaking, who presumes to give, as the characteristics of two celebrated orators, "The deep-mouthed rancour of Pulteney, and the yelping pertinacity of Pitt." *

* The following passage is from the Introduction to Arthur Murphy's edition of Johnson's Works.
"That Johnson was the author of the debates during that period was not generally known; but the secret transpired several years afterwards, and was avowed by himself on the following occasion. Mr. Wedderburne (now Lord Loughborough), Dr. Johnson, Dr. Francis (the translator of Horace), the present writer and others, dined with the late Mr. Foote. An important debate towards the end of Sir Robert Walpole's administration being mentioned, Dr. Francis observed 'That Mr. Pitt's speech on that occasion was the best he had ever read.' He added, 'That he had employed eight years of his life in the study of Demosthenes, and finished a trans-

§ 20

It does not appear that he wrote anything in 1744 for the "Gentleman's Magazine," but the Preface. His "Life of Barretier" was now re-published in a pamphlet by itself. But he produced one work this year, fully sufficient to maintain the high reputation which he had acquired. This was "THE LIFE OF RICHARD SAVAGE"; a man, of whom it is difficult to speak impartially, without wondering that he was for some time the intimate companion of Johnson; for his character was marked by profligacy, insolence and ingratitude : yet, as he undoubtedly had a warm and vigorous, though unregulated mind, had seen life in all its varieties, and been much in the company of the statesmen and wits of his time, he could communicate to Johnson an abundant supply of such materials as his philosophical curiosity most eagerly desired; and,

lation of that celebrated orator, with all the decorations of style and language within the reach of his capacity, but he had met with nothing equal to the speech above-mentioned.' Many of the company remembered the debate, and some passages were cited with the approbation and applause of all present. During the ardour of conversation Johnson remained silent. As soon as the warmth of praise subsided he opened with these words : 'That speech I wrote in a garret in Exeter-street.' The company were struck with astonishment. After staring at each other in silent amaze, Dr. Francis asked, 'How that speech could be written by him ?' 'Sir,' said Johnson, 'I wrote it in Exeter-street. I never had been in the gallery of the House of Commons but once. Cave had interest with the door-keeper. He, and the persons employed under him, gained admittance; they brought away the subject of discussion, the names of the speakers, the side they took and the order in which they rose, together with notes of the arguments advanced in the course of the debate. The whole was afterwards communicated to me, and I composed the speeches in the form which they now have in the Parliamentary debates.' To this discovery Dr. Francis made answer: 'Then, Sir, you have exceeded Demosthenes himself : for to say that you have exceeded Francis's Demosthenes would be to say nothing.' The rest of the company bestowed lavish encomiums on Johnson; one, in particular, praised his impartiality, observing that he dealt out reason and eloquence with an equal hand to both parties. 'That is not quite true,' said Johnson; 'I saved appearances tolerably well; but I took care that the WHIG DOGS should not have the best of it.'"

as Savage's misfortunes and misconduct had reduced
him to the lowest state of wretchedness as a writer for
his bread, his visit to St. John's Gate naturally brought
Johnson and him together.

It is melancholy to reflect, that Johnson and Savage
were sometimes in such extreme indigence, that they
could not pay for a lodging ; so that they have wan-
dered together whole nights in the streets. Yet in
these almost incredible scenes of distress, we may suppose that Savage mentioned many of the anecdotes
with which Johnson afterwards enriched the life of
this unhappy companion, and those of other poets.

He told Sir Joshua Reynolds, that one night in
particular, when Savage and he walked round St.
James's Square for want of a lodging, they were not
at all depressed by their situation ; but in high spirits
and brimful of patriotism, traversed the square for
several hours, inveighed against the minister, and
" resolved they would *stand by their country.*"

§ 21

This year his old pupil and friend, David Garrick,
having become joint patentee and manager of Drury-
lane theatre, Johnson honoured his opening of it with
a Prologue, which for just and manly dramatic criticism on the whole range of the English stage, as well
as for poetical excellence, is unrivalled. Like the celebrated Epilogue to " The Distressed Mother," it was,
during the season, often called for by the audience.
The most striking and brilliant passages of it have
been so often repeated, and are so well recollected by
all the lovers of the drama and of poetry, that it
would be superfluous to point them out.

§ 22

But the year 1747 is distinguished as the epoch,
when Johnson's arduous and important work, his

DICTIONARY OF THE ENGLISH LANGUAGE, was announced to the world, by the publication of its "Plan" or "Prospectus."

§ 23

Dr. Adams found him one day busy at his Dictionary, when the following dialogue ensued. "ADAMS: This is a great work, Sir. How are you to get all the etymologies? JOHNSON: Why, Sir, here is a shelf with Junius, and Skinner, and others; and there is a Welsh gentleman who has published a collection of Welsh proverbs, who will help me with the Welsh. ADAMS: But, Sir, how can you do this in three years? JOHNSON: Sir, I have no doubt that I can do it in three years. ADAMS: But the French Academy, which consists of forty members, took forty years to compile their Dictionary. JOHNSON: Sir, thus it is. This is the proportion. Let me see; forty times forty is sixteen hundred. As three to sixteen hundred, so is the proportion of an Englishman to a Frenchman." With so much ease and pleasantry could he talk of that prodigious labour which he had undertaken to execute.

§ 24

In January, 1749, he published "THE VANITY OF HUMAN WISHES, being the Tenth Satire of Juvenal imitated." He, I believe, composed it the preceding year. Mrs. Johnson, for the sake of country air, had lodgings at Hampstead, to which he resorted occasionally, and there the greatest part, if not the whole, of this Imitation was written. The fervid rapidity with which it was produced, is scarcely credible. I have heard him say, that he composed seventy lines of it in one day, without putting one of them upon paper till they were finished. I remember when I once regretted to him that he had not given us more of Juvenal's Satires, he said he probably should give more, for he had them all in his head; by which I understood, that he had the originals and correspondent allusions floating in his mind, which he could, when he pleased, embody and render permanent without much labour. Some of them, however, he observed, were too gross for imitation.

The profits of a single poem, however excellent, appear to have been very small in the last reign, compared with what a publication of the same size has since been known to yield. I have mentioned upon Johnson's own authority, that for his " LONDON " he had only ten guineas ; and now, after his fame was established, he got for his "Vanity of Human Wishes" but five guineas more, as is proved by an authentic document in my possession.

§ 25

Garrick being now vested with theatrical power by being manager of Drury-lane theatre, he kindly and generously made use of it to bring out Johnson's tragedy, which had been long kept back for want of encouragement. But in this benevolent purpose he met with no small difficulty from the temper of Johnson, which could not brook that a drama which he had formed with much study, and had been obliged to keep more than the nine years of Horace, should be revised and altered at the pleasure of an actor. Yet Garrick knew well, that without some alterations it would not be fit for the stage. A violent dispute having ensued between them, Garrick applied to the Reverend Dr. Taylor to interpose. Johnson was at first very obstinate. " Sir, said he, the fellow wants me to make Mahomet run mad, that he may have an opportunity of tossing his hands and kicking his heels." He was, however, at last, with difficulty, prevailed on to comply with Garrick's wishes, so as to allow of some changes ; but still there were not enough.

Dr. Adams was present the first night of the representation of " IRENE," and gave me the following account : " Before the curtain drew up, there were catcalls and whistling, which alarmed Johnson's friends. The Prologue, which was written by himself in a manly strain, soothed the audience, and the play went off tolerably, till it came to the conclusion, when Mrs. Pritchard, the heroine of the piece, was to be strangled upon the stage, and was to speak two lines with the bow-string round her neck. The audience cried out ' *Murder! Murder!* ' She several times attempted to speak ; but in vain. At last she was obliged to go off the stage alive." This passage was afterwards struck out, and she was carried off to be put to death behind the scenes, as the play now has it. The Epilogue, as Johnson informed me, was written by Sir William Yonge. I know not how his play came to be thus graced by the pen of a person then so eminent in the political world.

Notwithstanding all the support of such performers as Garrick, Barry, Mrs. Cibber, Mrs. Pritchard, and every advantage of dress and decoration, the tragedy of " Irene " did not please the public. Mr. Garrick's zeal carried it through for nine nights, so that the author had his three nights' profits ; and from a receipt signed by him, now in the hands of Mr. James Dodsley, it appears that his friend, Mr. Robert Dodsley, gave him 100*l.* for the copy, with his usual reservation of the right of one edition.

§ 26

The first paper of the " Rambler " was published on Tuesday the 20th of March, 1749–50 ; and its author was enabled to continue it, without interruption, every Tuesday and Saturday, till Saturday the 17th of March, 1752, on which day it closed. This is a strong confirmation of the truth of a remark of his, which I have had occasion to quote elsewhere, that " a man may write at any time, if he will set himself doggedly to it ; " for, notwithstanding his constitutional indolence, his depression of spirits, and his labour in carrying on his Dictionary, he answered the stated calls of the press twice a week from the stores of his mind during all that time ; having received no assistance, except four billets in No. 10, by Miss Mulso, now Mrs. Chapone ; No. 30, by Mrs. Catherine Talbot ; No. 97, by Mr. Samuel Richardson, whom he describes in an introductory note as " An author who has enlarged the knowledge of human nature and taught the passions to move at the command of virtue ; " and Nos. 44 and 100, by Mrs. Elizabeth Carter.

Posterity will be astonished when they are told, upon the authority of Johnson himself, that many of these discourses, which we should suppose had been laboured with all the slow attention of literary leisure, were written in haste as the moment pressed, without even being read over by him before they were printed. It can be accounted for only in this way ; that by reading and meditation, and a very close inspection of life, he had accumulated a great fund of miscellaneous knowledge, which by a peculiar promptitude of mind, was ever ready at his call, and which he had constantly accustomed himself to clothe in the most apt and energetic expression. Sir Joshua Reynolds once asked him by what means he had attained his extraordinary accuracy and flow of language. He told him, that he had early laid it down as a fixed rule to do his best on every occasion, and in every company : to impart whatever he knew in the most forcible language he could put it in ; and that by constant practice, and never suffering any careless expressions to escape him, or attempting to deliver his thoughts without arranging them in the clearest manner, it became habitual to him.

§ 27

Johnson told me, with an amiable fondness, a little pleasing circumstance relative to this work. Mrs. Johnson, in whose judgment and taste he had great confidence, said to him, after a few numbers of the " Rambler " had come out, " I thought very well of you before ; but I did not imagine you could have written anything equal to this." Distant praise, from whatever quarter, is not so delightful as that of a wife whom a man loves and esteems. Her approbation may be said to " come home to his *bosom ;* " and being so near, its effect is most sensible and permanent.

§ 28

That there should be a suspension of his literary labours during a part of the year 1752, will not seem strange, when it is considered that soon after closing his " Rambler," he suffered a loss which, there can be no doubt, affected him with the deepest distress. For on the 17th of March, O. S., his wife died.

§ 29

The following very solemn and affecting prayer was found after Dr. Johnson's decease, by his servant, Mr. Francis Barber, who delivered it to my worthy friend the Reverend Mr. Strahan, Vicar of Islington, who at my earnest request has obligingly favoured me with a copy of it, which he and I compared with the original. I present it to the world as an undoubted proof of a circumstance in the character of my illustrious friend, which, though some whose hard minds I never shall envy, may attack as superstitious, will I am sure endear him more to numbers of good men. I have an additional, and that a personal motive for presenting it, because it sanctions what I myself have always maintained and am fond to indulge :

"April 26, 1752, being after 12 at night of the 25th.

"O Lord ! Governor of heaven and earth, in whose hands are embodied and departed Spirits, if thou hast ordained the Souls of the Dead to minister to the Living, and appointed my departed Wife to have care of me, grant that I may enjoy the good effects of her attention and ministration, whether exercised by appearance, impulses, dreams, or in any other manner agreeable to thy Government. Forgive my presumption, enlighten my ignorance, and however meaner agents are employed, grant me the blessed influences of thy holy Spirit, through Jesus Christ our Lord. Amen."

What actually followed upon this most interesting piece of devotion by Johnson, we are not informed ; but I, whom it has pleased God to afflict in a similar manner to that which occasioned it, have certain experience of benignant communication by dreams.

That his love for his wife was of the most ardent kind, and, during the long period of fifty years, was unimpaired by the lapse of time, is evident from various passages in the series of his " Prayers and Meditations," published by the Reverend Mr. Strahan, as well as from other memorials, two of which I select, as strongly marking the tenderness and sensibility of his mind.

"March 28, 1753. I kept this day as the anniversary of my Tetty's death, with prayer and tears in the morning. In the evening I prayed for her conditionally, if it were lawful."

"April 23, 1753. I know not whether I do not too much indulge the vain longings of affection ; but I hope they intenerate my heart, and that when I die like my Tetty, this affection will be acknowledged in

a happy interview, and that in the meantime I am
incited by it to piety. I will, however, not deviate
too much from common and received methods of
devotion."

Her wedding-ring, when she became his wife, was,
after her death, preserved by him, as long as he lived,
with an affectionate care, in a little round wooden
box, in the inside of which he pasted a slip of paper,
thus inscribed by him in fair characters, as follows :

" Eheu !
Eliz. Johnson,
Nupta Jul. 9° 1736
Mortua, eheu !
Mart. 17° 1752."

§ 30

The circle of his friends, indeed, at this time, was
extensive and various, far beyond what has been
generally imagined. To trace his acquaintance with
each particular person, if it could be done, would be a
task, of which the labour would not be repaid by the
advantage. But exceptions are to be made ; one of
which must be a friend so eminent as Sir Joshua Reynolds, who was truly his *dulce decus*, and with whom
he maintained an uninterrupted intimacy to the last
hour of his life.

§ 31

Sir Joshua told me a pleasant characteristical anecdote of Johnson about the time of their first acquaintance. When they were one evening together at the
Miss Cotterells', the then Duchess of Argyle and
another lady of high rank came in. Johnson thinking
that the Miss Cotterells were too much engrossed by
them, and that he and his friend were neglected, as low
company of whom they were somewhat ashamed,

grew angry; and resolving to shock their supposed pride, by making their great visitors imagine that his friend and he were low indeed, he addressed himself in a loud tone to Mr. Reynolds, saying, "How much do you think you and I could get in a week, if we were to *work as hard* as we could?"—as if they had been common mechanics.

His acquaintance with Bennet Langton, Esq., of Langton, in Lincolnshire, another much valued friend, commenced soon after the conclusion of his "Rambler"; which that gentleman, then a youth, had read with so much admiration, that he came to London chiefly with a view of endeavouring to be introduced to its author. By a fortunate chance he happened to take lodgings in a house where Mr. Levett frequently visited; and having mentioned his wish to his landlady, she introduced him to Mr. Levett, who readily obtained Johnson's permission to bring Mr. Langton to him; as, indeed, Johnson, during the whole course of his life, had no shyness, real or affected, but was easy of access to all who were properly recommended, and even wished to see numbers at his *levée*, as his morning circle of company might, with strict propriety, be called. Mr. Langton was exceedingly surprised when the sage first appeared. He had not received the smallest intimation of his figure, dress, or manner. From perusing his writings, he fancied he should see a decent, well-drest, in short, a remarkably decorous philosopher. Instead of which, down from his bed-chamber, about noon, came, as newly risen, a huge uncouth figure, with a little dark wig which scarcely covered his head, and his clothes hanging loose about him. But his conversation was so rich, so animated, and so forcible, and his religious and political notions so congenial with those in which Langton had been educated, that he conceived for him that veneration and attachment which he ever preserved. Johnson was not the less ready to love Mr. Langton, for his being of a very ancient family ; for I have heard him say, with pleasure, " Langton, Sir, has a grant of free warren from Henry the Second ; and Cardinal Stephen Langton, in King John's reign, was of this family."

§ 32

Johnson was some time with Beauclerk at his house at Windsor, where he was entertained with experiments in natural philosophy. One Sunday, when the weather was very fine, Beauclerk enticed him, insensibly, to saunter about all the morning. They went into a churchyard, in the time of divine service, and Johnson laid himself down at his ease upon one of the tomb-stones. " Now, Sir," said Beauclerk, " you are like Hogarth's Idle Apprentice." When Johnson got his pension, Beauclerk said to him in the humorous phrase of Falstaff, " I hope you'll now purge and live cleanly like a gentleman."

One night when Beauclerk and Langton had supped at a tavern in London, and sat till about three in the morning, it came into their heads to go and knock up Johnson, and see if they could prevail on him to join them in a ramble. They rapped violently at the doors of his chambers in the Temple, till at last he appeared in his shirt, with his little black wig on the top of his head instead of a nightcap, and a poker in his hand, imagining, probably, that some ruffians were coming to attack him. When he discovered who they were, and was told their errand, he smiled, and with great good humour agreed to their proposal : " What, is it you, you dogs ! I'll have a frisk with you." He was soon drest, and they sallied forth together into Covent-Garden, where the green-grocers and fruiterers were beginning to arrange their hampers, just come in from the country. Johnson made some attempts to help them ; but the honest gardeners stared so at his figure and manner, and odd interference, that he soon saw his services were not relished. They then repaired to one of the neighbouring taverns, and made a bowl of that liquor called *Bishop*, which Johnson had always liked : while in joyous contempt of sleep, from which he had been roused, he repeated the festive lines,

> " Short, O short then be thy reign,
> And give us to the world again ! "

They did not stay long, but walked down to the Thames, took a boat, and rowed to Billingsgate. Beauclerk and Johnson were so well pleased with their amusement, that they resolved to persevere in dissipation for the rest of the day : but Langton deserted them, being engaged to breakfast with some young ladies. Johnson scolded him for " leaving his social friends, to go and sit with a set of wretched *un-idea'd* girls." Garrick being told of this ramble, said to him smartly, " I heard of your frolic t'other night. You'll be in the ' Chronicle.' " Upon which Johnson afterwards observed, " *He* durst not do such a thing. His *wife* would not *let* him ! "

§ 33

Lord Chesterfield, to whom Johnson had paid the high compliment of addressing to his Lordship the " Plan " of his Dictionary, had behaved to him in such a manner as to excite his contempt and indignation. The world has been for many years amused with a story confidently told, and as confidently repeated with additional circumstances, that a sudden disgust was taken by Johnson upon occasion of his having been one day kept long in waiting in his Lordship's antechamber, for which the reason assigned was, that he had company with him ; and that at last, when the door opened, out walked Colley Cibber ; and that Johnson was so violently provoked when he found for whom he had been so long excluded, that he went away in a passion, and never would return. I remember having mentioned this story to George Lord Lyttelton, who told me, he was very intimate with Lord Chesterfield ; and holding it as a well-known truth, defended Lord Chesterfield by saying, that " Cibber, who had been introduced familiarly by the back-stairs, had probably not been there above ten minutes." It may seem strange even to entertain a doubt concerning a story so long and so widely current, and thus implicitly adopted, if not sanctioned, by the authority which I have mentioned ; but Johnson himself assured me, that there was not the least foundation for it. He told me, that there never was any particular incident which produced a quarrel between Lord Chesterfield and him ; but that his Lordship's continued neglect was the reason why he resolved to have no connection with him. When the Dictionary was upon the eve of publication, Lord Chesterfield, who, it is said, had flattered himself with expectations that Johnson would dedicate the work to him, attempted, in a courtly manner, to soothe and insinuate himself with the Sage, conscious, as it should seem, of the cold indifference with which he had treated its learned author ; and further attempted to conciliate him, by writing two papers in " The World," in recommendation of the work ; and it must be confessed, that they contain some studied compliments, so finely turned, that if there had been no previous offence, it is probable that Johnson would have been highly delighted. Praise, in general, was pleasing to him ; but by praise from a man of rank and elegant accomplishments, he was peculiarly gratified.

§ 34

This courtly device failed of its effect. Johnson, who thought that " all was false and hollow," despised the honeyed words, and was even indignant that Lord Chesterfield should, for a moment, imagine that he could be the dupe of such an artifice. His expression to me concerning Lord Chesterfield, upon this occasion, was, " Sir, after making great professions, he had, for many years, taken no notice of me ; but when my Dictionary was coming out, he fell a scribbling in ' The World ' about it. Upon which, I wrote him a letter expressed in civil terms, but such as might show him that I did not mind what he said or wrote, and that I had done with him."

This is that celebrated letter of which so much has been said, and about which curiosity has been so long excited, without being gratified. I for many years solicited Johnson to favour me with a copy of it, that so excellent a composition might not be lost to posterity. He delayed from time to time to give it me ; till at last in 1781, when we were on a visit at Mr. Dilly's, at Southill in Bedfordshire, he was pleased to dictate it to me from memory. He afterwards found among his papers a copy of it, which he had dictated to Mr. Baretti, with its title and corrections, in his own handwriting. This he gave to Mr. Langton ; adding, that if it were to come into print, he wished it to be from that copy. By Mr. Langton's kindness, I am enabled to enrich my work with a perfect transcript of what the world has so eagerly desired to see.

" TO THE RIGHT HONOURABLE THE EARL OF CHESTERFIELD

" MY LORD,   " February 7, 1755.

" I HAVE been lately informed, by the proprietor of ' The World,' that two papers, in which my Dictionary is recommended to the public, were written by your Lordship. To be so distinguished, is an honour, which, being very little accustomed to favours from the great, I know not well how to receive, or in what terms to acknowledge.

" When, upon some slight encouragement, I first

visited your Lordship, I was overpowered, like the
rest of mankind, by the enchantment of your address,
and could not forbear to wish that I might boast myself *Le vainqueur du vainqueur de la terre ;*—that I
might obtain that regard for which I saw the world
contending ; but I found my attendance so little encouraged, that neither pride nor modesty would
suffer me to continue it.   When I had once addressed
your Lordship in public, I had exhausted all the art of
pleasing which a retired and uncourtly scholar can
possess. I had done all that I could ; and no man is well
pleased to have his all neglected, be it ever so little.

   "Seven years, my Lord, have now past, since I
waited in your outward rooms, or was repulsed from
your door ; during which time I have been pushing on
my work through difficulties, of which it is useless to
complain, and have brought it, at last, to the verge
of publication, without one act of assistance, one word
of encouragement, or one smile of favour. Such treatment I did not expect, for I never had a Patron before.

   "The shepherd in Virgil grew at last acquainted
with Love, and found him a native of the rocks.

   "Is not a Patron, my Lord, one who looks with
unconcern on a man struggling for life in the water,
and, when he has reached ground, encumbers him
with help ? The notice which you have been pleased
to take of my labours, had it been early, had been
kind ; but it has been delayed till I am indifferent,
and cannot enjoy it ; till I am solitary, and cannot
impart it ; till I am known, and do not want it.   I
hope it is no very cynical asperity not to confess
obligations where no benefit has been received, or to
be unwilling that the public should consider me as
owing that to a Patron, which Providence has enabled
me to do for myself.

   "Having carried on my work thus far with so little
obligation to any favourer of learning, I shall not be
disappointed though I should conclude it, if less be

possible, with less ; for I have been long wakened from that dream of hope, in which I once boasted myself with so much exultation, my Lord, your Lordship's most humble, most obedient servant,

"SAM. JOHNSON."

§ 35

On the 6th of March came out Lord Bolingbroke's works, published by Mr. David Mallet. The wild and pernicious ravings, under the name of " Philosophy," which were thus ushered into the world, gave great offence to all well-principled men. Johnson, hearing of their tendency, which nobody disputed, was roused with a just indignation, and pronounced this memorable sentence upon the noble author and his editor. " Sir, he was a scoundrel, and a coward : a scoundrel for charging a blunderbuss against religion and morality ; a coward, because he had no resolution to fire it off himself, but left half a crown to a beggarly Scotchman to draw the trigger after his death ! "

§ 36

Johnson this year found an interval of leisure to make an excursion to Oxford, for the purpose of consulting the libraries there.

§ 37

Of his conversation while at Oxford at this time, Mr. Warton preserved and communicated to me the following memorial :

. . . . . .

" In an evening we frequently took long walks from Oxford into the country, returning to supper. Once, in our way home, we viewed the ruins of the abbeys of Oseney and Rewley, near Oxford. After at least an hour's silence, Johnson said, ' I viewed them with indignation ! ' We had then a long conversation on

Gothic buildings ; and in talking of the form of old halls, he said, ' In these halls the fire-place was anciently always in the middle of the room, till the Whigs removed it on one side.'—About this time there had been an execution of two or three criminals at Oxford on a Monday. Soon afterwards, one day at dinner, I was saying that Mr. Swinton, the chaplain of the jail, and also a frequent preacher before the University, a learned man, but often thoughtless and absent, preached the condemnation sermon on repentance, before the convicts, on the preceding day, Sunday ; and that in the close he told his audience, that he should give them the remainder of what he had to say on the subject, the next Lord's Day. Upon which, one of our company, a Doctor of Divinity, and a plain matter-of-fact man, by way of offering an apology for Mr. Swinton, gravely remarked, that he had probably preached the same sermon before the University : ' Yes, Sir,' says Johnson, ' but the University were not to be hanged the next morning.' "

§ 38

Mr. Andrew Millar, bookseller in the Strand, took the principal charge of conducting the publication of Johnson's Dictionary ; and as the patience of the proprietors was repeatedly tried and almost exhausted by their expecting that the work would be completed within the time which Johnson had sanguinely supposed, the learned author was often goaded to dispatch, more especially as he had received all the copy-money, by different drafts, a considerable time before he had finished his task. When the messenger who carried the last sheet to Millar returned, Johnson asked him, " Well, what did he say ? "—" Sir," answered the messenger, " he said, ' Thank God I have done with him.' "—" I am glad," replied Johnson with a smile, " that he thanks GOD for anything."

§ 39

The Dictionary, with a Grammar and History of the English Language, being now at length published, in two volumes folio, the world contemplated with wonder so stupendous a work achieved by one man, while other countries had thought such undertakings fit only for whole academies. Vast as his powers were, I cannot but think that his imagination deceived him, when he supposed that by constant application he might have performed the task in three years. Let the Preface be attentively perused, in which is given, in a clear, strong, and glowing style, a comprehensive, yet particular view of what he had done ; and it will be evident, that the time he employed upon it was comparatively short.

§ 40

A few of his definitions must be admitted to be erroneous. Thus, *Windward* and *Leeward*, though directly of opposite meaning, are defined identically the same way ; as to which inconsiderable specks it is enough to observe, that his Preface announces that he was aware there might be many such in so immense a work ; nor was he at all disconcerted when an instance was pointed out to him. A lady once asked him how he came to define *Pastern* the *knee* of a horse : instead of making an elaborate defence, as she expected, he at once answered, " Ignorance, Madam, pure ignorance." His definition of *Network* has often been quoted with sportive malignity, as obscuring a thing in itself very plain. But to these frivolous censures no other answer is necessary than that with which we are furnished by his own Preface.

" To explain, requires the use of terms less abstruse than that which is to be explained, and such terms cannot always be found. For as nothing can be proved but by supposing something intuitively known, and evident without proof, so nothing can be defined but by the use of words too plain to admit of a definition. Sometimes easier words are changed into harder ; as, *burial*, into *sepulture* or *interment ; drier*, into *desiccative ; dryness*, into *siccity*, or *aridity ; fit*, into *paroxysm ;* for the *easiest* word, whatever it be, can never be translated into one more easy."

His introducing his own opinions, and even prejudices, under general definitions of words, while at the same time the original meaning of the words is not explained, as his *Tory, Whig, Pension, Oats, Excise,* and a few more, cannot be fully defended, and must be placed to the account of capricious and humorous indulgence. Talking to me upon this subject when we were at Ashbourne in 1777, he mentioned a still stronger instance of the predominance of his private feelings in the composition of this work, than any now to be found in it. " You know, Sir, Lord Gower forsook the old Jacobite interest. When I came to the word *Renegado,* after telling that it meant ' One who deserts to the enemy, a revolter,' I added, *Sometimes we say a* GOWER. Thus it went to the press : but the printer had more wit than I, and struck it out."

Let it, however, be remembered, that this indulgence does not display itself only in sarcasm towards others, but sometimes in playful allusion to the notions commonly entertained of his own laborious task. Thus : " *Grub-street,* the name of a street in London, much inhabited by writers of small histories, *dictionaries,* and temporary poems ; whence any mean production is called *Grub-street."*—" *Lexicographer,* a writer of dictionaries, a *harmless drudge."*

§ 41

It must undoubtedly seem strange, that the conclusion of his Preface should be expressed in terms so desponding, when it is considered that the author was then only in his forty-sixth year. But we must ascribe its gloom to that miserable dejection of spirits to which he was constitutionally subject, and which was aggravated by the death of his wife two years before. I have heard it ingeniously observed by a lady of rank and elegance, that " his melancholy was then at its meridian." It pleased GOD to grant him almost thirty years of life after this time ; and once when he was in a placid frame of mind, he was obliged to own to me that he had enjoyed happier days, and had many more friends, since that gloomy hour, than before.

It is a sad saying, that " most of those whom he wished to please had sunk into the grave ; " and his case at forty-five was singularly unhappy, unless the circle of his friends was very narrow. I have often thought, that as longevity is generally desired, and, I believe, generally expected, it would be wise to be continually adding to the number of our friends, that the loss of some may be supplied by others. Friendship, " the wine of life," should, like a well-stocked cellar, be thus continually renewed ; and it is consolatory to think, that although we can seldom add what will equal the generous *first-growths* of our youth, yet friendship becomes insensibly old in much less time than is commonly imagined, and not many years are required to make it very mellow and pleasant. *Warmth* will, no doubt, make a considerable difference. Men of affectionate temper and bright fancy will coalesce a great deal sooner than those who are cold and dull.

The proposition which I have now endeavoured to illustrate was, at a subsequent period of his life, the opinion of Johnson himself. He said to Sir Joshua Reynolds, " If a man does not make new acquaintance as he advances through life, he will soon find himself left alone. A man, Sir, should keep his friendship *in constant repair.*"

§ 42

He this year resumed his scheme of giving an edition of " Shakespeare " with notes. He issued Proposals of considerable length, in which he showed that he perfectly well knew what a variety of research such an undertaking required ; but his indolence prevented him from pursuing it with that diligence which alone can collect those scattered facts, that genius, however acute, penetrating, and luminous, cannot discover by its own force. It is remarkable, that at this time his fancied activity was for the moment so vigorous, that he promised his work should be published before Christmas, 1757. Yet nine years elapsed before it saw the light. His throes in bringing it forth had been severe and remittent ; and at last we may almost conclude that the Cæsarian operation was performed by the knife of Churchill, whose upbraiding satire, I dare say, made Johnson's friends urge him to dispatch.

" He for subscribers baits his hook,
And takes their cash ; but where's the book ?
No matter where ; wise fear, we know,
Forbids the robbing of a foe ;
But what, to serve our private ends,
Forbids the cheating of our friends ? "

(*The Ghost*, iii. 801.)

About this period he was offered a living of considerable value in Lincolnshire, if he were inclined to enter into holy orders. It was a rectory in the gift of Mr. Langton, the father of his much valued friend. But he did not accept of it ; partly I believe from a conscientious motive, being persuaded that his temper and habits rendered him unfit for that assiduous and familiar instruction of the vulgar and ignorant, which he held to be an essential duty in a clergyman ; and partly because his love of a London life was so strong, that he would have thought himself an exile in any

other place, particularly if residing in the country.
Whoever would wish to see his thoughts upon that
subject displayed in their full force, may peruse the
" Adventurer," Number 126.

§ 43

In 1759, in the month of January, his mother died
at the great age of ninety, an event which deeply
affected him ; not that " his mind had acquired no
firmness by the contemplation of mortality " (Hawkins's *Life of Johnson*, p. 395) ; but that his reverential
affection for her was not abated by years, as indeed he
retained all his tender feelings even to the latest period
of his life.

§ 44

" TO MRS. JOHNSON, IN LICHFIELD.

" HONOURED MADAM,
" THE account which Miss [Porter] gives me of
your health, pierces my heart. GOD comfort, and preserve you, and save you, for the sake of Jesus Christ.

" I would have Miss read to you from time to time
the Passion of our Saviour, and sometimes the sentences in the Communion Service, beginning—*Come
unto me, all ye that travail and are heavy laden, and I
will give you rest.*

" I have just now read a medical book, which inclines me to think that a strong infusion of the bark
would do you good. Do, dear Mother, try it.

" Pray, send me your blessing, and forgive all that
I have done amiss to you. And whatever you would
have done, and what debts you would have paid first,
or anything else that you would direct, let Miss put it
down ; I shall endeavour to obey you.

" I have got twelve guineas to send you, but unhappily am at a loss how to send it to-night. If I cannot send it to-night, it will come by the next post.

" Pray, do not omit anything mentioned in this letter. GOD bless you for ever and ever. I am, your dutiful Son,

" SAM. JOHNSON.

" Jan. 13, 1759."

§ 45

Soon after this event he wrote his " RASSELAS, PRINCE OF ABYSSINIA ; " concerning the publication of which Sir John Hawkins guesses vaguely and idly, instead of having taken the trouble to inform himself with authentic precision. Not to trouble my readers with a repetition of the Knight's reveries, I have to mention, that the late Mr. Strahan the printer told me, that Johnson wrote it, that with the profits he might defray the expense of his mother's funeral, and pay some little debts which she had left. He told Sir Joshua Reynolds, that he composed it in the evenings of one week, sent it to the press in portions as it was written, and had never since read it over. Mr. Strahan, Mr. Johnson, and Mr. Dodsley, purchased it for a hundred pounds, but afterwards paid him twenty-five pounds more when it came to a second edition.

Considering the large sums which have been received for compilations, and works requiring not much more genius than compilations, we cannot but wonder at the very low price which he was content to receive for this admirable performance ; which, though he had written nothing else, would have rendered his name immortal in the world of literature. None of his writings has been so extensively diffused over Europe ; for it has been translated into most, if not all, of the modern languages. This Tale, with all the charms of Oriental imagery, and all the force and beauty of which the English language is capable, leads us through the most important scenes of human life, and shows us that this stage of our being is full of "vanity and vexation of spirit." To those who look no farther than the present life, or who maintain that human nature has not fallen from the state in which it was created, the instruction of this sublime story will be of no avail. But they who think justly, and feel with strong sensibility, will listen with eagerness and admiration to its truth and wisdom. Voltaire's " CANDIDE," written to refute the system of Optimism, which it has accomplished with brilliant success, is wonderfully similar in its plan and conduct to Johnson's " RASSELAS " ; insomuch, that I have heard Johnson say, that if they had not been published so closely one after the other that there was not time for imitation, it would have been in vain to deny that the scheme of that which came latest was taken from the other. Though the proposition illustrated by both these works was the same, namely, that in our present state there is more evil than good, the intention of the writers was very different. Voltaire, I am afraid, meant only by wanton profaneness to obtain a sportive victory over religion, and to discredit the belief of a superintending Providence : Johnson meant, by showing the unsatisfactory nature of things temporal, to direct the hopes of man to things eternal. " Rasselas," as was observed to me by a very accomplished lady, may be considered as a more enlarged and more deeply philosophical discourse in prose, upon the interesting truth, which in his "Vanity of Human Wishes " he had so successfully enforced in verse.

The fund of thinking which this work contains is such, that almost every sentence of it may furnish a subject of long meditation. I am not satisfied if a year passes without my having read it through ; and at every perusal, my admiration of the mind which produced it is so highly raised, that I can scarcely believe that I had the honour of enjoying the intimacy of such a man.

§ 46

He now refreshed himself by an excursion to Oxford, of which the following short characteristical notice, in his own words, is preserved :—". . . is now making tea for me. I have been in my gown ever since I came here. It was, at my first coming, quite new and handsome. I have swum thrice, which I had disused for many years. I have proposed to Vansittart climbing over the wall, but he has refused me. And I have clapped my hands till they are sore, at Dr. King's speech."

His negro servant, Francis Barber, having left him, and been some time at sea, not pressed as has been supposed, but with his own consent, it appears from a letter to John Wilkes, Esq., from Dr. Smollett, that his master kindly interested himself in procuring his release from a state of life of which Johnson always expressed the utmost abhorrence. He said, " No man will be a sailor who has contrivance enough to get himself into a jail ; for being in a ship is being in a jail, with the chance of being drowned " (*Journal of a Tour to the Hebrides*). And at another time, " A man in a jail has more room, better food, and commonly better company " (*Ibid.*).

§ 47

This is to me a memorable year ; for in it I had the happiness to obtain the acquaintance of that extraordinary man whose memoirs I am now writing ; an acquaintance which I shall ever esteem as one of the most fortunate circumstances in my life. Though then but two-and-twenty, I had for several years read his works with delight and instruction, and had the highest reverence for their author, which had grown up in my fancy into a kind of mysterious veneration, by figuring to myself a state of solemn elevated abstraction, in which I supposed him to live in the immense metropolis of London. Mr. Gentleman, a native of Ireland, who passed some years in Scotland as a player, and as an instructor in the English language, a man whose talents and worth were depressed by misfortunes, had given me a representation of the figure and manner of DICTIONARY JOHNSON, as he was then generally called; and during my first visit to London, which was for three months in 1760, Mr. Derrick the poet, who was Gentleman's friend and countryman, flattered me with hopes that he would introduce me to Johnson, an honour of which I was very ambitious. But he never found an opportunity; which made me doubt that he had promised to do what was not in his power; till Johnson some years afterwards told me, " Derrick, Sir, might very well have introduced you. I had a kindness for Derrick, and am sorry he is dead."

§ 48

Mr. Thomas Davies the actor, who then kept a bookseller's shop in Russell Street, Covent Garden, told me that Johnson was very much his friend, and came frequently to his house, where he more than once invited me to meet him; but by some unlucky accident or other he was prevented from coming to us.

§ 49

At last, on Monday the 16th of May, when I was sitting in Mr. Davies's back-parlour, after having drunk tea with him and Mrs. Davies, Johnson unexpectedly came into the shop; and Mr. Davies having perceived him through the glass-door in the room in which we were sitting, advancing towards us, —he announced his awful approach to me, somewhat in the manner of an actor in the part of Horatio, when he addresses Hamlet on the appearance of his father's ghost, " Look, my lord, it comes." I found that I had a very perfect idea of Johnson's figure, from the portrait of him painted by Sir Joshua Reynolds soon after he had published his Dictionary, in the attitude of sitting in his easy chair in deep meditation; which was the first picture his friend did for him, which Sir Joshua very kindly presented to me. Mr. Davies mentioned my name, and respectfully introduced me to him. I was much agitated; and recollecting his prejudice against the Scotch, of which I had heard much, I said to Davies, " Don't tell where I come from."—" From Scotland," cried Davies, roguishly. " Mr. Johnson," said I, " I do indeed come from Scotland, but I cannot help it." I am willing to flatter myself that I meant this as light pleasantry to soothe and conciliate him, and not as a humiliating abasement at the expense of my country. But however that might be, this speech was somewhat unlucky; for with that quickness of wit for which he was so remarkable, he seized the expression " come from Scotland," which I used in the sense of being of that country; and, as if I had said that I had come away from it, or left it, retorted, " That, Sir, I find, is what a very great many of your countrymen cannot help." This stroke stunned me a good deal; and when we had sat down, I felt myself not a little embarrassed, and apprehensive of what might come next. He then addressed himself to Davies : " What do you think of Garrick ? He has refused me an order for the play for Miss Williams, because he knows the house will be full, and that an order would be worth three shillings." Eager to take any opening to get into conversation with him, I ventured to say, " O, Sir, I cannot think Mr. Garrick would grudge such a trifle to you."—" Sir," said he, with a stern look, " I have known David Garrick longer than you have done: and I know no right you have to talk to me on the subject." Perhaps I deserved this check ; for it was rather presumptuous in me, an entire stranger, to express any doubt of the justice of his animadversion upon his old acquaintance and pupil. I now felt myself much mortified, and began to think, that the hope which I had long indulged of obtaining his acquaintance was blasted. And, in truth, had not my ardour been uncommonly strong, and my resolution uncommonly persevering, so rough a reception might have deterred me for ever from making any farther attempts. Fortunately, however, I remained upon the field not wholly discomfited ; and was soon rewarded by hearing some of his conversation, of which I preserved the following short minute, without marking the questions and observations by which it was produced.

" People," he remarked, " may be taken in once, who imagine that an author is greater in private life than other men. Uncommon parts require uncommon opportunities for their exertion.

" In barbarous society, superiority of parts is of real consequence. Great strength or great wisdom is of much value to an individual. But in more polished times there are people to do everything for money; and then there are a number of other superiorities, such as those of birth and fortune, and rank, that dissipate men's attention, and leave no extraordinary share of respect for personal and intellectual superiority. This is wisely ordered by Providence, to preserve some equality among mankind."

" Sir, this book (' The Elements of Criticism,' which he had taken up) is a pretty essay, and deserves to be held in some estimation, though much of it is chimerical."

Speaking of one who with more than ordinary boldness attacked public measures and the royal family, he said, " I think he is safe from the law, but he is an abusive scoundrel ; and instead of applying

to my Lord Chief Justice to punish him, I would send
half a dozen footmen and have him well ducked."

" The notion of liberty amuses the people of England, and helps to keep off the *tædium vitæ*.   When a
butcher tells you that *his heart bleeds for his country*,
he has, in fact, no uneasy feeling."

"Sheridan will not succeed at Bath with his oratory.
Ridicule has gone down before him, and, I doubt,
Derrick is his enemy.

" Derrick may do very well, as long as he can outrun
his character ; but the moment his character gets up
with him, it is all over."

It is, however, but just to record, that some years
afterwards, when I reminded him of this sarcasm, he
said, " Well, but Derrick has now got a character that
he need not run away from."

I was highly pleased with the extraordinary vigour
of his conversation, and regretted that I was drawn
away from it by an engagement at another place.   I
had for a part of the evening been left alone with him,
and had ventured to make an observation now and
then, which he received very civilly ; so that I was
satisfied that though there was a roughness in his
manner, there was no ill-nature in his disposition.
Davies followed me to the door, and when I complained to him a little of the hard blows which the
great man had given me, he kindly took upon him to
console me by saying, " Don't be uneasy.   I can see
he likes you very well."

A few days afterwards I called on Davies, and asked
him if he thought I might take the liberty of waiting
on Mr. Johnson at his chambers in the Temple.   He
said I certainly might, and that Mr. Johnson would
take it as a compliment.   So upon Tuesday the 24th
of May, after having been enlivened by the witty
sallies of Messieurs Thornton, Wilkes, Churchill, and
Lloyd, with whom I had passed the morning, I boldly
repaired to Johnson.   His chambers were on the first

floor of No. 1, Inner Temple Lane, and I entered them with an impression given me by the Rev. Dr. Blair, of Edinburgh, who had been introduced to him not long before, and described his having " found the Giant in his den " ; an expression which, when I came to be pretty well acquainted with Johnson, I repeated to him, and he was diverted at this picturesque account of himself. Dr. Blair had been presented to him by Dr. James Fordyce. At this time the controversy concerning the pieces published by Mr. James Macpherson, as translations of Ossian, was at its height. Johnson had all along denied their authenticity ; and, what was still more provoking to their admirers, maintained that they had no merit. The subject having been introduced by Dr. Fordyce, Dr. Blair, relying on the internal evidence of their antiquity, asked Dr. Johnson whether he thought any man of a modern age could have written such poems ? Johnson replied, " Yes, Sir, many men, many women, and many children." Johnson, at this time, did not know that Dr. Blair had just published a Dissertation, not only defending their authenticity, but seriously ranking them with the poems of Homer and Virgil ; and when he was afterwards informed of this circumstance, he expressed some displeasure at Dr. Fordyce's having suggested the topic, and said, " I am not sorry that they got thus much for their pains. Sir, it was like leading one to talk of a book, when the author is concealed behind the door."

He received me very courteously ; but, it must be confessed, that his apartment, and furniture, and morning dress, were sufficiently uncouth. His brown suit of clothes looked very rusty ; he had on a little old shrivelled unpowdered wig, which was too small for his head ; his shirt-neck and knees of his breeches were loose ; his black worsted stockings ill drawn up ; and he had a pair of unbuckled shoes by way of slippers. But all these slovenly particularities were forgotten the moment that he began to talk. Some gentlemen, whom I do not recollect, were sitting with him ; and when they went away, I also rose ; but he said to me, " Nay, don't go."—" Sir," said I, " I am afraid that I intrude upon you. It is benevolent to allow me to sit and hear you." He seemed pleased with this compliment, which I sincerely paid him, and answered, " Sir, I am obliged to any man who visits me."

§ 50

He told me, that he generally went abroad at four in the afternoon, and seldom came home till two in the morning. I took the liberty to ask if he did not think it wrong to live thus, and not make more use of his great talents. He owned it was a bad habit. On reviewing, at the distance of many years, my journal of this period, I wonder how, at my first visit, I ventured to talk to him so freely, and that he bore it with so much indulgence.

Before we parted, he was so good as to promise to favour me with his company one evening at my lodgings ; and as I took my leave, shook me cordially by the hand. It is almost needless to add, that I felt no little elation at having now so happily established an acquaintance of which I had been so long ambitious.

§ 51

Finding him in a placid humour, and wishing to avail myself of the opportunity which I fortunately had of consulting a sage, to hear whose wisdom, I conceived in the ardour of youthful imagination, that men filled with a noble enthusiasm for intellectual improvement would gladly have resorted from distant lands ;—I opened my mind to him ingenuously, and gave him a little sketch of my life, to which he was pleased to listen with great attention.

I acknowledged, that though educated very strictly in the principles of religion, I had for some time been misled into a certain degree of infidelity; but that I was come now to a better way of thinking, and was fully satisfied of the truth of the Christian revelation, though I was not clear as to every point considered to be orthodox. Being at all times a curious examiner of the human mind, and pleased with an undisguised display of what had passed in it, he called to me with warmth, " Give me your hand; I have taken a liking to you." He then began to descant upon the force of testimony, and the little we could know of final causes; so that the objections of, Why was it so? or, Why was it not so? ought not to disturb us: adding that he himself had at one period been guilty of a temporary neglect of religion, but that it was not the result of argument, but mere absence of thought.

After having given credit to reports of his bigotry, I was agreeably surprised when he expressed the following very liberal sentiment, which has the additional value of obviating an objection to our holy religion, founded upon the discordant tenets of Christians themselves: " For my part, Sir, I think all Christians, whether Papists or Protestants, agree in the essential articles, and that their differences are trivial, and rather political than religious."

§ 52

On Tuesday the 5th of July, I again visited Johnson. He told me he had looked into the poems of a pretty voluminous writer, Mr. (now Dr.) John Ogilvie, one of the Presbyterian ministers of Scotland, which had lately come out, but could find no thinking in them. BOSWELL: " Is there not imagination in them, Sir? " JOHNSON: " Why, Sir, there is in them what *was* imagination, but it is no more imagination in *him*, than sound is sound in the echo. And his diction too is not his own. We have long ago seen *white-robed innocence*, and *flower-bespangled meads.*"

Talking of London, he observed, " Sir, if you wish to have a just notion of the magnitude of this city, you must not be satisfied with seeing its great streets and squares, but must survey the innumerable little lanes and courts. It is not in the showy evolutions of buildings, but in the multiplicity of human habitations which are crowded together, that the wonderful immensity of London consists."—I have often amused myself with thinking how different a place London is to different people. They, whose narrow minds are contracted to the consideration of some one particular pursuit, view it only through that medium. A politician thinks of it merely as the seat of government in its different departments ; a grazier, as a vast market for cattle ; a mercantile man, as a place where a prodigious deal of business is done upon 'Change ; a dramatic enthusiast, as the grand scene of theatrical entertainments ; a man of pleasure, as an assemblage of taverns, and the great emporium for ladies of easy virtue. But the intellectual man is struck with it, as comprehending the whole of human life in all its variety, the contemplation of which is inexhaustible.

On Wednesday, July 6th, he was engaged to sup with me at my lodgings in Downing Street, Westminster. But on the preceding night my landlord having behaved very rudely to me and some company who were with me, I had resolved not to remain another night in his house. I was exceedingly uneasy at the awkward appearance I supposed I should make to Johnson and the other gentlemen whom I had invited, not being able to receive them at home, and being obliged to order supper at the Mitre. I went to Johnson in the morning, and talked of it as of a serious distress. He laughed, and said, " Consider, Sir, how insignificant this will appear a twelvemonth hence."—Were this consideration to be applied

to most of the little vexatious incidents of life, by
which our quiet is too often disturbed, it would
prevent many painful sensations. I have tried it
frequently with good effect. "There is nothing," continued he, " in this mighty misfortune ; nay, we shall
be better at the Mitre." I told him that I had been at
Sir John Fielding's office, complaining of my landlord,
and had been informed, that though I had taken my
lodgings for a year, I might, upon proof of his bad
behaviour, quit them when I pleased, without being
under an obligation to pay rent for any longer time
than while I possessed them. The fertility of Johnson's mind could show itself even upon so small a
matter as this. "Why, Sir," said he, "I suppose this
must be the law, since you have been told so in Bow
Street. But, if your landlord could hold you to your
bargain, and the lodgings should be yours for a year,
you may certainly use them as you think fit. So,
Sir, you may quarter two life-guardsmen upon him ;
or you may send the greatest scoundrel you can find
into your apartments ; or you may say that you want
to make some experiments in natural philosophy, and
may burn a large quantity of assafœtida in his house."

I had as my guests this evening at the Mitre tavern,
Dr. Johnson, Dr. Goldsmith, Mr. Thomas Davies, Mr.
Eccles, an Irish gentleman, for whose agreeable company I was obliged to Mr. Davies, and the Reverend
Mr. John Ogilvie, who was desirous of being in company with my illustrious friend, while I, in my turn,
was proud to have the honour of showing one of my
countrymen upon what easy terms Johnson permitted
me to live with him.

§ 53

Mr. Ogilvie was unlucky enough to choose for the
topic of his conversation the praises of his native
country. He began with saying, that there was very
rich land around Edinburgh. Goldsmith, who had

studied physic there, contradicted this, very untruly, with a sneering laugh. Disconcerted a little by this, Mr. Ogilvie then took new ground, where, I suppose, he thought himself perfectly safe ; for he observed, that Scotland had a great many noble wild prospects. JOHNSON : "I believe, Sir, you have a great many. Norway, too, has noble wild prospects ; and Lapland is remarkable for prodigious noble wild prospects. But, Sir, let me tell you, the noblest prospect which a Scotchman ever sees, is the high road that leads him to England !" This unexpected and pointed sally produced a roar of applause. After all, however, those who admire the rude grandeur of Nature, cannot deny it to Caledonia.

§ 54

To such a degree of unrestrained frankness had he now accustomed me, that in the course of this evening I talked of the numerous reflections which had been thrown out against him on account of his having accepted a pension from his present Majesty. " Why, Sir," said he, with a hearty laugh, "it is a mighty foolish noise that they make. I have accepted of a pension as a reward which has been thought due to my literary merit ; and now that I have this pension, I am the same man in every respect that I have ever been ; I retain the same principles. It is true, that I cannot now curse (smiling) the House of Hanover ; nor would it be decent for me to drink King James's health in the wine that King George gives me money to pay for. But, Sir, I think that the pleasure of cursing the House of Hanover, and drinking King James's health, are amply over balanced by 300*l.* a year."

§ 55

Yet there is no doubt that at earlier periods he was wont often to exercise both his pleasantry and ingenuity in talking Jacobitism. My much respected friend, Dr. Douglas, now Bishop of Salisbury, has favoured me with the following admirable instance from his Lordship's own recollection. One day when dining at old Mr. Langton's, where Miss Roberts, his niece, was one of the company, Johnson, with his usual complacent attention to the fair sex, took her by the hand and said, " My dear, I hope you are a Jacobite." Old Mr. Langton, who, though a high and steady Tory, was attached to the present Royal Family, seemed offended, and asked Johnson, with great warmth, what he could mean by putting such a question to his niece ? " Why, Sir," said Johnson, " I meant no offence to your niece, I meant her a great compliment. A Jacobite, Sir, believes in the divine right of Kings. He that believes in the divine right of Kings believes in a Divinity. A Jacobite believes in the divine right of Bishops. He that believes in the divine right of Bishops believes in the divine authority of the Christian religion. Therefore, Sir, a Jacobite is neither an Atheist nor a Deist. That cannot be said of a Whig ; for *Whiggism is a negation of all principle*."

§ 56

I said, I considered distinction or rank to be of so much importance in civilized society, that if I were asked on the same day to dine with the first duke in England, and with the first man in Britain for genius, I should hesitate which to prefer. JOHNSON : " To be sure, Sir, if you were to dine only once, and it were never to be known where you dined, you would choose rather to dine with the first man of genius ; but to gain most respect, you should dine with the first duke in England. For nine people in ten that you meet with, would have a higher opinion of you for having dined with a duke ; and the great genius himself would receive you better, because you had been with the great duke."

§ 57

He again insisted on the duty of maintaining subordination of rank. " Sir, I would no more deprive a nobleman of his respect, than of his money. I consider myself as acting a part in the great system of society, and I do to others as I would have them do to me. I would behave to a nobleman as I should expect he would behave to me, were I a nobleman and he Sam. Johnson. Sir, there is one Mrs. Macaulay in this town, a great republican. One day when I was at her house, I put on a very grave countenance, and said to her, ' Madam, I am now become a convert to your way of thinking. I am convinced that all mankind are upon an equal footing ; and to give you an unquestionable proof, Madam, that I am in earnest, here is a very sensible, civil, well-behaved fellow-citizen, your footman ; I desire that he may be allowed to sit down and dine with us.' I thus, Sir, showed her the absurdity of the levelling doctrine. She has never liked me since. Sir, your levellers wish to level *down* as far as themselves ; but they cannot bear levelling *up* to themselves. They would all have some people under them ; why not then have some people above them ? " I mentioned a certain author who disgusted me by his forwardness, and by showing no deference to noblemen into whose company he was admitted. JOHNSON : " Suppose a shoemaker should claim an equality with him, as he does with a lord : how he would stare. ' Why, Sir, do you stare ? (says the shoemaker ;) I do great service to society. 'Tis true, I am paid for doing it ; but so are you, Sir ; and I am sorry to say it, better paid than I am, for doing something not so necessary. For mankind could do better without your books, than without my shoes.' Thus, Sir, there would be a perpetual struggle for precedence, were there no fixed invariable rules for the distinction of rank, which creates no jealousy, as it is allowed to be accidental."

§ 58

On Saturday, July 30, Dr. Johnson and I took a sculler at the Temple-stairs, and set out for Greenwich. I asked him if he really thought a knowledge of the Greek and Latin languages an essential requisite to a good education. JOHNSON: "Most certainly, Sir; for those who know them have a very great advantage over those who do not. Nay, Sir, it is wonderful what a difference learning makes upon people even in the common intercourse of life, which does not appear to be much connected with it."— "And yet," said I, "people go through the world very well, and carry on the business of life to good advantage, without learning." JOHNSON: "Why, Sir, that may be true in cases where learning cannot possibly be of any use; for instance, this boy rows us as well without learning, as if he could sing the song of Orpheus to the Argonauts, who were the first sailors." He then called to the boy, "What would you give, my lad, to know about the Argonauts?" "Sir," said the boy, "I would give what I have." Johnson was much pleased with his answer, and we gave him a double fare. Dr. Johnson then turning to me, "Sir," said he, "a desire of knowledge is the natural feeling of mankind; and every human being, whose mind is not debauched, will be willing to give all that he has to get knowledge."

We landed at the Old Swan, and walked to Billingsgate, where we took oars and moved smoothly along the silver Thames. It was a very fine day. We were entertained with the immense number and variety of ships that were lying at anchor, and with the beautiful country on each side of the river.

§ 59

Next day, Sunday, July 31, I told him I had been that morning at a meeting of the people called

Quakers, where I had heard a woman preach. JOHNSON : " Sir, a woman's preaching is like a dog's walking on his hinder legs. It is not done well; but you are surprised to find it done at all."

§ 60

On Wednesday, August 3, we had our last social evening at the Turk's Head coffee-house, before my setting out for foreign parts. I had the misfortune, before we parted, to irritate him unintentionally. I mentioned to him how common it was in the world to tell absurd stories of him, and to ascribe to him very strange sayings. JOHNSON : " What do they make me say, Sir ? " BOSWELL : " Why, Sir, as an instance very strange indeed (laughing heartily as I spoke), David Hume told me, you said that you would stand before a battery of cannon to restore the Convocation to its full powers."—Little did I apprehend that he had actually said this : but I was soon convinced of my error ; for, with a determined look, he thundered out " And would I not, Sir ? Shall the Presbyterian *Kirk* of Scotland have its General Assembly, and the Church of England be denied its Convocation ? " He was walking up and down the room, while I told him the anecdote ; but when he uttered this explosion of High Church zeal, he had come close to my chair, and his eyes flashed with indignation. I bowed to the storm, and diverted the force of it, by leading him to expatiate on the influence which religion derived from maintaining the Church with great external respectability.

§ 61

On Friday, August 5, we set out early in the morning in the Harwich stage-coach. A fat, elderly gentlewoman, and a young Dutchman, seemed the most inclined among us to conversation. At the inn where we dined, the gentlewoman said that she had done her best to educate her children; and, particularly, that she had never suffered them to be a moment idle. JOHNSON: "I wish, Madam, you would educate me too: for I have been an idle fellow all my life." "I am sure, Sir," said she, "you have not been idle." JOHNSON: "Nay, Madam, it is very true; and that gentleman there," pointing to me, "has been idle. He was idle at Edinburgh. His father sent him to Glasgow, where he continued to be idle. He then came to London, where he has been very idle; and now he is going to Utrecht, where he will be as idle as ever." I asked him privately how he could expose me so. JOHNSON: "Poh, poh!" said he, "they knew nothing about you, and will think of it no more." In the afternoon the gentlewoman talked violently against the Roman Catholics, and of the horrors of the Inquisition. To the utter astonishment of all the passengers but myself, who knew that he could talk upon any side of a question, he defended the Inquisition, and maintained, that "False doctrine should be checked on its first appearance; that the Civil Power should unite with the Church in punishing those who dared to attack the established religion, and that such only were punished by the Inquisition." He had in his pocket "Pomponius Mela de Situ Orbis," in which he read occasionally, and seemed very intent upon ancient geography. Though by no means niggardly, his attention to what was generally right was so minute, that having observed at one of the stages that I ostentatiously gave a shilling to the coachman, when the custom was for each passenger to give only six-pence, he took me aside and scolded me, saying that what I had done would make the coachman dissatisfied with all the rest of the passengers who gave him no more than his due. This was a just reprimand; for in whatever way a man may indulge his generosity or his vanity in spending his money, for the sake of others he ought not to raise the price of any article for which there is a constant demand.

§ 62

At supper this night he talked of good eating with uncommon satisfaction. " Some people," said he, " have a foolish way of not minding, or pretending not to mind, what they eat. For my part, I mind my belly very studiously, and very carefully ; for I look upon it, that he who does not mind his belly will hardly mind anything else." He now appeared to me *Jean Bull philosophe*, and he was for the moment, not only serious but vehement. Yet I have heard him, upon other occasions, talk with great contempt of people who were anxious to gratify their palates ; and the 206th number of his " Rambler " is a masterly essay against gulosity. His practice, indeed, I must acknowledge, may be considered as casting the balance of his different opinions upon this subject ; for I never knew any man who relished good eating more than he did. When at table, he was totally absorbed in the business of the moment ; his looks seemed riveted to his plate ; nor would he, unless when in very high company, say one word, or even pay the least atten-tion to what was said by others, till he had satisfied his appetite ; which was so fierce, and indulged with such intenseness, that while in the act of eating, the veins of his forehead swelled, and generally a strong perspiration was visible. To those whose sensations were delicate, this could not but be disgusting ; and it was doubtless not very suitable to the character of a philosopher, who should be distinguished by self-command. But it must be owned, that Johnson, though he could be rigidly *abstemious*, was not a *temperate* man either in eating or drinking. He could refrain, but he could not use moderately. He told me, that he had fasted two days without inconvenience, and that he had never been hungry but once. They who beheld with wonder how much he eat upon all occasions when his dinner was to his taste, could not easily conceive what he must have meant by hunger ; and not only was he remarkable for the extraordinary quantity which he eat, but he was, or affected to be, a man of very nice discernment in the science of cookery. He used to descant critically on the dishes which had been at table where he had dined or supped, and to recollect very minutely what he had liked. I remember when he was in Scotland, his praising " *Gordon's palates* " (a dish of palates at the Honourable Alexander Gordon's) with a warmth of expression which might have done honour to more important subjects. " As for Maclaurin's imitation of a *made dish*, it was a wretched attempt." He about the same time was so much displeased with the performance of a nobleman's French cook, that he exclaimed with vehemence, " I'd throw such a rascal into the river ; " and he then proceeded to alarm a lady at whose house he was to sup, by the following manifesto of his skill : " I, Madam, who live at a variety of good tables, am a much better judge of cookery, than any person who has a very tolerable cook, but lives much at home ; for his palate is gradually adapted to the taste of his cook ; whereas, Madam, in trying by a wider range, I can more exquisitely judge." When invited to dine even with an intimate friend, he was not pleased if something better than a plain dinner was not prepared for him. I have heard him say on such an occasion, " This was a good dinner enough, to be sure ; but it was not a dinner to *ask* a man to." On the other hand, he was wont to express, with great glee, his satisfaction when he had been entertained quite to his mind. One day when he had dined with his neighbour and landlord in Bolt Court, Mr. Allen, the printer, whose old housekeeper had studied his taste in everything, he pronounced this eulogy : " Sir, we could not have had a better dinner had there been a *Synod of Cooks.*"

§ 63

Next day we got to Harwich to dinner ; and my passage in the packet-boat to Helvoetsluys being secured, and my baggage put on board, we dined at our inn by ourselves. I happened to say it would be terrible if he should not find a speedy opportunity of returning to London, and be confined in so dull a place. JOHNSON : " Don't, Sir, accustom yourself to use big words for little matters. It would *not* be *terrible,* though I *were* to be detained some time here." The practice of using words of disproportionate magnitude, is, no doubt, too frequent everywhere ; but I think most remarkable among the French, of which, all who have travelled in France must have been struck with innumerable instances.

We went and looked at the church, and having gone into it and walked up to the altar, Johnson, whose piety was constant and fervent, sent me to my knees, saying, " Now that you are going to leave your native country, recommend yourself to the protection of your CREATOR and REDEEMER."

§ 64

This year was distinguished by his being introduced into the family of Mr. Thrale, one of the most eminent brewers in England, and Member of Parliament for the borough of Southwark. Foreigners are not a little amazed when they hear of brewers, distillers, and men in similar departments of trade, held forth as persons of considerable consequence. In this great commercial country it is natural that a situation which produces much wealth should be considered as very respectable ; and, no doubt, honest industry is entitled to esteem. But, perhaps, the too rapid ad-

vances of men of low extraction tends to lessen the
value of that distinction by birth and gentility, which
has ever been found beneficial to the grand scheme of
subordination. Johnson used to give this account of
the rise of Mr. Thrale's father : " He worked at six
shillings a week for twenty years in the great brewery,
which afterwards was his own. The proprietor of it
had an only daughter, who was married to a nobleman. It was not fit that a peer should continue the
business. On the old man's death, therefore, the
brewery was to be sold. To find a purchaser for so
large a property was a difficult matter ; and, after
some time, it was suggested, that it would be advisable
to treat with Thrale, a sensible, active, honest man,
who had been employed in the house, and to transfer
the whole to him for 30,000l., security being taken
upon the property. This was accordingly settled. In
eleven years Thrale paid the purchase-money. He
acquired a large fortune, and lived to be a Member of
Parliament for Southwark. But what was most remarkable was the liberality with which he used his
riches. He gave his son and daughters the best education. The esteem which his good conduct procured
him from the nobleman who had married his master's
daughter, made him be treated with much attention ;
and his son, both at school and at the University of
Oxford, associated with young men of the first rank.
His allowance from his father, after he left college, was
splendid ; not less than a thousand a year. This, in
a man who had risen as old Thrale did, was an extraordinary instance of generosity. He used to say,
' If this young dog does not find so much after I am
gone as he expects, let him remember that he has had
a great deal in my own time.' "

The son, though in affluent circumstances, had good
sense enough to carry on his father's trade, which was
of such extent, that I remember he once told me, he
would not quit it for an annuity of ten thousand a

year; "Not," said he, "that I get ten thousand a year by it, but it is an estate to a family." Having left daughters only, the property was sold for the immense sum of 135,000*l*.; a magnificent proof of what may be done by fair trade in a long period of time.

§ 65

Mr. Thrale had married Miss Hesther Lynch Salusbury, of good Welsh extraction, a lady of lively talents, improved by education. That Johnson's introduction into Mr. Thrale's family, which contributed so much to the happiness of his life, was owing to her desire for his conversation, is a very probable and the general supposition : but it is not the truth. Mr. Murphy, who was intimate with Mr. Thrale, having spoken very highly of Dr. Johnson, he was requested to make them acquainted. This being mentioned to Johnson, he accepted an invitation to dinner at Thrale's, and was so much pleased with his reception, both by Mr. and Mrs. Thrale, and they so much pleased with him, that his invitations to their house were more and more frequent, till at last he became one of the family, and an apartment was appropriated to him, both in their house at Southwark and in their villa at Streatham.

Johnson had a very sincere esteem for Mr. Thrale, as a man of excellent principles, a good scholar, well skilled in trade, of a sound understanding, and of manners such as presented the character of a plain independent English Squire. As this family will frequently be mentioned in the course of the following pages, and as a false notion has prevailed that Mr. Thrale was inferior, and in some degree insignificant, compared with Mrs. Thrale, it may be proper to give a true state of the case from the authority of Johnson himself in his own words.

" I know no man," said he, " who is more master of

his wife and family than Thrale. If he but holds up a finger, he is obeyed. It is a great mistake to suppose that she is above him in literary attainments. She is more flippant ; but he has ten times her learning : he is a regular scholar ; but her learning is that of a schoolboy in one of the lower forms." My readers may naturally wish for some representation of the figures of this couple. Mr. Thrale was tall, well proportioned, and stately. As for *Madam*, or *my Mistress*, by which epithets Johnson used to mention Mrs. Thrale, she was short, plump, and brisk. She has herself given us a lively view of the idea which Johnson had of her person, on her appearing before him in a dark-coloured gown : " You little creatures should never wear those sort of clothes, however ; they are unsuitable in every way. What ! have not all insects gay colours ? " (*Anecdotes*, p. 279). Mr. Thrale gave his wife a liberal indulgence, both in the choice of their company, and in the mode of entertaining them. He understood and valued Johnson, without remission, from their first acquaintance to the day of his death. Mrs. Thrale was enchanted with Johnson's conversation for its own sake, and had also a very allowable vanity in appearing to be honoured with the attention of so celebrated a man.

Nothing could be more fortunate for Johnson than this connection. He had at Mr. Thrale's all the comforts and even luxuries of life ; his melancholy was diverted, and his irregular habits lessened by association with an agreeable and well-ordered family. He was treated with the utmost respect, and even affection. The vivacity of Mrs. Thrale's literary talk roused him to cheerfulness and exertion, even when they were alone. But this was not often the case ; for he found here a constant succession of what gave him the highest enjoyment, the society of the learned, the witty, and the eminent in every way ; who were assembled in numerous companies, called forth his wonderful powers, and gratified him with admiration, to which no man could be insensible.

§ 66

I told him that a foreign friend of his, whom I had met with abroad, was so wretchedly perverted to infidelity, that he treated the hopes of immortality with brutal levity ; and said, " As man dies like a dog, let him lie like a dog." JOHNSON : " *If* he dies like a dog, *let* him lie like a dog." I added, that this man said to me, " I hate mankind, for I think myself one of the best of them, and I know how bad I am." JOHNSON : " Sir, he must be very singular in his opinion, if he thinks himself one of the best of men ; for none of his friends think him so."—He said, " No, honest man could be a Deist ; for no man could be so after a fair examination of the proofs of Christianity." I named Hume. JOHNSON : " No, Sir ; Hume owned to a clergyman in the bishopric of Durham, that he had never read the New Testament with attention."—I mentioned Hume's notion, that all who are happy are equally happy ; a little miss with a new gown at a dancing-school ball, a general at the head of a victorious army, and an orator after having made an eloquent speech in a great assembly. JOHNSON : " Sir, that all who are happy, are equally happy, is not true. A peasant and a philosopher may be equally *satisfied*, but not equally *happy*. Happiness consists in the multiplicity of agreeable consciousness. A peasant has not capacity for having equal happiness with a philosopher." I remember this very question very happily illustrated in opposition to Hume, by the Reverend Mr. Robert Brown, at Utrecht. " A small drinking-glass and a large one," said he, " may be equally full ; but the large one holds more than the small."

§ 67

Our next meeting at the Mitre was on Saturday the 15th of February, when I presented to him my old and most intimate friend, the Reverend Mr. Temple, then of Cambridge. I having mentioned that I had passed some time with Rousseau in his wild retreat, and having quoted some remark made by Mr. Wilkes, with whom I had spent many pleasant hours in Italy, Johnson said (sarcastically), " It seems, Sir, you have kept very good company abroad, Rousseau and Wilkes ! " Thinking it enough to defend one at a time, I said nothing as to my gay friend, but answered with a smile, " My dear Sir, you don't call Rousseau bad company. Do you really think *him* a bad man ? " JOHNSON : " Sir, if you are talking jestingly of this, I don't talk with you. If you mean to be serious, I think him one of the worst of men ; a rascal, who ought to be hunted out of society, as he has been. Three or four nations have expelled him : and it is a shame that he is protected in this country." BOSWELL : " I don't deny, Sir, but that his novel may, perhaps, do harm ; but I cannot think his intention was bad." JOHNSON : " Sir, that will not do. We cannot prove any man's intention to be bad. You may shoot a man through the head, and say you intended to miss him ; but the judge will order you to be hanged. An alleged want of intention, when evil is committed, will not be allowed in a court of justice. Rousseau, Sir, is a very bad man. I would sooner sign a sentence for his transportation, than that of any felon who has gone from the Old Bailey these many years. Yes, I should like to have him work in the plantations." BOSWELL : " Sir, do you think him as bad a man as Voltaire ? " JOHNSON : " Why, Sir, it is difficult to settle the proportion of iniquity between them."

§ 68

One evening, when a young gentleman teased him with an account of the infidelity of his servant, who, he said, would not believe the Scriptures, because he could not read them in the original tongues, and be sure that they were not invented. " Why, foolish fellow," said Johnson, " has he any better authority for almost everything that he believes ? " BOSWELL : " Then the vulgar, Sir, never can know they are right, but must submit themselves to the learned." JOHNSON : " To be sure, Sir. The vulgar are the children of the State, and must be taught like children." BOSWELL : " Then, Sir, a poor Turk must be a Mahometan, just as a poor Englishman must be a Christian ? " JOHNSON : " Why, yes, Sir ; and what then ? This now is such stuff as I used to talk to my mother, when I first began to think myself a clever fellow ; and she ought to have whipped me for it."

§ 69

In February, 1767, there happened one of the most remarkable incidents of Johnson's life, which gratified his monarchical enthusiasm, and which he loved to relate with all its circumstances, when requested by his friends.   This was his being honoured by a private conversation with his Majesty, in the library at the Queen's house.   He had frequently visited those splendid rooms and noble collection of books, which he used to say was more numerous and curious than he supposed any person could have made in the time which the King had employed.   Mr. Barnard, the librarian, took care that he should have every accommodation that could contribute to his ease and convenience, while indulging his literary taste in that place ; so that he had here a very agreeable resource at leisure hours.

His Majesty having been informed of his occasional visits, was pleased to signify a desire that he should be told when Dr. Johnson came next to the library. Accordingly, the next time that Johnson did come, as soon as he was fairly engaged with a book, on which, while he sat by the fire, he seemed quite intent, Mr. Barnard stole round to the apartment where the King was, and, in obedience to his Majesty's commands, mentioned that Dr. Johnson was then in the library. His Majesty said he was at leisure, and would go to him ; upon which Mr. Barnard took one of the candles that stood on the King's table, and lighted his Majesty through a suite of rooms, till they came to a private door into the library, of which his Majesty had the key. Being entered, Mr. Barnard stepped forward hastily to Dr. Johnson, who was still in a profound study, and whispered him, " Sir, here is the King." Johnson started up, and stood still. His Majesty approached him, and at once was courteously easy.

His Majesty began by observing, that he understood he came sometimes to the library ; and then mentioned his having heard that the Doctor had been lately at Oxford, and asked him if he was not fond of going thither. To which Johnson answered, that he was indeed fond of going to Oxford sometimes, but was likewise glad to come back again. The King then asked him what they were doing at Oxford. Johnson answered, he could not much commend their diligence, but that in some respects they were mended, for they had put their press under better regulations, and were at that time printing Polybius. He was then asked whether there were better libraries at Oxford or Cambridge. He answered, he believed the Bodleian was larger than any they had at Cambridge ; at the same time adding, " I hope, whether we have more books or not than they have at Cambridge, we shall make as good use of them as they do." Being asked whether

All Souls or Christ Church library was the largest, he answered, " All Souls library is the largest we have, except the Bodleian." " Ay," said the King, " that is the public library."

His Majesty inquired if he was then writing anything. He answered, he was not, for he had pretty well told the world what he knew, and must now read to acquire more knowledge. The King, as it should seem with a view to urge him to rely on his own stores as an original writer, and to continue his labours, then said, " I do not think you borrow much from anybody." Johnson said, he thought he had already done his part as a writer. " I should have thought so too," said the King, " if you had not written so well." —Johnson observed to me, upon this, that " No man could have paid a handsomer compliment ; and it was fit for a King to pay. It was decisive." When asked by another friend, at Sir Joshua Reynolds's, whether he made any reply to this high compliment, he answered, " No, Sir. When the King had said it, it was to be so. It was not for me to bandy civilities with my Sovereign." Perhaps no man who had spent his whole life in courts could have shown a more nice and dignified sense of true politeness, than Johnson did in this instance.

§ 70

During the whole of this interview, Johnson talked to his Majesty with profound respect, but still in his firm manly manner, with a sonorous voice, and never in that subdued tone which is commonly used at the levee and in the drawing-room. After the King withdrew, Johnson showed himself highly pleased with his Majesty's conversation, and gracious behaviour. He said to Mr. Barnard, " Sir, they may talk of the King as they will ; but he is the finest gentleman I have ever seen." And he afterward observed to Mr. Langton, " Sir, his manners are those of as fine a gentleman as we may suppose Lewis the Fourteenth or Charles the Second."

§ 71

I received no letter from Johnson this year; nor have I discovered any of the correspondence he had, except the two letters to Mr. Drummond, which have been inserted, for the sake of connection with that to the same gentleman in 1776. His diary affords no light as to his employment at this time. He passed three months at Lichfield: and I cannot omit an affecting and solemn scene there, as related by himself:

" Sunday, Oct. 18, 1767. Yesterday, Oct. 17, at about ten in the morning, I took my leave for ever of my dear old friend, Catharine Chambers, who came to live with my mother about 1724, and has been but little parted from us since. She buried my father, my brother, and my mother. She is now fifty-eight years old.

" I desired all to withdraw, then told her that we were to part for ever; that as Christians, we should part with prayer; and that I would, if she was willing, say a short prayer beside her. She expressed great desire to hear me; and held up her poor hands, as she lay in bed, with great fervour, while I prayed, kneeling by her, nearly in the following words:

" Almighty and most merciful Father, whose loving-kindness is over all thy works, behold, visit, and relieve this thy servant, who is grieved with sickness. Grant that the sense of her weakness may add strength to her faith, and seriousness to her repentance. And grant that by the help of thy Holy Spirit, after the pains and labours of this short life, we may all obtain everlasting happiness, through JESUS CHRIST our Lord, for whose sake hear our prayers. Amen. Our father, &c.

" I then kissed her. She told me, that to part was the greatest pain that she had ever felt, and that she hoped we should meet again in a better place. I expressed, with swelled eyes, and great emotion of tenderness, the same hopes. We kissed, and parted. I humbly hope to meet again, and to part no more " (*Pr. and Med.*, pp. 77–8).

By those who have been taught to look upon Johnson as a man of a harsh and stern character, let this tender and affectionate scene be candidly read ; and let them then judge whether more warmth of heart, and grateful kindness, is often found in human nature.

§ 72

I asked him whether, as a moralist, he did not think that the practice of the law, in some degree, hurt the nice feeling of honesty. JOHNSON : " Why no, Sir, if you act properly. You are not to deceive your clients with false representations of your opinion : you are not to tell lies to a judge." BOSWELL : " But what do you think of supporting a cause which you know to be bad ? " JOHNSON : " Sir, you do not know it to be good or bad till the judge determines it. I have said that you are to state facts fairly ; so that your thinking, or what you call knowing, a cause to be bad, must be from reasoning, must be from your supposing your arguments to be weak and inconclusive. But, Sir, that is not enough. An argument which does not convince yourself, may convince the judge to whom you urge it : and if it does convince him, why, then, Sir, you are wrong, and he is right. It is his business to judge ; and you are not to be confident in your own opinion that a cause is bad, but to say all you can for your client, and then hear the judge's opinion." BOSWELL : " But, Sir, does not affecting a warmth when you have no warmth, and appearing to be clearly of one opinion when you are in reality of another opinion, does not such dissimulation impair one's honesty ? Is there not some danger that a lawyer may put on the same mask in common life, in the intercourse with his friends ? " JOHNSON : " Why no, Sir. Everybody knows you are paid for affecting warmth for your client ; and it is, therefore, properly no dissimulation : the moment you come from the bar you resume your usual behaviour. Sir, a man will no more carry the artifice of the bar into the common intercourse of society, than a man who is paid for tumbling upon his hands will continue to tumble upon his hands when he should walk on his feet."

§ 73

An essay, written by Mr. Deane, a divine of the Church of England, maintaining the future life of brutes by an explication of certain parts of the Scriptures, was mentioned, and the doctrine insisted on by a gentleman who seemed fond of curious speculation. Johnson, who did not like to hear of anything concerning a future state which was not authorized by the regular canons of orthodoxy, discouraged this talk ; and being offended at its continuation, he watched an opportunity to give the gentleman a blow of reprehension. So, when the poor speculatist, with a serious metaphysical pensive face, addressed him, " But really, Sir, when we see a very sensible dog, we don't know what to think of him." Johnson, rolling with joy at the thought which beamed in his eye, turned quickly round, and replied, " True, Sir : and when we see a very foolish *fellow*, we don't know what to think of *him*." He then rose up, strided to the fire, and stood for some time laughing and exulting.

§ 74

He remained at Oxford a considerable time ; I was obliged to go to London, where I received his letter, which had been returned from Scotland.

" TO JAMES BOSWELL, ESQ.

" MY DEAR BOSWELL,

" I HAVE omitted a long time to write to you, without knowing very well why. I could not tell why I should not write : for who would write to men who publish the letters of their friends, without their leave ? Yet I write to you in spite of my caution, to tell you that I shall be glad to see you, and that I wish you would empty your head of Corsica, which I think has filled it rather too long. But, at all events, I shall be glad, very glad, to see you. I am, Sir, yours affectionately,

" SAM. JOHNSON.

" Oxford, March 23, 1768."

I answered thus :

" TO MR. SAMUEL JOHNSON.

" London, 26th April, 1768.

" MY DEAR SIR,

" I HAVE received your last letter, which, though very short, and by no means complimentary, yet gave me real pleasure, because it contains these words, ' I shall be glad, very glad to see you.'—Surely you have no reason to complain of my publishing a single paragraph of one of your letters ; the temptation to it was so strong. An irrevocable grant of your friendship, and your dignifying my desire of visiting Corsica with the epithet of ' a wise and noble curiosity,' are to me more valuable than many of the grants of kings.

" But how can you bid me ' empty my head of

Corsica '? My noble-minded friend, do you not feel
for an oppressed nation bravely struggling to be free?
Consider fairly what is the case. The Corsicans never
received any kindness from the Genoese. They never
agreed to be subject to them. They owe them nothing,
and when reduced to an abject state of slavery by
force, shall they not rise in the great cause of liberty,
and break the galling yoke? And shall not every
liberal soul be warm for them? Empty my head of
Corsica! Empty it of honour, empty it of humanity,
empty it of friendship, empty it of piety. No! while
I live, Corsica and the cause of the brave islanders
shall ever employ much of my attention, shall ever
interest me in the sincerest manner.

" I am, &c.
" JAMES BOSWELL."

§ 75

When I called upon Dr. Johnson next morning, I
found him highly satisfied with his colloquial prowess
the preceding evening. "Well," said he, "we had
good talk." BOSWELL: "Yes, Sir; you tossed and
gored several persons."

§ 76

The late Alexander Earl of Eglinton, who loved wit
more than wine, and men of genius more than syco-
phants, had a great admiration of Johnson; but from the
remarkable elegance of his own manners, was, perhaps,
too delicately sensible of the roughness which sometimes appeared in Johnson's behaviour. One evening
about this time, when his Lordship did me the honour
to sup at my lodgings with Dr. Robertson and several
other men of literary distinction, he regretted that Johnson had not been educated with more refinement, and
lived more in polished society. "No, no, my Lord,"

said Signor Baretti, " do with him what you would, he would always have been a bear." "True," answered the Earl, with a smile, "but he would have been a *dancing* bear.'

To obviate all the reflections which have gone round the world to Johnson's prejudice, by applying to him the epithet of a *bear*, let me impress upon my readers a just and happy saying of my friend Goldsmith, who knew him well : " Johnson, to be sure, has a roughness in his manner ; but no man alive has a more tender heart. *He has nothing of the bear but his skin.*"

§ 77

On the 30th of September we dined together at the Mitre. I attempted to argue for the superior happiness of the savage life, upon the usual fanciful topics. JOHNSON : " Sir, there can be nothing more false. The savages have no bodily advantages beyond those of civilized men. They have not better health ; and as to care or mental uneasiness, they are not above it, but below it, like bears. No, Sir ; you are not to talk such paradox : let me have no more on't. It cannot entertain, far less can it instruct. Lord Monboddo, one of your Scotch judges, talked a great deal of such nonsense. I suffered *him ;* but I will not suffer *you.*"—BOSWELL : " But, Sir, does not Rousseau talk such nonsense ? " JOHNSON : " True, Sir, but Rousseau *knows* he is talking nonsense, and laughs at the world for staring at him." BOSWELL : " How so, Sir ? " JOHNSON : " Why, Sir, a man who talks nonsense so well, must know that he is talking nonsense. But I am *afraid* (chuckling and laughing), Monboddo does *not* know that he is talking nonsense." BOSWELL : " Is it wrong then, Sir, to affect singularity, in order to make people stare ? " JOHNSON : " Yes, if you do it by propagating error : and, indeed, it is wrong in any way. There is in human nature a general inclination to make people stare ; and every wise man has himself to cure of it, and does cure himself. If you wish to make people stare by doing better than others, why, make them stare till they stare their eyes out. But consider how easy it is to make people stare, by being absurd. I may do it by going into a drawing-room without my shoes. You remember the gentleman in ' The Spectator,' who had a commission of lunacy taken out against him for his extreme singularity, such as never wearing a wig, but a night-cap. Now, Sir, abstractedly, the night-cap was best : but, relatively, the advantage was overbalanced by his making the boys run after him."

Talking of a London life, he said, " The happiness of London is not to be conceived but by those who have been in it. I will venture to say, there is more learning and science within the circumference of ten miles from where we now sit, than in all the rest of the kingdom." BOSWELL : " The only disadvantage is the great distance at which people live from one another." JOHNSON : " Yes, Sir ; but that is occasioned by the largeness of it, which is the cause of all the other advantages." BOSWELL : " Sometimes I have been in the humour of wishing to retire to a desert." JOHNSON : " Sir, you have desert enough in Scotland."

§ 78

I had last year the pleasure of seeing Mrs. Thrale at Dr. Johnson's one morning, and had conversation enough with her to admire her talents ; and to show her that I was as Johnsonian as herself. Dr. Johnson had probably been kind enough to speak well of me, for this evening he delivered me a very polite card from Mr. Thrale and her, inviting me to Streatham.

On the 6th of October I complied with this obliging invitation, and found, at an elegant villa, six miles from town, every circumstance that can make society pleasing. Johnson, though quite at home, was yet looked up to with an awe, tempered by affection, and seemed to be equally the care of his host and hostess. I rejoiced at seeing him so happy.

He played off his wit against Scotland with a good-humoured pleasantry, which gave me, though no bigot to national prejudices, an opportunity for a little contest with him. I having said that England was obliged to us for gardeners, almost all their good gardeners being Scotsmen ;—JOHNSON : " Why, Sir, that is because gardening is much more necessary amongst you than with us, which makes so many of your people learn it. It is *all* gardening with you. Things which grow wild here, must be cultivated with great care in Scotland. Pray now (throwing himself back in his chair, and laughing), are you ever able to bring the *sloe* to perfection ? "

I boasted that we had the honour of being the first to abolish the unhospitable, troublesome, and ungracious custom of giving vails to servants. JOHNSON : " Sir, you abolished vails, because you were too poor to be able to give them."

§ 79

Dr. Johnson shunned to-night any discussion of the perplexed question of fate and free-will, which I attempted to agitate : " Sir," said he, " we *know* our will is free, and *there's* an end on't."

He honoured me with his company at dinner on the 16th of October, at my lodgings in Old Bond Street, with Sir Joshua Reynolds, Mr. Garrick, Dr. Goldsmith, Mr. Murphy, Mr. Bickerstaff, and Mr. Thomas Davies. Garrick played round him with a fond vivacity, taking hold of the breasts of his coat, and looking up in his face with a lively archness, complimented him on the good health which he seemed then to enjoy ; while the Sage, shaking his head, beheld him with a gentle complacency. One of the company not being come at the appointed hour, I proposed, as usual upon such occasions, to order dinner to be served ; adding, " Ought six people to be kept waiting for one ? " " Why, yes," answered Johnson, with a delicate humanity, " if the one will suffer more by your sitting down, than the six will do by waiting." Goldsmith, to divert the tedious minutes, strutted about, bragging of his dress, and I believe was seriously vain of it, for his mind was wonderfully prone to such impressions. " Come, come," said Garrick, " talk no more of that. You are, perhaps, the worst—eh, eh ! "—Goldsmith was eagerly attempting to interrupt him, when Garrick went on, laughing ironically, " Nay, you will always *look* like a gentleman ; but I am talking of being well or *ill drest*." " Well, let me tell you," said Goldsmith, " when my tailor brought home my bloom-coloured coat, he said, ' Sir, I have a favour to beg of you. When anybody asks you who made your clothes, be pleased to mention John Filby, at the Harrow, in Water Lane.' " JOHNSON : " Why, Sir, that was because he knew the strange colour would attract crowds to gaze at it, and thus they might hear of him, and see how well he could make a coat even of so absurd a colour."

§ 80

I mentioned to him that I had seen the execution of several convicts at Tyburn, two days before, and that none of them seemed to be under any concern. JOHNSON : " Most of them, Sir, have never thought at all." BOSWELL : " But is not the fear of death natural to man ? " JOHNSON : " So much so, Sir, that the whole of life is but keeping away the thoughts of it." He then, in a low and earnest tone, talked of his meditating upon the awful hour of his own dissolution, and in what manner he should conduct himself upon that occasion : " I know not," said he, " whether I should wish to have a friend by me, or have it all between God and myself."

Talking of our feeling for the distresses of others ;— JOHNSON : " Why, Sir, there is much noise made about it, but it is greatly exaggerated. No, Sir, we have a certain degree of feeling to prompt us to do good ; more than that, Providence does not intend. It would be misery to no purpose." BOSWELL : " But suppose now, Sir, that one of your intimate friends were apprehended for an offence for which he might be hanged." JOHNSON : " I should do what I could to bail him, and give him any other assistance ; but if he were once fairly hanged, I should not suffer." BOSWELL : " Would you eat your dinner that day, Sir ? " JOHNSON : " Yes, Sir ; and eat it as if he were eating with me. Why, there's Baretti, who is to be tried for his life to-morrow, friends have risen up for him on every side ; yet if he should be hanged, none of them will eat a slice of plum-pudding the less. Sir, that sympathetic feeling goes a very little way in depressing the mind."

I told him that I had dined lately at Foote's, who showed me a letter which he had received from Tom Davies, telling him that he had not been able to sleep, from the concern he felt on account of " *This sad affair of Baretti*," begging of him to try if he could suggest anything that might be of service ; and, at the same time, recommending to him an industrious young man who kept a pickle-shop. JOHNSON : " Ay, Sir, here you have a specimen of human sympathy ; a friend hanged, and a cucumber pickled. We know not whether Baretti or the pickle-man has kept Davies from sleep : nor does he know himself. And as to his not sleeping, Sir ; Tom Davies is a very great man ; Tom has been upon the stage, and knows how to do those things. I have not been upon the stage, and cannot do those things." BOSWELL : " I have often blamed myself, Sir, for not feeling for others as sensibly as many say they do." JOHNSON : " Sir, don't be duped by them any more. You will find these very feeling people are not very ready to do you good. They *pay* you by *feeling*."

BOSWELL : " Foote has a great deal of humour." JOHNSON : " Yes, Sir." BOSWELL : " He has a singular talent of exhibiting character." JOHNSON : " Sir, it is not a talent ; it is a vice ; it is what others abstain from. It is not comedy, which exhibits the character of a species, as that of a miser gathered from many misers : it is farce which exhibits individuals." BOSWELL : " Did not he think of exhibiting you, Sir ? " JOHNSON : " Sir, fear restrained him ; he knew I would have broken his bones. I would have saved him the trouble of cutting off a leg ; I would not have left him a leg to cut off." BOSWELL : " Pray, Sir, is not Foote an infidel ? " JOHNSON : " I do not know, Sir, that the fellow is an infidel ; but if he be an infidel, he is an infidel as a dog is an infidel ; that is to say, he has never thought upon the subject." BOSWELL : " I suppose, Sir, he has thought superficially, and seized the first notions which occurred to his mind." JOHNSON : " Why then, Sir, still he is like a dog, that snatches the piece next him. Did you never observe that dogs have not the power of comparing ? A dog will take a small bit of meat as readily as a large, when both are before him."

§ 81

I know not how so whimsical a thought came into my mind, but I asked, " If, Sir, you were shut up in a castle, and a new-born child with you, what would you do ? " JOHNSON : " Why, Sir, I should not much like my company." BOSWELL : " But would you take the trouble of rearing it ? " He seemed, as may be supposed, unwilling to pursue the subject : but upon my persevering in my question, replied, " Why yes,

Sir, I would; but I must have all conveniences. If I had no garden, I would make a shed on the roof, and take it there for fresh air. I should feed it, and wash it much, and with warm water, to please it, not with cold water to give it pain." Boswell: "But, Sir, does not heat relax?" Johnson: "Sir, you are not to imagine the water is to be very hot. I would not *coddle* the child. No, Sir, the hardy method of treating children does no good. I'll take you five children from London, who shall cuff five Highland children. Sir, a man bred in London will carry a burden, or run or wrestle, as well as a man brought up in the hardest manner in the country." Boswell: "Good living, I suppose, makes the Londoners strong." Johnson: "Why, Sir, I don't know that it does. Our chairmen from Ireland, who are as strong men as any, have been brought up upon potatoes. Quantity makes up for quality." Boswell: "Would you teach this child that I have furnished you with, anything?" Johnson: "No, I should not be apt to teach it." Boswell: "Would not you have a pleasure in teaching it?" Johnson: "No, Sir, I should *not* have a pleasure in teaching it." Boswell: "Have you not a pleasure in teaching men?—*There* I have you. You have the same pleasure in teaching men, that I should have in teaching children." Johnson: "Why, something about that."

§ 82

Boswell: "But, to consider the state of our own country;—does not throwing a number of farms into one hand hurt population?" Johnson: "Why no, Sir; the same quantity of food being produced, will be consumed by the same number of mouths, though the people may be disposed of in different ways. We see, if corn be dear, and butchers' meat cheap, the farmers all apply themselves to the raising of corn, till it becomes plentiful and cheap, and then butchers' meat becomes dear ; so that an equality is always preserved. No, Sir, let fanciful men do as they will, depend upon it, it is difficult to disturb the system of life." Boswell : " But, Sir, is it not a very bad thing for landlords to oppress their tenants by raising their rents ? " Johnson : " Very bad. But, Sir, it never can have any general influence ; it may distress some individuals. For, consider this : landlords cannot do without tenants. Now tenants will not give more for land than land is worth. If they can make more of their money by keeping a shop, or any other way, they'll do it, and so oblige landlords to let land come back to a reasonable rent, in order that they may get tenants. Land, in England, is an article of commerce. A tenant who pays his landlord his rent, thinks himself no more obliged to him than you think yourself obliged to a man in whose shop you buy a piece of goods. He knows the landlord does not let him have his land for less than he can get from others, in the same manner as the shopkeeper sells his goods. No shopkeeper sells a yard of riband for sixpence when sevenpence is the current price." Boswell : " But, Sir, is it not better that tenants should be dependent on landlords ? " Johnson : " Why, Sir, as there are many more tenants than landlords, perhaps strictly speaking, we should wish not. But if you please you may let your lands cheap, and so get the value, part in money and part in homage. I should agree with you in that." Boswell : " So, Sir, you laugh at schemes of political improvement." Johnson : " Why, Sir, most schemes of political improvement are very laughable things."

§ 83

I had hired a Bohemian as my servant while I remained in London, and being much pleased with him, I asked Dr. Johnson whether his being a Roman Catholic should prevent my taking him with me to

Scotland. JOHNSON : " Why no, Sir. If *he* has no objection, you can have none." BOSWELL : " So, Sir, you are no great enemy to the Roman Catholic religion." JOHNSON : " No more, Sir, than to the Presbyterian religion." BOSWELL : " You are joking." JOHNSON : " No, Sir, I really think so. Nay, Sir, of the two, I prefer the Popish." BOSWELL : " How so, Sir ? " JOHNSON : " Why, Sir, the Presbyterians have no church, no apostolical ordination." BOSWELL : " And do you think that absolutely essential, Sir ? " JOHNSON : " Why, Sir, as it was an apostolic institution, I think it is dangerous to be without it. And, Sir, the Presbyterians have no public worship : they have no form of prayer in which they know they are to join. They go to hear a man pray, and are to judge whether they will join with him." BOSWELL : " But, Sir, their doctrine is the same with that of the Church of England. Their Confession of Faith, and the Thirty-Nine Articles, contain the same points, even the doctrine of predestination." JOHNSON : " Why yes, Sir ; predestination was a part of the clamour of the times, so it is mentioned in our articles, but with as little positiveness as could be." BOSWELL : " Is it necessary, Sir, to believe all the thirty-nine articles ? " JOHNSON : " Why, Sir, that is a question which has been much agitated. Some have thought it necessary that they should all be believed ; others have considered them to be only articles of peace, that is to say, you are not to preach against them." BOSWELL : " It appears to me, Sir, that predestination, or what is equivalent to it, cannot be avoided, if we hold a universal prescience in the Deity." JOHNSON : " Why, Sir, does not GOD every day see things going on without preventing them ? " BOSWELL : " True, Sir, but if a thing be *certainly* foreseen, it must be fixed, and cannot happen otherwise ; and if we apply this consideration to the human mind, there is no free will, nor do I see how prayer can be of any avail." He mentioned Dr. Clarke, and Bishop Bramhall on Liberty and Necessity, and bid me read South's " Sermons on Prayer " ; but avoided the question which has excruciated philosophers and divines beyond any other. I did not press it farther, when I perceived that he was displeased, and shrunk from any abridgment of an attribute usually ascribed to the Divinity, however irreconcilable in its full extent with the grand system of moral government. His supposed orthodoxy here cramped the vigorous powers of his understanding. He was confined by a chain which early imagination and long habit made him think massy and strong, but which, had he ventured to try, he could at once have snapt asunder.

I proceeded : " What do you think, Sir, of Purgatory, as believed by the Roman Catholics ? " Johnson : " Why, Sir, it is a very harmless doctrine. They are of opinion that the generality of mankind are neither so obstinately wicked as to deserve everlasting punishment, nor so good as to merit being admitted into the society of blessed spirits ; and therefore that God is graciously pleased to allow of a middle state, where they may be purified by certain degrees of suffering. You see, Sir, there is nothing unreasonable in this." Boswell : " But then, Sir, their masses for the dead ? " Johnson : " Why, Sir, if it be once established that there are souls in purgatory, it is as proper to pray for *them*, as for our brethren of mankind who are yet in this life." Boswell : " The idolatry of the Mass ? " Johnson : " Sir, there is no idolatry in the Mass. They believe God to be there, and they adore him." Boswell : " The worship of Saints ? " Johnson : " Sir, they do not worship saints ; they invoke them ; they only ask their prayers. I am talking all this time of the *doctrines* of the Church of Rome. I grant you that in *practice*, Purgatory is made a lucrative imposition, and that the people do become idolatrous as they recommend themselves to the tute-

lary protection of particular saints. I think their giving
the sacrament only in one kind is criminal, because it
is contrary to the express institution of CHRIST, and
I wonder how the Council of Trent admitted it."
BOSWELL: "Confession?" JOHNSON: "Why, I don't
know but that is a good thing. The Scripture says,
'Confess your faults one to another,' and the priests confess as well as the laity. Then it must be considered
that their absolution is only upon repentance, and often
upon penance also. You think your sins may be for-
given without penance, upon repentance alone."

I thus ventured to mention all the common objections against the Roman Catholic Church, that I might
hear so great a man upon them. What he said is here
accurately recorded. But it is not improbable that if
one had taken the other side, he might have reasoned
differently.

§ 84

On Thursday, April 9, I called on him to beg he
would go and dine with me at the Mitre tavern. He
had resolved not to dine with me at all this day, I
know not for what reason; and I was so unwilling to
be deprived of his company, that I was content to
submit to suffer a want, which was at first somewhat
painful, but he soon made me forget it; and a man is
always pleased with himself, when he finds his intellectual inclinations predominate.

He observed, that to reason philosophically on the
nature of prayer, was very unprofitable.

Talking of ghosts, he said he knew one friend, who
was an honest man and a sensible man, who told him
he had seen a ghost; old Mr. Edward Cave, the printer
at St. John's Gate. He said Mr. Cave did not like to
talk of it, and seemed to be in great horror whenever it
was mentioned. BOSWELL: "Pray, Sir, what did he
say was the appearance?" JOHNSON: "Why, Sir,
something of a shadowy being."

(2,601)

7

§ 85

The subject of ghosts being introduced, Johnson repeated what he had told me of a friend of his, an honest man, and a man of sense, having asserted to him, that he had seen an apparition. Goldsmith told us, he was assured by his brother, the Reverend Mr. Goldsmith, that he also had seen one. General Oglethorpe told us that Prendergast, an officer in the Duke of Marlborough's army, had mentioned to many of his friends that he should die on a particular day: that upon that day a battle took place with the French ; that after it was over, and Prendergast was still alive, his brother officers, while they were yet in the field, jestingly asked him, where was his prophecy now. Prendergast gravely answered, " I shall die, notwithstanding what you see." Soon afterwards, there came a shot from a French battery, to which the orders for a cessation of arms had not yet reached, and he was killed upon the spot. Colonel Cecil, who took possession of his effects, found in his pocket-book the following solemn entry : [Here the date.] " Dreamt —or———— Sir John Friend meets me : " (here the very day on which he was killed was mentioned). Prendergast had been connected with Sir John Friend, who was executed for high-treason. General Oglethorpe said, he was with Colonel Cecil, when Pope came and inquired into the truth of this story, which made a great noise at the time, and was then confirmed by the Colonel.

§ 86

I talked of the recent expulsion of six students from the University of Oxford, who were Methodists, and would not desist from publicly praying and exhorting. JOHNSON : " Sir, that expulsion was extremely just and proper. What have they to do at a University, who are not willing to be taught, but will presume to teach ? Where is religion to be learnt, but at a University ? Sir, they were examined, and found to be mighty ignorant fellows." BOSWELL : " But, was it not hard, Sir, to expel them, for I am told they were good beings ? " JOHNSON : " I believe they might be good beings ; but they were not fit to be in the University of Oxford. A cow is a very good animal in the field ; but we turn her out of a garden." Lord Elibank used to repeat this as an illustration uncommonly happy.

Desirous of calling Johnson forth to talk, and exercise his wit, though I should myself be the object of it, I resolutely ventured to undertake the defence of convivial indulgence in wine, though he was not to-night in the most genial humour. After urging the common plausible topics, I at last had recourse to the maxim, *in vino veritas*, a man who is well warmed with wine will speak truth. JOHNSON : " Why, Sir, that may be an argument for drinking, if you suppose men in general to be liars. But, Sir, I would not keep company with a fellow, who lies as long as he is sober, and whom you must make drunk before you can get a word of truth out of him."

Mr. Langton told us, he was about to establish a school upon his estate, but it had been suggested to him that it might have a tendency to make the people less industrious. JOHNSON : " No, Sir. While learning to read and write is a distinction, the few who have that distinction may be the less inclined to work ; but when everybody learns to read and write, it is no longer a distinction. A man who has a laced waistcoat is too fine a man to work ; but if everybody had laced waistcoats, we should have people working in laced waistcoats. There are no people whatever more industrious, none who work more, than our manufacturers ; yet they have all learnt to read and write. Sir, you must not neglect doing a thing immediately good, from fear of remote evil ;—from fear of its being abused. A man who has candles may sit up too late, which he would not do if he had not candles; but nobody will deny that the art of making candles, by which light is continued to us beyond the time that the sun gives us light, is a valuable art, and ought to be preserved." BOSWELL : " But, Sir, would it not be better to follow nature; and go to bed and rise just as nature gives us light or witholds it ? " JOHNSON : " No, Sir; for then we should have no kind of equality in the partition of our time between sleeping and waking. It would be very different in different seasons and in different places. In some of the northern parts of Scotland how little light is there in the depth of winter ! "

§ 87

A learned gentleman who in the course of conversation wished to inform us of this simple fact, that the counsel upon the circuit at Shrewsbury were much bitten by fleas, took, I suppose, seven or eight minutes in relating it circumstantially. He in a plenitude of phrase told us that large bales of woollen cloth were lodged in the town-hall ;—that by reason of this, fleas nestled there in prodigious numbers; that the lodgings of the counsel were near the town-hall ;—and that those little animals moved from place to place with wonderful agility. Johnson sat in great impatience till the gentleman had finished his tedious narrative, and then burst out (playfully however), " It is a pity, Sir, that you have not seen a lion ; for a flea has taken you such a time, that a lion must have served you a twelvemonth."

He would not allow Scotland to derive any credit from Lord Mansfield ; for he was educated in England. " Much," said he, " may be made of a Scotchman, if he be *caught* young."

§ 88

On the 9th of April, being Good Friday, I breakfasted with him on tea and cross-buns; *Doctor* Levett, as Frank called him, making the tea. He carried me with him to the church of St. Clement Danes, where he had his seat; and his behaviour was, as I had imaged to myself, solemnly devout. I never shall forget the tremulous earnestness with which he pronounced the awful petition in the Litany: " In the hour of death, and in the day of judgment, good LORD deliver us."

We went to church both in the morning and evening. In the interval between the two services we did not dine; but he read in the Greek New Testament, and I turned over several of his books.

§ 89

To my great surprise he asked me to dine with him on Easter-day. I never supposed that he had a dinner at his house; for I had not then heard of any one of his friends having been entertained at his table. He told me, " I generally have a meat-pie on Sunday: it is baked at a public oven, which is very properly allowed, because one man can attend it; and thus the advantage is obtained of not keeping servants from church to dress dinners."

April 11, being Easter Sunday, after having attended Divine Service at St. Paul's, I repaired to Dr. Johnson's. I had gratified my curiosity much in dining with JEAN JACQUES ROUSSEAU, while he lived in the wilds of Neufchatel: I had as great a curiosity to dine with DR. SAMUEL JOHNSON, in the dusky recess of a court in Fleet Street. I supposed we should scarcely have knives and forks, and only some strange, uncouth, ill-drest dish; but I found everything in very good order. We had no other company but Mrs. Williams and a young woman whom I did not know.

As a dinner here was considered as a singular phenomenon, and as I was frequently interrogated on the subject, my readers may perhaps be desirous to know our bill of fare. Foote, I remember, in allusion to Francis, the *negro*, was willing to suppose that our repast was *black broth*. But the fact was that we had a very good soup, a boiled leg of lamb and spinach, a veal pie, and a rice pudding.

§ 90

I again solicited him to communicate to me the particulars of his early life. He said, " You shall have them all for twopence. I hope you shall know a great deal more of me before you write my Life." He mentioned to me this day many circumstances, which I wrote down when I went home, and have interwoven in the former part of this narrative.

On Tuesday, April 13, he and Dr. Goldsmith and I dined at General Oglethorpe's. Goldsmith expatiated on the common topic, that the race of our people was degenerated, and that this was owing to luxury. JOHNSON : " Sir, in the first place, I doubt the fact. I believe there are as many tall men in England now, as ever there were. But, secondly, supposing the stature of our people to be diminished, that is not owing to luxury ; for, Sir, consider to how very small a proportion of our people luxury can reach. Our soldiery, surely, are not luxurious, who live on sixpence a day ; and the same remark will apply to almost all the other classes. Luxury, so far as it reaches the poor, will do good to the race of people ; it will strengthen and multiply them. Sir, no nation was ever hurt by luxury ; for, as I said before, it can reach but to a very few. I admit that the great increase of commerce and manufactures hurts the military spirit of a people ; because it produces a competition for something else than martial honours,—a competition for riches. It also hurts the bodies of the people ; for you will observe, there is no man who works at any particular trade, but you may know him from his appearance to do so. One part or the other of his body being more used than the rest, he is in some degree deformed : but, Sir, that is not luxury. A tailor sits cross-legged ; but that is not luxury." GOLDSMITH : " Come, you're just going to the same place by another road." JOHNSON : " Nay, Sir, I say that is not *luxury*. Let us take a walk from Charing Cross to Whitechapel, through, I suppose, the greatest series of shops in the world, what is there in any of these shops (if you except gin-shops) that can do any human being any harm ? " GOLDSMITH : " Well, Sir, I'll accept your challenge. The very next shop to Northumberland House is a pickle-shop." JOHNSON : " Well, Sir : do we not know that a maid can in one afternoon make pickles sufficient to serve a whole family for a year ? nay, that five pickle-shops can serve all the kingdom ? Besides, Sir, there is no harm done to anybody by the making of pickles, or the eating of pickles."

We drank tea with the ladies ; and Goldsmith sung Tony Lumpkin's song in his comedy, " She Stoops to Conquer," and a very pretty one, to an Irish tune, which he had designed for Miss Hardcastle, but as Mrs. Bulkeley, who played the part, could not sing, it was left out. He afterwards wrote it down for me, by which means it was preserved, and now appears amongst his poems. Dr. Johnson, in his way home, stopped at my lodgings in Piccadilly, and sat with me, drinking tea a second time, till a late hour.

I told him that Mrs. Macaulay said, she wondered how he could reconcile his political principles with his moral ; his notions of inequality and subordination with wishing well to the happiness of all mankind, who might live so agreeably, had they all their portions of land, and none to domineer over another. JOHNSON :

" Why, Sir, I reconcile my principles very well, because mankind are happier in a state of inequality and subordination. Were they to be in this pretty state of equality, they would soon degenerate into brutes ;— they would become Monboddo's nation ;—their tails would grow. Sir, all would be losers, were all to work for all :—they would have no intellectual improvement. All intellectual improvement arises from leisure : all leisure arises from one working for another."

§ 91

The modes of living in different countries, and the various views with which men travel in quest of new scenes, having been talked of, a learned gentleman who holds a considerable office in the law, expatiated on the happiness of a savage life ; and mentioned an instance of an officer who had actually lived for some time in the wilds of America, of whom, when in that state, he quoted this reflection with an air of admiration, as if it had been deeply philosophical : " Here am I, free and unrestrained, amidst the rude magnificence of Nature, with this Indian woman by my side, and this gun, with which I can procure food when I want it : what more can be desired for human happiness ? " It did not require much sagacity to foresee that such a sentiment would not be permitted to pass without due animadversion. JOHNSON : " Do not allow yourself, Sir, to be imposed upon by such gross absurdity. It is sad stuff ; it is brutish. If a bull could speak, he might as well exclaim,—Here am I with this cow and this grass ; what being can enjoy greater felicity ? "

§ 92

On Friday, April 30, I dined with him at Mr. Beauclerk's, where were Lord Charlemont, Sir Joshua Reynolds, and some more members of the LITERARY CLUB, whom he had obligingly invited to meet me, as I was this evening to be balloted for as candidate for admission into that distinguished society. Johnson had done me the honour to propose me, and Beauclerk was very zealous for me.

Goldsmith being mentioned; JOHNSON: " It is amazing how little Goldsmith knows. He seldom comes where he is not more ignorant than any one else." SIR JOSHUA REYNOLDS: " Yet there is no man whose company is more liked." JOHNSON: " To be sure, Sir. When people find a man of the most distinguished abilities as a writer, their inferior while he is with them, it must be highly gratifying to them. What Goldsmith comically says of himself is very true, —he always gets the better when he argues alone; meaning, that he is master of a subject in his study, and can write well upon it ; but when he comes into company, grows confused, and unable to talk. Take him as a poet, his ' Traveller ' is a very fine performance ; ay, and so is his ' Deserted Village,' were it not sometimes too much the echo of his ' Traveller.' Whether, indeed, we take him as a poet, as a comic writer, or as an historian, he stands in the first class."

§ 93

JOHNSON : " I remember once being with Goldsmith in Westminster Abbey. While we surveyed the Poets' Corner, I said to him,

' Forsitan et nostrum nomen miscebitur istis.'   (Ovid, *Art. Am.* iii. 339.)

When we got to Temple Bar he stopped me, pointed to the heads upon it, and slily whispered me,

' Forsitan et nostrum nomen miscebitur ISTIS.' "

JOHNSON praised John Bunyan highly. " His ' Pil-grim's Progress ' has great merit, both for invention, imagination, and the conduct of the story ; and it has had the best evidence of its merit, the general and continued approbation of mankind. Few books, I believe, have had a more extensive sale. It is remark-able, that it begins very much like the poem of Dante ; yet there was no translation of Dante when Bunyan wrote. There is reason to think that he had read Spenser."

§ 94

The gentlemen went away to their club, and I was left at Beauclerk's till the fate of my election should be announced to me. I sat in a state of anxiety which even the charming conversation of Lady Di Beau-clerk could not entirely dissipate. In a short time I received the agreeable intelligence that I was chosen. I hastened to the place of meeting, and was introduced to such a society as can seldom be found. Mr. Ed-mund Burke, whom I then saw for the first time, and whose splendid talents had long made me ardently wish for his acquaintance ; Dr. Nugent, Mr. Garrick, Dr. Goldsmith, Mr. (afterwards Sir William) Jones, and the company with whom I had dined. Upon my entrance, Johnson placed himself behind a chair, on which he leaned as on a desk or pulpit, and with humorous formality gave me a *charge*, pointing out the conduct expected from me as a good member of this club.

§ 95

BOSWELL : " Pray, Mr. Dilly, how does Dr. Le-land's ' History of Ireland ' sell ? " JOHNSON (burst-ing forth with a generous indignation) : " The Irish are in a most unnatural state ; for we see there the minority prevailing over the majority. There is no instance, even in the ten persecutions, of such severity as that which the Protestants of Ireland have exercised against the Catholics. Did we tell them we have conquered them, it would be above board : to punish them by confiscation and other penalties, as rebels, was monstrous injustice. King William was not their lawful sovereign : he had not been acknowledged by the Parliament of Ireland, when they appeared in arms against him."

I here suggested something favourable of the Roman Catholics. TOPLADY : " Does not their invocation of saints suppose omnipresence in their saints ? " JOHNSON : " No, Sir ; it supposes only pluri-presence ; and when spirits are divested of matter, it seems probable that they should see with more extent than when in an embodied state. There is, therefore, no approach to an invasion of any of the divine attributes, in the invocation of saints. But I think it is will-worship, and presumption. I see no command for it, and therefore think it safer not to practise it."

He and Mr. Langton and I went together to THE CLUB, where we found Mr. Burke, Mr. Garrick, and some other members, and amongst them our friend Goldsmith, who sat silently brooding over Johnson's reprimand to him after dinner. Johnson perceived this, and said aside to some of us : " I'll make Goldsmith forgive me ; " and then called to him in a loud voice, " Dr. Goldsmith,—something passed to-day where you and I dined ; I ask your pardon." Goldsmith answered placidly, " It must be much from you, Sir, that I take ill." And so at once the difference was over, and they were on as easy terms as ever, and Goldsmith rattled away as usual.

§ 96

On Monday, May 9, as I was to set out on my return to Scotland next morning, I was desirous to see as

much of Dr. Johnson as I could.   But I first called on
Goldsmith to take leave of him.   The jealousy and
envy which, though possessed of many most amiable
qualities, he frankly avowed, broke out violently at
this interview.   Upon another occasion, when Goldsmith confessed himself to be of an envious disposition,
I contended with Johnson that we ought not to be
angry with him, he was so candid in owning it.   " Nay,
Sir," said Johnson, "we must be angry that a man has
such a superabundance of an odious quality, that he
cannot keep it within his own breast, but it boils
over."   In my opinion, however, Goldsmith had not
more of it than other people have, but only talked of
it freely.

He now seemed very angry that Johnson was going
to be a traveller ; said " He would be a dead weight
for me to carry, and that I should never be able to lug
him along through the Highlands and Hebrides."   Nor
would he patiently allow me to enlarge upon Johnson's wonderful abilities ; but exclaimed, " Is he like
Burke, who winds into a subject like a serpent ? "
" But," said I, " Johnson is the Hercules who strangled
serpents in his cradle."

I dined with Dr. Johnson at General Paoli's.   He
was obliged, by indisposition, to leave the company
early ; he appointed me, however, to meet him in the
evening at Mr. (now Sir Robert) Chambers's in the
Temple, where he accordingly came, though he continued to be very ill.   Chambers, as is common on
such occasions, prescribed various remedies to him.
Johnson (fretted by pain) : " Pr'ythee don't teaze
me.   Stay till I am well, and then you shall tell me
how to cure myself."   He grew better, and talked
with a noble enthusiasm of keeping up the representation of respectable families.   His zeal on this subject
was a circumstance in his character exceedingly remarkable, when it is considered that he himself had
no pretensions to blood.   I heard him once say, " I

have great merit in being zealous for subordination and the honours of birth; for I can hardly tell who was my grandfather." He maintained the dignity and propriety of male succession, in opposition to the opinion of one of our friends, who had that day employed Mr. Chambers to draw his will, devising his estate to his three sisters, in preference to a remote heir male. Johnson called them " three *dowdies*," and said, with as high a spirit as the boldest baron in the most perfect days of the feudal system : " An ancient estate should always go to males. It is mighty foolish to let a stranger have it because he marries your daughter, and takes your name. As for an estate newly acquired by trade, you may give it, if you will, to the dog *Towser*, and let him keep his *own* name."

I have known him at times exceedingly diverted at what seemed to others a very small sport. He now laughed immoderately, without any reason that we could perceive, at our friend's making his will ; called him the *testator*, and added : " I dare say, he thinks he has done a mighty thing, He won't stay till he gets home to his seat in the country, to produce this wonderful deed : he'll call up the landlord of the first inn on the road ; and, after a suitable preface upon mortality and the uncertainty of life, will tell him that he should not delay making his will ; and here, Sir, will he say, is my will, which I have just made, with the assistance of one of the ablest lawyers in the kingdom ; and he will read it to him (laughing all the time). He believes he has made this will ; but he did not make it : you, Chambers, made it for him. I trust you have had more conscience than to make him say, ' being of sound understanding ; ' ha, ha, ha ! I hope he has left me a legacy. I'd have his will turned into verse, like a ballad."

In this playful manner did he run on, exulting in his own pleasantry, which certainly was not such as might be expected from the author of the " Rambler," but which is here preserved, that my readers may be acquainted even with the slightest occasional characteristics of so eminent a man.

Mr. Chambers did not by any means relish this jocularity upon a matter of which *pars magna fuit,* and seemed impatient till he got rid of us. Johnson could not stop his merriment, but continued it all the way till he got without the Temple-gate. He then burst into such a fit of laughter, that he appeared to be almost in a convulsion ; and, in order to support himself, laid hold of one of the posts at the side of the foot pavement, and sent forth peals so loud, that in the silence of the night his voice seemed to resound from Temple Bar to Fleet Ditch.

This most ludicrous exhibition of the awful, melancholy, and venerable Johnson, happened well to counteract the feelings of sadness which I used to experience when parting with him for a considerable time. I accompanied him to his door, where he gave me his blessing.

§ 97

On the 5th of March I wrote to him, requesting his counsel whether I should this spring come to London. I stated to him on the one hand some pecuniary embarrassments, which, together with my wife's situation at that time, made me hesitate ; and, on the other, the pleasure and improvement which my annual visit to the metropolis always afforded me ; and particularly mentioned a peculiar satisfaction which I experienced in celebrating the festival of Easter in St. Paul's Cathedral ; that to my fancy it appeared like going up to Jerusalem at the feast of the Passover; and that the strong devotion which I felt on that occasion diffused its influence on my mind through the rest of the year.

" TO JAMES BOSWELL, ESQ.

[Not dated, but written about the 15th of March.]

" DEAR SIR,

" I AM ashamed to think that since I received your letter I have passed so many days without answering it.

" I think there is no great difficulty in resolving your doubts. The reasons for which you are inclined to visit London, are, I think, not of sufficient strength to answer the objections. That you should delight to come once a year to the fountain of intelligence and pleasure, is very natural ; but both information and pleasure must be regulated by propriety. Pleasure, which cannot be obtained but by unseasonable or unsuitable expense, must always end in pain ; and pleasure, which must be enjoyed at the expense of another's pain, can never be such as a worthy mind can fully delight in.

" What improvement you might gain by coming to London, you may easily supply or easily compensate, by enjoining yourself some particular study at home, or opening some new avenue to information. Edinburgh is not yet exhausted ; and I am sure you will find no pleasure here which can deserve either that you should anticipate any part of your future fortune, or that you should condemn yourself and your lady to penurious frugality for the rest of the year.

" I need not tell you what regard you owe to Mrs. Boswell's entreaties ; or how much you ought to study the happiness of her who studies yours with so much diligence, and of whose kindness you enjoy such good effects. Life cannot subsist in society but by reciprocal concessions. She permitted you to ramble last year, you must permit her now to keep you at home.

" Your last reason is so serious, that I am unwilling to oppose it. Yet you must remember, that your image of worshipping once a year in a certain place, in imitation of the Jews, is but a comparison ; and *simile non est idem ;* if the annual resort to Jerusalem was a duty to the Jews, it was a duty because it was commanded ; and you have no such command, therefore no such duty. It may be dangerous to receive too readily, and indulge too fondly, opinions, from which, perhaps, no pious mind is wholly disengaged, of local sanctity and local devotion. You know what strange effects they have produced over a great part of the Christian world. I am now writing, and you, when you read this, are reading under the Eye of Omnipresence.

" To what degree fancy is to be admitted into religious offices, it would require much deliberation to determine. I am far from intending totally to exclude it. Fancy is a faculty bestowed by our Creator, and it is reasonable that all His gifts should be used to His glory, that all our faculties should co-operate in His worship ; but they are to co-operate according to the will of Him that gave them, according to the order which His wisdom has established. As ceremonies prudential or convenient are less obligatory than positive ordinances, as bodily worship is only the token to others or ourselves of mental adoration, so Fancy is always to act in subordination to Reason. We may take Fancy for a companion, but must follow Reason as our guide. We may allow Fancy to suggest certain ideas in certain places ; but Reason must always be heard, when she tells us, that those ideas and those places have no natural or necessary relation. When we enter a church we habitually recall to mind the duty of adoration, but we must not omit adoration for want of a temple ; because we know, and ought to remember, that the Universal Lord is everywhere present ; and that, therefore, to come to Iona, or to

Jerusalem, though it may be useful, cannot be necessary.

" Thus I have answered your letter, and have not answered it negligently. I love you too well to be careless when you are serious.

" I think I shall be very diligent next week about our travels, which I have too long neglected. I am, dear Sir, your most, &c.

" SAM. JOHNSON.

" Compliments to Madam and Miss."

§ 98

What words were used by Mr. Macpherson in his letter to the venerable Sage, I have never heard ; but they are generally said to have been of a nature very different from the language of literary contest. Dr. Johnson's answer appeared in the newspapers of the day, and has since been frequently republished ; but not with perfect accuracy. I give it as dictated to me by himself, written down in his presence, and authenticated by a note in his own handwriting. " *This, I think, is a true copy.*"

" MR. JAMES MACPHERSON,

" I received your foolish and impudent letter. Any violence offered me I shall do my best to repel ; and what I cannot do for myself, the law shall do for me. I hope I shall not be deterred from detecting what I think a cheat by the menaces of a ruffian.

" What would you have me retract ? I thought your book an imposture ; I think it an imposture still. For this opinion I have given my reasons to the public, which I here dare you to refute. Your rage I defy. Your abilities, since your Homer, are not so formidable : and what I hear of your morals inclines me to pay regard not to what you shall say, but to what you shall prove. You may print this if you will.

" SAM. JOHNSON."

Mr. Macpherson little knew the character of Dr. Johnson, if he supposed that he could be easily intimidated ; for no man was ever more remarkable for personal courage. He had, indeed, an awful dread of death, or rather, " of something after death ; " and what rational man, who seriously thinks of quitting all that he has ever known, and going into a new and unknown state of being, can be without that dread ? But his fear was from reflection ; his courage natural. His fear, in that one instance, was the result of philosophical and religious consideration. He feared death, but he feared nothing else, not even what might occasion death. Many instances of his resolution may be mentioned. One day at Mr. Beauclerk's house in the country, when two large dogs were fighting, he went up to them, and beat them till they separated ; and at another time, when told of the danger there was that a gun might burst if charged with many balls, he put in six or seven, and fired it off against a wall. Mr. Langton told me, that when they were swimming together near Oxford, he cautioned Dr. Johnson against a pool, which was reckoned particularly dangerous ; upon which Johnson directly swam into it. He told me himself that one night he was attacked in the street by four men, to whom he would not yield, but kept them all at bay, till the watch came up, and carried both him and them to the round-house. In the play-house at Lichfield, as Mr. Garrick informed me, Johnson having for a moment quitted a chair which was placed for him between the side-scenes, a gentleman took possession of it, and when Johnson on his return civilly demanded his seat, rudely refused to give it up ; upon which Johnson laid hold of it, and tossed him and the chair into the pit. Foote, who so successfully revived the old comedy by exhibiting living characters, had resolved to imitate Johnson on the stage, expecting great profits from his ridicule of so celebrated a man.

Johnson being informed of his intention, and being at dinner at Mr. Thomas Davies's the bookseller, from whom I had the story, he asked Mr. Davies, " What was the common price of an oak stick ; " and being answered sixpence, " Why then, Sir," said he, " give me leave to send your servant to purchase me a shilling one. I'll have a double quantity ; for I am told Foote means to *take me off,* as he calls it, and I am determined the fellow shall not do it with impunity." Davies took care to acquaint Foote of this, which effectually checked the wantonness of the mimic. Mr. Macpherson's menaces made Johnson provide himself with the same implement of defence ; and had he been attacked, I have no doubt that, old as he was, he would have made his corporal prowess be felt as much as his intellectual.

§ 99

On Tuesday, March 21, I arrived in London ; and on repairing to Dr. Johnson's before dinner, found him in his study, sitting with Mr. Peter Garrick, the elder brother of David, strongly resembling him in countenance and voice, but of more sedate and placid manners. Johnson informed me, that though Mr. Beauclerk was in great pain, it was hoped he was not in danger, and that he now wished to consult Dr. Heberden, to try the effect of a " *new understanding.*" Both at this interview, and in the evening at Mr. Thrale's, where he and Mr. Peter Garrick and I met again, he was vehement on the subject of the Ossian controversy ; observing : " We do not know that there are any ancient Erse manuscripts ; and we have no other reason to disbelieve that there are men with three heads, but that we do not know that there are any such men." He also was outrageous, upon his supposition that my countrymen " loved Scotland better than truth," saying, " All of them,—nay, not all,—but *droves* of them, would come up, and attest

anything for the honour of Scotland." He also persevered in his wild allegation, that he questioned if
there was a tree between Edinburgh and the English
border older than himself. I assured him he was mistaken, and suggested that the proper punishment
would be that he should receive a stripe at every tree
above a hundred years old, that was found within
that space. He laughed, and said, " I believe I might
submit to it for a *baubee.*"

The doubts which, in my correspondence with him,
I had ventured to state as to the justice and wisdom
of the conduct of Great Britain towards the American
colonies, while I at the same time requested that he
would enable me to inform myself upon that mo-
mentous subject, he had altogether disregarded ; and
had recently published a pamphlet, entitled, " Taxation no Tyranny ; an answer to the Resolutions and
Address of the American Congress."

He had long before indulged most unfavourable
sentiments of our fellow-subjects in America. For,
as early as 1769, I was told by Dr. John Campbell,
that he had said of them, " Sir, they are a race of
convicts, and ought to be thankful for anything we
allow them short of hanging."

Of this performance I avoided to talk with him ;
for I had now formed a clear and settled opinion, that
the people of America were well warranted to resist
a claim that their fellow-subjects in the mother-
country should have the entire command of their
fortunes, by taxing them without their own consent ;
and the extreme violence which it breathed, appeared
to me so unsuitable to the mildness of a Christian
philosopher, and so directly opposite to the principles
of peace which he had so beautifully recommended in
his pamphlet respecting Falkland's Islands, that I was
sorry to see him appear in so unfavourable a light.
Besides, I could not perceive in it that agility of argument, or that felicity of expression, for which he was,

upon other occasions, so eminent. Positive assertion, sarcastical severity, and extravagant ridicule, which he himself reprobated as a test of truth, were united in this rhapsody.

§ 100

Mr. Strahan talked of launching into the great ocean of London, in order to have a chance for rising into eminence ; and, observing that many men were kept back from trying their fortunes there, because they were born to a competency, said, " Small certainties are the bane of men of talents ; " which Johnson confirmed. Mr. Strahan put Johnson in mind of a remark which he had made to him : " There are few ways in which a man can be more innocently employed than in getting money." " The more one thinks of this," said Strahan, " the juster it will appear."

Mr. Strahan had taken a poor boy from the country as an apprentice, upon Johnson's recommendation. Johnson having inquired after him, said, " Mr. Strahan, let me have five guineas on account, and I'll give this boy one. Nay, if a man recommends a boy, and does nothing for him, it is sad work. Call him down."

I followed him into the court-yard, behind Mr. Strahan's house ; and there I had a proof of what I had heard him profess, that he talked alike to all. " Some people tell you that they let themselves down to the capacity of their hearers. I never do that. I speak uniformly, in as intelligible a manner as I can."

" Well, my boy, how do you go on ? "—" Pretty well, Sir ; but they are afraid I an't strong enough for some parts of the business." JOHNSON : " Why, I shall be sorry for it ; for when you consider with how little mental power and corporeal labour a printer can get a guinea a week, it is a very desirable occupation for you. Do you hear—take all the pains you

can ; and if this does not do, we must think of some
other way of life for you.　There's a guinea."

Here was one of the many, many instances of his
active benevolence.　At the same time, the slow and
sonorous solemnity with which, while he bent himself down, he addressed a little thick, short-legged boy,
contrasted with the boy's awkwardness and awe,
could not but excite some ludicrous emotions.

§ 101

On Friday, March 31, I supped with him and some
friends at a tavern.　One of the company attempted,
with too much forwardness, to rally him on his late
appearance at the theatre ; but had reason to repent
of his temerity.　" Why, Sir, did you go to Mrs.
Abington's benefit ?　Did you see ? " JOHNSON :
" No, Sir."　" Did you hear ? " JOHNSON : " No, Sir."
" Why then, Sir, did you go ? " JOHNSON : " Because,
Sir, she is a favourite of the public ; and when the
public cares the thousandth part for you that it does
for her, I will go to your benefit too."

§ 102

I talked of the cheerfulness of Fleet Street, owing
to the constant quick succession of people which we
perceive passing through it.　JOHNSON : " Why, Sir,
Fleet Street has a very animated appearance ; but I
think the full tide of human existence is at Charing
Cross."

He made the common remark on the unhappiness
which men who have led a busy life experience, when
they retire in expectation of enjoying themselves at
ease, and that they generally languish for want of their
habitual occupation, and wish to return to it.　He
mentioned as strong an instance of this as can well

be imagined. " An eminent tallow-chandler in London, who had acquired a considerable fortune, gave up the trade in favour of his foreman, and went to live at a country-house near town. He soon grew weary, and paid frequent visits to his old shop, where he desired they might let him know their *melting-days*, and he would come and assist them ; which he accordingly did. Here, Sir, was a man, to whom the most disgusting circumstance in the business to which he had been used, was a relief from idleness."

§ 103

" The Beggar's Opera," and the common question whether it was pernicious in its effects, having been introduced ;—JOHNSON : " As to this matter, which has been very much contested, I myself am of opinion that more influence has been ascribed to ' The Beggar's Opera,' than it in reality ever had ; for I do not believe that any man was ever made a rogue by being present at its representation. At the same time I do not deny that it may have some influence, by making the character of a rogue familiar, and in some degree pleasing." Then collecting himself, as it were, to give a heavy stroke : " There is in it such a *labe-factation* of all principles, as may be injurious to morality."

While he pronounced this response, we sat in a comical sort of restraint, smothering a laugh, which we were afraid might burst out. In his life of Gay, he has been still more decisive as to the inefficiency of " The Beggar's Opera " in corrupting society. But I have ever thought somewhat differently ; for, indeed, not only are the gaiety and heroism of a highwayman very captivating to a youthful imagination, but the arguments for adventurous depredation are so plausible, the allusions so lively, and the contrasts with the ordinary and more painful modes of acquiring property are so artfully displayed, that it requires a cool and strong judgment to resist so imposing an aggregate : yet, I own, I should be very sorry to have " The Beggar's Opera " suppressed ; for there is in it so much of real London life, so much of brilliant wit, and such a variety of airs, which, from early association of ideas, engage, soothe, and enliven the mind, that no performance which the theatre exhibits delights me more.

The late " *worthy* " Duke of Queensberry, as Thomson, in his " Seasons," justly characterizes him, told me, that when Gay showed him " The Beggar's Opera," his Grace's observation was, " This is a very odd thing, Gay ; I am satisfied that it is either a very good thing, or a very bad thing." It proved the former, beyond the warmest expectations of the author or his friends. Mr. Cambridge, however, showed us to-day that there was good reason enough to doubt concerning its success. He was told by Quin, that during the first night of its appearance it was long in a very dubious state ; that there was a disposition to damn it, and that it was saved by the song,

" Oh, ponder well ! be not severe ! "

the audience being much affected by the innocent looks of Polly, when she came to those two lines, which exhibit at once a painful and ridiculous image,

" For on the rope that hangs my Dear,
Depends poor Polly's life."

Quin himself had so bad an opinion of it, that he refused the part of Captain Macheath, and gave it to Walker, who acquired great celebrity by his grave yet animated performance of it.

§ 104

When I met him in London the following year, the account which he gave me of his French tour, was: "Sir, I have seen all the visibilities of Paris, and around it; but to have formed an acquaintance with the people there, would have required more time than I could stay. I was just beginning to creep into acquaintance by means of Colonel Drumgold, a very high man, Sir, head of *L'Ecole Militaire*, a most complete character, for he had first been a professor of rhetoric, and then became a soldier. And, Sir, I was very kindly treated by the English Benedictines, and have a cell appropriated to me in their convent."

He observed: "The great in France live very magnificently, but the rest very miserably. There is no happy middle state as in England. The shops of Paris are mean: the meat in the markets is such as would be sent to a gaol in England; and Mr. Thrale justly observed, that the cookery of the French was forced upon them by necessity; for they could not eat their meat, unless they added some taste to it. The French are an indelicate people; they will spit upon any place. At Madame [Du Bocage's], a literary lady of rank, the footman took the sugar in his fingers, and threw it into my coffee. I was going to put it aside: but hearing it was made on purpose for me, I e'en tasted Tom's finger. The same lady would needs make tea *à l'anglaise*. The spout of the teapot did not pour freely; she bade the footman blow into it. France is worse than Scotland in everything but climate. Nature has done more for the French; but they have done less for themselves than the Scotch have done."

It happened that Foote was at Paris at the same time with Dr. Johnson, and his description of my friend while there was abundantly ludicrous. He told me, that the French were quite astonished at his figure and manner, and at his dress, which he obstinately continued exactly as in London ;—his brown clothes, black stockings, and plain shirt. He mentioned, that an Irish gentleman said to Johnson, " Sir, you have not seen the best French players." JOHNSON : " Players, Sir ! I look on them as no better than creatures set upon tables and joint stools to make faces and produce laughter, like dancing dogs."— " But, Sir, you will allow that some players are better than others ? " JOHNSON : " Yes, Sir, as some dogs dance better than others."

§ 105

Having arrived in London late on Friday, the 15th of March, I hastened next morning to wait on Dr. Johnson, at his house ; but found he was removed from Johnson's Court, No. 7, to Bolt Court, No. 8, still keeping to his favourite Fleet Street. My reflection at the time upon this change as marked in my Journal, is as follows: " I felt a foolish regret that he had left a court which bore his name ; but it was not foolish to be affected with some tenderness of regard for a place in which I had seen him a great deal, from whence I had often issued a better and a happier man than when I went in, and which had often appeared to my imagination while I trod its pavement, in the solemn darkness of the night, to be sacred to wisdom and piety." Being informed that he was at Mr. Thrale's, in the Borough, I hastened thither, and found Mrs. Thrale and him at breakfast. I was kindly welcomed. In a moment he was in a full glow of conversation and I felt myself elevated as if brought into another state of being. Mrs. Thrale and I looked to each other while he talked, and our looks expressed our congenial admiration and affection for him. I shall ever recollect this scene with great pleasure. I exclaimed to her, " I am now intellectually, *Hermippus*

Redivivus, I am quite restored by him, by transfusion of *mind*." "There are many," she replied, " who admire and respect Mr. Johnson ; but you and I *love* him."

§ 106

We got into a boat to cross over to Blackfriars ; and as we moved along the Thames, I talked to him of a little volume, which, altogether unknown to him, was advertised to be published in a few days, under the title of " Johnsoniana, or Bon-Mots of Dr. Johnson." JOHNSON : " Sir, it is a mighty impudent thing." BOSWELL : " Pray, Sir, could you have no redress if you were to prosecute a publisher for bringing out, under your name, what you never said, and ascribing to you dull stupid nonsense, or making you swear profanely, as many ignorant relaters of your *bon-mots* do ? " JOHNSON : " No, Sir ; there will always be some truth mixed with the falsehood, and how can it be ascertained how much is true and how much is false ? Besides, Sir, what damages would a jury give me for having been represented as swearing ? " BOSWELL : " I think, Sir, you should at least disavow such a publication, because the world and posterity might with much plausible foundation say, ' Here is a volume which was publicly advertised and came out in Dr. Johnson's own time, and, by his silence, was admitted by him to be genuine.' " JOHNSON : " I shall give myself no trouble about the matter."

He was, perhaps, above suffering from such spurious publications ; but I could not help thinking, that many men would be much injured in their reputation, by having absurd and vicious sayings imputed to them ; and that redress ought in such cases to be given.

He said, " The value of every story depends on its being true. A story is a picture either of an individual or of human nature in general : if it be false, it is a picture of nothing. For instance : suppose a man should tell that Johnson, before setting out for Italy, as he had to cross the Alps, sat down to make himself wings. This many people would believe ; but it would be a picture of nothing. . . . . . (naming a worthy friend of ours) used to think a story, a story, till I showed him that truth was essential to it." I observed, that Foote entertained us with stories which were not true ; but that, indeed, it was properly not as narratives that Foote's stories pleased us, but as collections of ludicrous images. JOHNSON : " Foote is quite impartial, for he tells lies of everybody."

The importance of strict and scrupulous veracity cannot be too often inculcated. Johnson was known to be so rigidly attentive to it, that even in his common conversation the slightest circumstance was mentioned with exact precision. The knowledge of his having such a principle and habit made his friends have a perfect reliance on the truth of everything that he told, however it might have been doubted if told by many others. As an instance of this, I may mention an odd incident which he related as having happened to him one night in Fleet Street. " A gentlewoman," said he, " begged I would give her my arm to assist her in crossing the street, which I accordingly did ; upon which she offered me a shilling, supposing me to be the watchman. I perceived that she was somewhat in liquor." This, if told by most people, would have been thought an invention ; when told by Johnson, it was believed by his friends as much as if they had seen what passed.

We landed at the Temple Stairs, where we parted.

I found him in the evening in Mrs. Williams's room. We talked of religious orders. He said : " It is as unreasonable for a man to go into a Carthusian convent for fear of being immoral, as for a man to cut off his hands for fear he should steal. There is, indeed, great resolution in the immediate act of dismembering himself ; but when that is once done, he has no longer any merit : for though it is out of his power to steal, yet he may all his life be a thief in his heart. So when a man has once become a Carthusian, he is obliged to continue so, whether he chooses it or not. Their silence, too, is absurd. We read in the Gospel of the Apostles being sent to preach, but not to hold their tongues. All severity that does not tend to increase good, or prevent evil, is idle. I said to the Lady Abbess of a convent, ' Madam, you are here, not for the love of virtue, but the fear of vice.' She said, ' She should remember this as long as she lived.' " I thought it hard to give her this view of her situation, when she could not help it ; and, indeed, I wondered at the whole of what he now said ; because, both in his " Rambler " and " Idler," he treats religious austerities with much solemnity of respect.

Finding him still persevering in his abstinence from wine, I ventured to speak to him of it.—JOHNSON : " Sir, I have no objection to a man's drinking wine, if he can do it in moderation. I found myself apt to go to excess in it, and therefore, after having been for some time without it, on account of illness, I thought it better not to return to it. Every man is to judge for himself, according to the effects which he experiences. One of the fathers tells us, he found fasting made him so peevish that he did not practise it."

§ 107

I again visited him on Monday. He took occasion to enlarge, as he often did, upon the wretchedness of a sea-life. " A ship is worse than a jail. There is, in a jail, better air, better company, better conveniency of every kind ; and a ship has the additional disadvantage of being in danger. When men come to like a sea-life, they are not fit to live on land."—" Then," said I, " it would be cruel in a father to breed his son to the sea." JOHNSON : " It would be cruel in a father who thinks as I do. Men go to sea before they know the unhappiness of that way of life : and when they have come to know it, they cannot escape from it, because it is then too late to choose another profession; as indeed is generally the case with men, when they have once engaged in any particular way of life."

§ 108

Upon our arrival at Oxford, Dr. Johnson and I went directly to University College, but were disappointed on finding that one of the fellows, his friend Mr. Scott, who accompanied him from Newcastle to Edinburgh, was gone to the country. We put up at the Angel Inn, and passed the evening by ourselves in easy and familiar conversation. Talking of constitutional melancholy, he observed, " A man so afflicted, Sir, must divert distressing thoughts, and not combat with them." BOSWELL : " May not he think them down, Sir ? " JOHNSON : " No, Sir. To attempt to *think them down* is madness. He should have a lamp constantly burning in his bed-chamber during the night, and if wakefully disturbed, take a book and read, and compose himself to rest. To have the management of the mind is a great art, and it may be attained in a considerable degree by experience and habitual exercise." BOSWELL : " Should not he provide amusements for himself ? Would it not, for instance, be right for him to take a course of chemistry ? " JOHNSON : " Let him take a course of chemistry, or a course of rope-dancing, or a course of anything to which he is inclined at the time. Let him contrive to have as many retreats for his mind as he can, as many things to which it can fly from itself. Burton's 'Anatomy of Melancholy ' is a valuable work. It is, perhaps, overloaded with quotation. But there is a great spirit and great power in what Burton says, when he writes from his own mind."

Next morning we visited Dr. Wetherell, Master of University College, with whom Dr. Johnson conferred on the most advantageous mode of disposing of the books printed at the Clarendon press. I often had occasion to remark, Johnson loved business, loved to have his wisdom actually operate on real life. Dr. Wetherell and I talked of him without reserve in his own presence. WETHERELL : " I would have given him a hundred guineas if he would have written a preface to his ' Political Tracts,' by way of a Discourse on the British Constitution." BOSWELL : " Dr. Johnson, though in his writings, and upon all occasions a great friend to the Constitution both in Church and State, has never written expressly in support of either. There is really a claim upon him for both. I am sure he could give a volume of no great bulk upon each, which would comprise all the substance, and with his spirit would effectually maintain them. He should erect a fort on the confines of each." I could perceive that he was displeased with this dialogue. He burst out, " Why should *I* be always writing ? " I hoped he was conscious that the debt was just, and meant to discharge it, though he disliked being dunned.

We then went to Pembroke College, and waited on his old friend Dr. Adams, the Master of it, whom I found to be a most polite, pleasing communicative man. Before his advancement to the headship of his college, I had intended to go and visit him at Shrewsbury, where he was rector of St. Chad's, in order to get from him what particulars he could recollect of Johnson's academical life. He now obligingly gave me part of that authentic information, which, with what I afterwards owed to his kindness, will be found incorporated in its proper place in this work.

§ 109

I censured some ludicrous fantastic dialogues between two coach-horses and other such stuff, which Baretti had lately published. He joined with me, and said, " Nothing odd will do long. ' Tristram Shandy ' did not last." I expressed a desire to be acquainted with a lady who had been much talked of, and universally celebrated for extraordinary address and insinuation. JOHNSON: "Never believe extraordinary characters which you hear of people. Depend upon it, Sir, they are exaggerated. You do not see one man shoot a great deal higher than another." I mentioned Mr. Burke. JOHNSON : " Yes ; Burke *is* an extraordinary man. His stream of mind is perpetual." It is very pleasing to me to record, that Johnson's high estimation of the talents of this gentleman was uniform from their early acquaintance. Sir Joshua Reynolds informs me, that when Mr. Burke was first elected a Member of Parliament, and Sir John Hawkins expressed a wonder at his attaining a seat, Johnson said, " Now we who know Mr. Burke, know that he will be one of the first men in the country." And once, when Johnson was ill, and unable to exert himself as much as usual without fatigue, Mr. Burke having been mentioned, he said, " That fellow calls forth all my powers. Were I to see Burke now it would kill me." So much was he accustomed to consider conversation as a contest, and such was his notion of Burke as an opponent.

Next morning, Thursday, March 21, we set out in a post-chaise to pursue our ramble. It was a delightful day and we rode through Blenheim Park. When I looked at the magnificent bridge built by John Duke of Marlborough, over a small rivulet, and recollected the epigram made upon it—

" The lofty arch his high ambition shows,
　　The stream, an emblem of his bounty flows : "

and saw that now, by the genius of Brown, a magnificent body of water was collected, I said, " They have *drowned* the epigram." I observed to him, while in the midst of the noble scene around us, " You and I, Sir, have, I think, seen together the extremes of what can be seen in Britain—the wild rough island of Mull, and Blenheim Park."

We dined at an excellent inn at Chapel House, where he expatiated on the felicity of England in its taverns and inns, and triumphed over the French for not having, in any perfection, the tavern life. " There is no private house," said he, " in which people can enjoy themselves so well as in a capital tavern. Let there be ever so great plenty of good things, ever so much grandeur, ever so much elegance, ever so much desire that everybody should be easy ; in the nature of things it cannot be : there must always be some degree of care and anxiety. The master of the house is anxious to entertain his guests ; the guests are anxious to be agreeable to him : and no man, but a very impudent dog indeed, can as freely command what is in another man's house, as if it were his own. Whereas, at a tavern, there is a general freedom from anxiety. You are sure you are welcome : and the more noise you make, the more trouble you give, the more good things you call for, the welcomer you are. No servants will attend you with the alacrity which waiters do, who are incited by the prospect of an immediate reward in proportion as they please. No, Sir ; there is nothing which has yet been contrived by man, by which so much happiness is produced as by a good tavern or inn." He then repeated, with great emotion, Shenstone's lines :

> " Whoe'er has travell'd life's dull round
> Where'er his stages may have been,
> May sigh to think he still has found
> The warmest welcome at an inn."

§ 110

On Friday, March 22, having set out early from Henley, where we had lain the preceding night, we arrived at Birmingham about nine o'clock, and, after breakfast, went to call on his old schoolfellow Mr. Hector. A very stupid maid, who opened the door, told us that " her master was gone out ; he was gone to the country ; she could not tell when he would return." In short, she gave us a miserable reception ; and Johnson observed, " She would have behaved no better to people who wanted him in the way of his profession." He said to her, " My name is Johnson ; tell him I called. Will you remember the name ? " She answered with rustic simplicity in the Warwickshire pronunciation, " I don't understand you, Sir." —" Blockhead," said he, " I'll write." I never heard the word *blockhead* applied to a woman before, though I do not see why it should not, when there is evident occasion for it. He, however, made another attempt to make her understand him, and roared loud in her ear, " *Johnson*," and then she catched the sound.

We next called on Mr. Lloyd, one of the people called Quakers. He too was not at home, but Mrs. Lloyd was, and received us courteously, and asked us to dinner. Johnson said to me, " After the uncertainty of all human things at Hector's, this invitation came very well." We walked about the town, and he was pleased to see it increasing.

§ 111

Mr. Lloyd joined us in the street ; and in a little while we met *Friend Hector*, as Mr. Lloyd called him. It gave me pleasure to observe the joy which Johnson and he expressed at seeing each other again. Mr. Lloyd and I left them together, while he obligingly showed me some of the manufactures of this very curious assemblage of artificers. We all met at dinner at Mr. Lloyd's, where we were entertained with great hospitality. Mr. and Mrs. Lloyd had been married the same year with their Majesties, and like them had been blessed with a numerous family of fine children, their numbers being exactly the same. Johnson said, " Marriage is the best state for man in general ; and every man is a worse man in proportion as he is unfit for the married state."

§ 112

From Mr. Hector I now learnt many particulars of Dr. Johnson's early life, which, with others that he gave me at different times since, have contributed to the formation of this work.

Dr. Johnson said to me in the morning, " You will see, Sir, at Mr. Hector's, his sister, Mrs. Careless, a clergyman's widow. She was the first woman with whom I was in love. It dropt out of my head imperceptibly ; but she and I shall always have a kindness for each other." He laughed at the notion that a man can never be really in love but once, and considered it as a mere romantic fancy.

On our return from Mr. Bolton's, Mr. Hector took me to his house, where we found Johnson sitting placidly at tea, with his *first love ;* who though now advanced in years, was a genteel woman, very agreeable and well bred.

Johnson lamented to Mr. Hector the state of one of their schoolfellows, Mr. Charles Congreve, a clergyman, which he thus described : " He obtained, I believe, considerable preferment in Ireland, but now lives in London, quite as a valetudinarian, afraid to go into any house but his own. He takes a short airing in his post-chaise every day. He has an elderly woman, whom he calls cousin, who lives with him, and jogs his elbow when his glass has stood too long empty, and encourages him in drinking, in which he

is very willing to be encouraged ; not that he gets
drunk, for he is a very pious man, but he is always
muddy. He confesses to one bottle of port every day,
and he probably drinks more. He is quite unsocial ;
his conversation is quite mono-syllabical ; and when,
at my last visit, I asked him what a clock it was ?
that signal of my departure had so pleasing an effect
on him, that he sprung up to look at his watch, like a
greyhound bounding at a hare." When Johnson took
leave of Mr. Hector, he said, " Don't grow like Congreve ; nor let me grow like him, when you are near
me."

When he again talked of Mrs. Careless to-night he
seemed to have had his affection revived ; for he said,
" If I had married her, it might have been as happy
for me." BOSWELL : " Pray, Sir, do you not suppose that there are fifty women in the world, with any
one of whom a man may be as happy, as with any one
woman in particular ? " JOHNSON : " Ay, Sir, fifty
thousand." BOSWELL : " Then, Sir, you are not of
opinion with some who imagine that certain men and
certain women are made for each other ; and that they
cannot be happy if they miss their counterparts."
JOHNSON : " To be sure not, Sir. I believe mar-
riages would in general be as happy, and often more
so, if they were all made by the Lord Chancellor, upon
a due consideration of the characters and circumstances, without the parties having any choice in the
matter."

§ 113

We dined at our inn, and had with us a Mr. Jackson,
one of Johnson's schoolfellows, whom he treated with
much kindness, though he seemed to be a low man,
dull and untaught. He had a coarse grey coat, black
waistcoat, greasy leather breeches, and yellow un-
curled wig ; and his countenance had the ruddiness
which betokens one who is in no haste to " leave his

can." He drank only ale. He had tried to be a cutler at Birmingham, but had not succeeded ; and now he lived poorly at home, and had some scheme of dressing leather in a better manner than common : to his indistinct account of which Dr. Johnson listened with patient attention, that he might assist him with his advice. Here was an instance of genuine humanity and real kindness in this great man, who has been most unjustly represented as altogether harsh and destitute of tenderness. A thousand such instances might have been recorded in the course of his long life : though that his temper was warm and hasty, and his manner often rough, cannot be denied.

§ 114

On Monday, March 25, we breakfasted at Mrs. Lucy Porter's. Johnson had sent an express to Dr. Taylor's acquainting him of our being at Lichfield, and Taylor had returned an answer that his post-chaise should come for us this day. While we sat at breakfast, Dr. Johnson received a letter by the post, which seemed to agitate him very much. When he had read it, he exclaimed, " One of the most dreadful things that has happened in my time." The phrase *my time*, like the word *age*, is usually understood to refer to an event of a public or general nature. I imagined something like an assassination of the King—like a gun-powder-plot carried into execution—or like another fire of London. When asked, " What is it, Sir ? " he answered, " Mr. Thrale has lost his only son ! " This was, no doubt, a very great affliction to Mr. and Mrs. Thrale, which their friends would consider accordingly; but from the manner in which the intelligence of it was communicated by Johnson, it appeared for the moment to be comparatively small. I, however, soon felt a sincere concern, and was curious to observe, how Dr. Johnson would be affected. He said, " This is a total extinction to their family, as much as if they were sold into captivity." Upon my mentioning that Mr. Thrale had daughters, who might inherit his wealth;—" Daughters," said Johnson warmly, " he'll no more value his daughters than—" I was going to speak.—" Sir," said he, " don't you know how you yourself think ? Sir, he wishes to propagate his name." In short, I saw male succession strong in his mind, even where there was no name, no family of any long standing. I said, it was lucky he was not present when this misfortune happened. JOHNSON : " It is lucky for *me*. People in distress never think that you feel enough." BOSWELL : " And, Sir, they will have the hope of seeing you, which will be a relief in the meantime ; and when you get to them, the pain will be so far abated, that they will be capable of being consoled by you, which, in the first violence of it, I believe, would not be the case." JOHNSON : " No, Sir ; violent pain of mind, like violent pain of body, *must* be severely felt." BOSWELL : " I own, Sir, I have not so much feeling for the distress of others, as some people have, or pretend to have : but I know this, that I would do all in my power to relieve them." JOHNSON : " Sir, it is affectation to pretend to feel the distress of others, as much as they do themselves. It is equally so, as if one should pretend to feel as much pain while a friend's leg is cutting off, as he does. No, Sir ; you have expressed the rational and just nature of sympathy. I would have gone to the extremity of the earth to have preserved this boy."

He was soon quite calm. The letter was from Mr. Thrale's clerk, and concluded, " I need not say how much they wish to see you in London." He said, " We shall hasten back from Taylor's."

Mrs. Lucy Porter and some other ladies of the place talked a great deal of him when he was out of the room, not only with veneration but affection. It pleased me to find that he was so much *beloved* in his native city.

§ 115

On Tuesday, March 26, there came for us an equipage properly suited to a wealthy well-beneficed clergyman : Dr. Taylor's large, roomy post-chaise, drawn by four stout plump horses, and driven by two steady jolly postilions, which conveyed us to Ashbourne ; where I found my friend's schoolfellow living upon an establishment perfectly corresponding with his substantial creditable equipage ; his house, garden, pleasure grounds, table, in short everything good, and no scantiness, appearing. Every man should form such a plan of living as he can execute completely. Let him not draw an outline wider than he can fill up. I have seen many skeletons of show and magnificence which excite at once ridicule and pity. Dr. Taylor had a good estate of his own, and good preferment in the Church, being a prebendary of Westminster, and rector of Bosworth. He was a diligent justice of the peace, and presided over the town of Ashbourne, to the inhabitants of which I was told he was very liberal ; and as a proof of this it was mentioned to me, he had, the preceding winter, distributed two hundred pounds among such of them as stood in need of his assistance. He had consequently a considerable political interest in the county of Derby, which he employed to support the Devonshire family ; for though the schoolfellow and friend of Johnson, he was a Whig. I could not perceive in his character much congeniality of any sort with that of Johnson, who, however, said to me, " Sir, he has a very strong understanding." His size, and figure, and countenance, and manner, were that of a hearty English squire, with the parson superinduced : and I took particular notice of his upper servant, Mr. Peters, a decent grave man, in purple clothes, and a large white wig, like the butler or *major-domo* of a bishop.

Dr. Johnson and Dr. Taylor met with great cordiality ; and Johnson soon gave him the same sad account of their schoolfellow, Congreve, that he had given to Mr. Hector ; adding a remark of such moment to the rational conduct of a man in the decline of life, that it deserves to be imprinted upon every mind : " There is nothing against which an old man should be so much upon his guard as putting himself to nurse." Innumerable have been the melancholy instances of men once distinguished for firmness, resolution, and spirit, who in their latter days have been governed like children, by interested female artifice.

Dr. Taylor commended a physician who was known to him and Dr. Johnson, and said : " I fight many battles for him, as many people in the country dislike him." JOHNSON : " But you should consider, Sir, that by every one of your victories he is a loser ; for, every man of whom you get the better, will be very angry, and resolve not to employ him ; whereas if people get the better of you in argument about him, they'll think, ' We'll send for Dr. [Butler] nevertheless.' " This was an observation deep and sure in human nature.

§ 116

On Wednesday, April 3, in the morning I found him very busy putting his books in order, and as they were generally very old ones, clouds of dust were flying around him. He had on a pair of large gloves such as hedgers use. His present appearance put me in mind of my uncle Dr. Boswell's description of him, " A robust genius, born to grapple with whole libraries."

I gave him an account of a conversation which had passed between me and Captain Cook, the day before, at dinner at Sir John Pringle's ; and he was much pleased with the conscientious accuracy of that celebrated circumnavigator, who set me right as to many of the exaggerated accounts given by Dr. Hawkesworth of his Voyages. I told him that while

I was with the Captain, I catched the enthusiasm of
curiosity and adventure, and felt a strong inclination
to go with him on his next voyage. JOHNSON : " Why,
Sir, a man *does* feel so, till he considers how very little
he can learn from such voyages." BOSWELL : " But
one is carried away with the general grand and indistinct notion of A VOYAGE ROUND THE WORLD."
JOHNSON : " Yes, Sir, but a man is to guard himself
against taking a thing in general." I said I was
certain that a great part of what we are told by the
travellers to the South Sea must be conjecture, because
they had not enough of the language of those countries
to understand so much as they have related. Objects
falling under the observation of the senses might be
clearly known ; but everything intellectual, everything abstract—politics, morals, and religion, must be
darkly guessed. Dr. Johnson was of the same opinion.
He upon another occasion, when a friend mentioned
to him several extraordinary facts, as communicated
to him by the circumnavigators, slily observed : " Sir,
I never before knew how much I was respected by
these gentlemen ; they told *me* none of these things."

§ 117

Volumes would be required to contain a list of his
numerous and various acquaintance, none of whom
he ever forgot ; and could describe and discriminate
them all with precision and vivacity. He associated
with persons the most widely different in manners,
abilities, rank, and accomplishments. He was at once
the companion of the brilliant Colonel Forrester of the
Guards, who wrote " The Polite Philosopher," and of
the awkward and uncouth Robert Levett ; of Lord
Thurlow, and Mr. Sastres, the Italian master : and
has dined one day with the beautiful, gay, and fasci-
nating Lady Craven, and the next with good Mrs.
Gardiner, the tallow-chandler on Snow Hill.

§ 118

I said, I disliked the custom which some people had of bringing their children into company, because it in a manner forced us to pay foolish compliments to please their parents. JOHNSON : " You are right, Sir. We may be excused for not caring much about other people's children, for there are many who care very little about their own children. It may be observed that men, who from being engaged in business, or from their course of life in whatever way, seldom see their children, do not care much about them. I myself should not have had much fondness for a child of my own." MRS. THRALE : " Nay, Sir, how can you talk so ? " JOHNSON : " At least I never wished to have a child."

§ 119

On Thursday, April 11, I dined with him at General Paoli's, in whose house I now resided, and where I had ever afterwards the honour of being entertained with the kindest attention as his constant guest, while I was in London, till I had a house of my own there. I mentioned my having that morning introduced to Mr. Garrick, Count Neni, a Flemish nobleman of great rank and fortune, to whom Garrick talked of Abel Drugger as *a small part ;* and related, with pleasant vanity, that a Frenchman who had seen him in one of his low characters, exclaimed, " *Comment ! je ne le crois pas. Ce n'est pas, Monsieur Garrick, ce grand homme !* " Garrick added, with an appearance of grave recollection, " If I were to begin life again, I think I should not play these low characters." Upon which I observed, " Sir, you would be in the wrong ; for your great excellence is your variety of playing, your representing so well characters so very different." JOHNSON : " Garrick, Sir, was not in earnest in what he said ; for to be sure his peculiar excellence is his variety : and, perhaps there is not any one character which has not been as well acted by somebody else, as he could do it." BOSWELL : " Why then, Sir, did he talk so ? " JOHNSON : " Why, Sir, to make you answer as you did." BOSWELL : " I don't know, Sir ; he seemed to dip deep into his mind for the reflection." JOHNSON : " He had not far to dip, Sir ; he had said the same thing, probably, twenty times before."

Of a nobleman raised at a very early period to high office, he said, " His parts, Sir, are pretty well for a Lord ; but would not be distinguished in a man who had nothing else but his parts."

A journey to Italy was still in his thoughts. He said, " A man who has not been in Italy, is always conscious of an inferiority, from his not having seen what it is expected a man should see. The grand object of travelling is to see the shores of the Mediterranean. On those shores were the four great empires of the world : the Assyrian, the Persian, the Grecian, and the Roman.—All our religion, almost all our law, almost all our arts, almost all that sets us above savages, has come to us from the shores of the Mediterranean." The General observed, that " THE MEDITERRANEAN would be a noble subject for a poem."

We talked of translation. I said I could not define it, nor could I think of a similitude to illustrate it ; but that it appeared to me the translation of poetry could be only imitation. JOHNSON : " You may translate books of science exactly. You may also translate history, in so far as it is not embellished with oratory, which is poetical. Poetry, indeed, cannot be translated ; and, therefore, it is the poets that preserve the languages ; for we would not be at the trouble to learn a language, if we could have all that is written in it just as well in a translation. But as the beauties of poetry cannot be preserved in any language except that in which it was originally written, we learn the language."

§ 120

He said, that for general improvement, a man should read whatever his immediate inclination prompts him to ; though to be sure, if a man has a science to learn, he must regularly and resolutely advance. He added : " What we read with inclination makes a much stronger impression. If we read without inclination, half the mind is employed in fixing the attention ; so there is but one half to be employed on what we read." He told us, he read Fielding's " Amelia " through without stopping. He said : " If a man begins to read in the middle of a book, and feels an inclination to go on, let him not quit it, to go to the beginning. He may perhaps not feel again the inclination.

§ 121

A gentleman expressed a wish to go and live three years at Otaheité, or New Zealand, in order to obtain a full acquaintance with people, so totally different from all that we have ever known, and be satisfied what pure nature can do for man. JOHNSON : " What could you learn, Sir ? What can savages tell, but what they themselves have seen ? Of the past, or the invisible, they can tell nothing. The inhabitants of Otaheité and New Zealand are not in a state of pure nature ; for it is plain they broke off from some other people. Had they grown out of the ground, you might have judged of a state of pure nature. Fanciful people may talk of a mythology being amongst them ; but it must be invention. They have once had religion, which has been gradually debased. And what account of your religion can you suppose to be learnt from savages ? Only consider, Sir, our own state : our religion is in a book ; we have an order of men whose duty it is to teach it ; we have one day in the week set apart for it, and this is in general pretty well observed.   Yet ask the first ten gross men you meet, and hear what they can tell of their religion."

On Monday, April 29, he and I made an excursion to Bristol, where I was entertained with seeing him inquire upon the spot, into the authenticity of Rowley's poetry, as I had seen him inquire upon the spot into the authenticity of Ossian's poetry.   George Catcot the pewterer, who was as zealous for Rowley, as Hugh Blair was for Ossian (I trust my reverend friend will excuse the comparison), attended us at our inn, and with a triumphant air of lively simplicity called out, " I'll make Dr. Johnson a convert."   Dr. Johnson, at his desire, read aloud some of Chatterton's fabricated verses, while Catcot stood at the back of his chair, moving himself like a pendulum, and beating time with his feet, and now and then looking into Dr. Johnson's face, wondering that he was not yet convinced.   We called on Mr. Barret, the surgeon, and saw some of the *originals* as they were called, which were executed very artificially ; but from a careful inspection of them and a consideration of the circumstances with which they were attended we were quite satisfied of the imposture, which, indeed, has been clearly demonstrated from internal evidence, by several able critics.

Honest Catcot seemed to pay no attention whatever to any objections, but insisted as an end of all controversy, that we should go with him to the tower of the church of St. Mary Redcliffe, and *view with our own eyes* the ancient chest in which the manuscripts were found.   To this, Dr. Johnson good-naturedly agreed ; and though troubled with a shortness of breathing, laboured up a long flight of steps, till we came to the place where the wondrous chest stood.   " *There,*" said Catcot, with a bouncing confident credulity, " *there* is the very chest itself."   After this *ocular demonstration,* there was no more to be said.   He brought to my recollection a Scotch Highlander, a man of learning too, and who had seen the world, attesting, and at the same time giving his reasons for the authenticity of Fingal :—" I have heard all that poem when I was young."—" Have you, Sir ? Pray what have you heard ? "—" I have heard Ossian, Oscar, and *every one of them.*"

Johnson said of Chatterton, "This is the most extraordinary young man that has encountered my knowledge. It is wonderful how the whelp has written such things."

We were by no means pleased with our inn at Bristol.

" Let us see now," said I, " how we should describe it." Johnson was ready with his raillery. " Describe it, Sir ?—Why, it was so bad that Boswell wished to be in Scotland ! "

§ 122

I am now to record a very curious incident in Dr. Johnson's Life, which fell under my own observation ; of which *pars magna fui*, and which I am persuaded will, with the liberal-minded, be much to his credit.

My desire of being acquainted with celebrated men of every description, had made me, much about the same time, obtain an introduction to Dr. Samuel Johnson and to John Wilkes, Esq. Two men more different could perhaps not be selected out of all mankind. They had even attacked one another with some asperity in their writings ; yet I lived in habits of friendship with both. I could fully relish the excellence of each ; for I have ever delighted in that intellectual chemistry which can separate good qualities from evil in the same person.

Sir John Pringle, " mine own friend and my father's friend," between whom and Dr. Johnson I in vain wished to establish an acquaintance, as I respected and lived in intimacy with both of them, observed to me once, very ingeniously : " It is not in friendship as in mathematics, where two things, each equal to a third, are equal between themselves. You agree with Johnson as a middle quality, and you agree with me as a middle quality ; but Johnson and I should not agree." Sir John was not sufficiently flexible ; so I desisted ; knowing, indeed, that the repulsion was equally strong on the part of Johnson ; who, I know not from what cause, unless his being a Scotchman, had formed a very erroneous opinion of Sir John. But I conceived an irresistible wish, if possible, to bring Dr. Johnson and Mr. Wilkes together. How to manage it, was a nice and difficult matter.

My worthy booksellers and friends Messieurs Dilly in the Poultry, at whose hospitable and well-covered table I have seen a greater number of literary men than at any other except that of Sir Joshua Reynolds, had invited me to meet Mr. Wilkes and some more gentlemen, on Wednesday, May 15. " Pray," said I, " let us have Dr. Johnson."—" What, with Mr. Wilkes ? not for the world," said Mr. Edward Dilly : " Dr. Johnson would never forgive me."—" Come," said I, " if you'll let me negotiate for you I will be answerable that all shall go well." DILLY : " Nay, if you will take it upon you, I am sure I shall be very happy to see them both here."

Notwithstanding the high veneration which I entertained for Dr. Johnson, I was sensible that he was sometimes a little actuated by the spirit of contradiction, and by means of that I hoped I should gain my point. I was persuaded, that if I had come upon him with a direct proposal, " Sir, will you dine in company with Jack Wilkes ? " he would have flown into a passion, and would probably have answered, " Dine with Jack Wilkes, Sir ! I'd as soon dine with Jack Ketch." I therefore, while we were sitting quietly by ourselves at his house in an evening, took occasion to open my plan thus :—" Mr. Dilly, Sir, sends his respectful compliments to you, and would be happy if you would do him the honour to dine with him on Wednesday next along with me, as I must soon go to Scotland." JOHNSON : " Sir, I am obliged to Mr. Dilly. I will wait upon him—" BOSWELL : " Provided, Sir, I suppose, that the company which he is to have, is agreeable to you." JOHNSON : " What do you mean, Sir ? What do you take me for ? Do you think I am so ignorant of the world, as to imagine that I am to prescribe to a gentleman what company he is to have at his table ? " BOSWELL : " I beg your pardon, Sir, for wishing to prevent you from meeting people whom you might not like. Perhaps he may have some of what he calls his patriotic friends with him." JOHNSON : " Well, Sir, and what then ? What care I for his *patriotic friends ?* Poh ! " BOSWELL : " I should not be surprised to find Jack Wilkes there." JOHNSON : " And if Jack Wilkes *should* be there, what is that to *me,* Sir ? My dear friend, let us have no more of this. I am sorry to be angry with you ; but really it is treating me strangely to talk to me as if I could not meet any company whatever, occasionally." BOSWELL : " Pray forgive me, Sir : I meant well. But you shall meet whoever comes, for me." Thus I secured him, and told Dilly that he would find him very well pleased to be one of his guests, on the day appointed.

Upon the much expected Wednesday, I called on him about half an hour before dinner, as I often did when we were to dine out together, to see that he was ready in time, and to accompany him. I found him buffeting his books, as upon a former occasion, covered with dust, and making no preparation for going abroad. " How is this, Sir ? " said I. " Don't you recollect that you are to dine at Mr. Dilly's ? " JOHNSON : " Sir, I did not think of going to Dilly's : it went out of my head. I have ordered dinner at home with Mrs. Williams." BOSWELL : " But, my dear Sir, you know you were engaged to Mr. Dilly, and I told him so. He will expect you, and will be much disappointed if you don't come." JOHNSON : " You must talk to Mrs. Williams about this."

Here was a sad dilemma. I feared that what I was so confident I had secured would yet be frustrated. He had accustomed himself to show Mrs. Williams such a degree of humane attention as frequently imposed some restraint upon him ; and I knew that if she should be obstinate, he would not stir. I hastened downstairs to the blind lady's room, and told her I was in great uneasiness, for Dr. Johnson had engaged to me to dine this day at Mr. Dilly's, but that he had told me he had forgotten his engagement, and had ordered dinner at home. " Yes, Sir," said she, pretty peevishly, " Dr. Johnson is to dine at home."—" Madam," said I, " his respect for you is such, that I know he will not leave you, unless you absolutely desire it. But as you have so much of his company, I hope you will be good enough to forego it for a day ; as Mr. Dilly is a very worthy man, has frequently had agreeable parties at his house for Dr. Johnson, and will be vexed if the Doctor neglects him to-day. And then, Madam, be pleased to consider my situation ; I carried the message, and I assured Mr. Dilly that Dr. Johnson was to come ; and no doubt he has made a dinner, and invited a company, and boasted of the honour he expected to have. I shall be quite disgraced if the Doctor is not there." She gradually softened to my solicitations, which were certainly as earnest as most entreaties to ladies upon any occasion, and was graciously pleased to empower me to tell Dr. Johnson, " That all things considered, she thought he should certainly go." I flew back to him, still in dust, and careless of what should be the event, " Indifferent in his choice to go or stay ; " but as soon as I had announced to him Mrs. Williams's consent he roared, " Frank, a clean shirt," and was very soon dressed. When I had him fairly seated in a hackney coach with me, I exulted as much as a fortune-hunter, who has got an heiress into a post-chaise with him, to set out for Gretna Green.

When we entered Mr. Dilly's drawing-room, he found himself in the midst of a company he did not know. I kept myself snug and silent, watching how he would conduct himself. I observed him whispering to Mr. Dilly, " Who is that gentleman, Sir ? "—" Mr. Arthur Lee."—JOHNSON : " Too, too, too " (under his breath), which was one of his habitual mutterings. Mr. Arthur Lee could not but be very obnoxious to Johnson, for he was not only a *patriot* but an *American*. He was afterwards minister from the United States at the court of Madrid. " And who is the gentleman in lace ? "—" Mr. Wilkes, Sir." This information confounded him still more ; he had some difficulty to restrain himself, and taking up a book, sat down upon a window-seat and read, or at least kept his eye upon it intently for some time, till he composed himself. His feelings, I dare say, were awkward enough. But he no doubt recollected his having rated me, for supposing that he could be at all disconcerted by any company, and he, therefore, resolutely set himself to behave quite as an easy man of the world, who could adapt himself at once to the disposition and manners of those whom he might chance to meet.

The cheering sound of, " Dinner is upon the table," dissolved his reverie, and we *all* sat down without any symptom of ill humour. There were present, beside Mr. Wilkes, and Mr. Arthur Lee, who was an old companion of mine when he studied physic at Edinburgh, Mr. (now Sir John) Miller, Dr. Lettsom, and Mr. Slater the druggist. Mr. Wilkes placed himself next to Dr. Johnson, and behaved to him with so much attention and politeness, that he gained upon him insensibly. No man ate more heartily than Johnson, or loved better what was nice and delicate.

Mr. Wilkes was very assiduous in helping him to some fine veal. " Pray give me leave, Sir ;—It is better here—A little of the brown—Some fat, sir—A little of the stuffing—Some gravy—Let me have the pleasure of giving you some butter—Allow me to recommend a squeeze of this orange ;—or the lemon, perhaps, may have more zest."—" Sir, Sir, I am obliged to you, Sir," cried Johnson, bowing and turning his head to him with a look for some time of " surly virtue," but, in a short while, of complacency.

Foote being mentioned, Johnson said, " He is not a good mimic." One of the company added, " A merry-Andrew, a buffoon." JOHNSON : " But he has wit too, and is not deficient in ideas, or in fertility and variety of imagery, and not empty of reading ; he has knowledge enough to fill up his part. One species of wit he has in an eminent degree, that of escape. You drive him into a corner with both hands ; but he's gone, Sir, when you think you have got him—like an animal that jumps over your head. Then he has a great range for wit ; he never lets truth stand between him and a jest, and he is sometimes mighty coarse. Garrick is under many restraints from which Foote is free." WILKES : " Garrick's wit is more like Lord Chesterfield's." JOHNSON : " The first time I was in company with Foote, was at Fitzherbert's. Having no good opinion of the fellow, I was resolved not to be pleased ; and it is very difficult to please a man against his will. I went on eating my dinner pretty sullenly, affecting not to mind him. But the dog was so very comical that I was obliged to lay down my knife and fork, throw myself back upon my chair, and fairly laugh it out. No, Sir, he was irresistible. He upon one occasion experienced, in an extraordinary degree, the efficacy of his powers of entertaining. Amongst the many and various modes which he tried of getting money, he became a partner with a small-beer brewer, and he was to have a share of the profits for procuring

customers amongst his numerous acquaintance. Fitzherbert was one who took his small-beer; but it was
so bad that the servants resolved not to drink it. They
were at some loss how to notify their resolution, being
afraid of offending their master, who they knew liked
Foote much as a companion. At last they fixed upon
a little black boy, who was rather a favourite, to be
their deputy, and deliver their remonstrance; and
having invested him with the whole authority of the
kitchen, he was to inform Mr. Fitzherbert, in all their
names, upon a certain day, that they would drink
Foote's small-beer no longer. On that day Foote
happened to dine at Fitzherbert's, and this boy served
at table; he was so delighted with Foote's stories,
and merriment, and grimace, that when he went downstairs, he told them: " This is the finest man I have
ever seen. I will not deliver your message. I will
drink his small-beer."

Somebody observed that Garrick could not have
done this. WILKES: " Garrick would have made the
small-beer still smaller. He is now leaving the stage;
but he will play *Scrub* all his life." I knew that Johnson would let nobody attack Garrick but himself, as
Garrick said to me, and I had heard him praise his
liberality; so to bring out his commendation of his
celebrated pupil, I said, loudly, " I have heard Garrick is liberal." JOHNSON: " Yes, Sir, I know that
Garrick has given away more money than any man in
England that I am acquainted with, and that not
from ostentatious views. Garrick was very poor when
he began life; so when he came to have money, he
probably was very unskilful in giving away, and saved
when he should not. But Garrick began to be liberal
as soon as he could; and I am of opinion, the reputation of avarice which he has had, has been very
lucky for him, and prevented his having many enemies. You despise a man for avarice, but do not hate
him. Garrick might have been much better attacked

for living with more splendour than is suitable to a player : if they had had the wit to have assaulted him in that quarter, they might have galled him more. But they have kept clamouring about his avarice, which has rescued him from much obloquy and envy."

Talking of the great difficulty of obtaining authentic information for biography, Johnson told us, " When I was a young fellow I wanted to write the ' Life of Dryden,' and in order to get materials, I applied to the only two persons then alive who had seen him ; these were old Swinney, and old Cibber. Swinney's information was no more than this, ' That at Will's coffee-house Dryden had a particular chair for himself, which was set by the fire in winter, and was then called his winter-chair ; and that it was carried out for him to the balcony in summer, and was then called his summer-chair.' Cibber could tell no more but ' That he remembered him a decent old man, arbiter of critical disputes at Will's.' You are to consider that Cibber was then at a great distance from Dryden, had perhaps one leg only in the room, and durst not draw in the other." BOSWELL : " But Cibber was a man of observation ? " JOHNSON : " I think not." BOSWELL : " You will allow his 'Apology' to be well done." JOHNSON : " Very well done, to be sure, Sir. That book is a striking proof of the justice of Pope's remark :

' Each might his several province well command,
   Would all but stoop to what they understand.' "

BOSWELL : " And his plays are good." JOHNSON : " Yes ; but that was his trade ; *l'esprit de corps ;* he had been all his life among players and play-writers. I wondered that he had so little to say in conversation, for he had kept the best company, and learnt all that can be got by the ear. He abused Pindar to me, and then showed me an ode of his own, with an absurd couplet, making a linnet soar on an eagle's wing. I told him that when the ancients made a simile, they always made it like something real."

Mr. Wilkes remarked that, "Among all the bold flights of Shakespeare's imagination, the boldest was making Birnam-wood march to Dunsinane; creating a wood where there never was a shrub; a wood in Scotland! ha! ha! ha!" And he also observed that, "The clannish slavery of the Highlands of Scotland was the single exception to Milton's remark of 'The Mountain Nymph, sweet Liberty,' being worshipped in all hilly countries."—"When I was at Inveraray," said he, "on a visit to my old friend, Archibald, Duke of Argyle, his dependents congratulated me on being such a favourite of his Grace. I said, 'It is then, gentlemen, truly lucky for me; for if I had displeased the Duke, and he had wished it, there is not a Campbell among you but would have been ready to bring John Wilkes's head to him in a charger. It would have been only

Off with his head! So much for *Aylesbury*.'

I was then Member for Aylesbury."

Dr. Johnson and Mr. Wilkes talked of the contested passage in Horace's "Art of Poetry," "*Difficile est proprie communia dicere.*" Mr. Wilkes, according to my note, gave the interpretation thus: "It is difficult to speak with propriety of common things; as, if a poet had to speak of Queen Caroline drinking tea, he must endeavour to avoid the vulgarity of cups and saucers." But upon reading my note he tells me that he meant to say, that "The word *communia* being a Roman law-term, signifies here things *communis juris*, that is to say, what have never yet been treated by anybody;" and this appears clearly from what followed,

" ——————tuque
Rectius Iliacum carmen deducis in actus,
Quam si proferres ignota indictaque primus."

You will easier make a tragedy out of the " Iliad "
than on any subject not handled before. JOHNSON :
" He means that it is difficult to appropriate to particular persons qualities which are common to all
mankind, as Homer has done."

WILKES : " We have no City-Poet now : that is an
office which has gone into disuse. The last was
Elkanah Settle. There is something in *names* which
one cannot help feeling. Now *Elkanah Settle* sounds
so *queer*, who can expect much from that name ? We
should have no hesitation to give it for John Dryden,
in preference to Elkanah Settle, from the names only,
without knowing their different merits." JOHNSON :
" I suppose, Sir, Settle did as well for Aldermen in his
time, as John Home could do now. Where did Beck-
ford and Trecothick learn English ? "

Mr. Arthur Lee mentioned some Scotch who had
taken possession of a barren part of America, and
wondered why they should choose it. JOHNSON :
" Why, Sir, all barrenness is comparative. The
Scotch would not know it to be barren." BOSWELL :
" Come, come, he is flattering the English. You
have now been in Scotland, Sir, and say if you did
not see meat and drink enough there ? " JOHNSON :
" Why yes, Sir ; meat and drink enough to give the
inhabitants sufficient strength to run away from
home." All these quick and lively sallies were said
sportively, quite in jest, and with a smile which
showed that he meant only wit. Upon this topic, he
and Mr. Wilkes could perfectly assimilate ; here was
a bond of union between them, and I was conscious
that as both of them had visited Caledonia, both were
fully satisfied of the strange narrow ignorance of those
who imagine that it is a land of famine. But they

amused themselves with persevering in the old jokes.
When I claimed a superiority for Scotland over England in one respect, that no man can be arrested there
for a debt, merely because another swears it against
him ; but there must first be the judgment of a court
of law ascertaining its justice ; and that a seizure of
the person, before judgment is obtained, can take
place only, if his creditor should swear that he is about
to fly from the country, or, as it is technically expressed, is *in meditatione fugæ :* WILKES : " That, I
should think, may be safely sworn of all the Scotch
nation." JOHNSON (to Mr. Wilkes) : " You must
know, Sir, I lately took my friend Boswell, and showed
him genuine civilized life in an English provincial
town. I turned him loose at Lichfield, my native
city, that he might see for once real civility : for you
know he lives among savages in Scotland, and among
rakes in London." WILKES : " Except when he is
with grave, sober, decent people, like you and me."
JOHNSON (smiling) : " And we ashamed of him."

They were quite frank and easy. Johnson told the
story of his asking Mrs. Macaulay to allow her footman to sit down with them, to prove the ridiculous-
ness of the argument for the equality of mankind ;
and he said to me afterwards, with a nod of satisfaction, " You saw Mr. Wilkes acquiesced." Wilkes
talked with all imaginable freedom of the ludicrous
title given to the Attorney-General, *Diabolus Regis ;*
adding, " I have reason to know something about that
officer ; for I was prosecuted for a libel." Johnson,
who many people would have supposed must have
been furiously angry at hearing this talked of so
lightly, said not a word. He was now, *indeed,* " a
good-humoured fellow."

After dinner, we had an accession of Mrs. Knowles,
the Quaker lady, well known for her various talents,
and of Mr. Alderman Lee. Amidst some patriotic
groans, somebody, I think the Alderman, said, " Poor

old England is lost." JOHNSON : " Sir, it is not so much to be lamented that Old England is lost, as that the Scotch have found it." WILKES : " Had Lord Bute governed Scotland only, I should not have taken the trouble to write his eulogy, and dedicate ' MORTIMER ' to him."

Mr. Wilkes held a candle to show a fine print of a beautiful female figure which hung in the room, and pointed out the elegant contour of the bosom, with the finger of an arch connoisseur. He afterwards, in a conversation with me, waggishly insisted, that all the time Johnson showed visible signs of a fervent admiration of the corresponding charms of the fair Quaker.

This record, though by no means so perfect as I could wish, will serve to give a notion of a very curious interview, which was not only pleasing at the time, but had the agreeable and benignant effect of reconciling any animosity, and sweetening any acidity, which in the various bustle of political contest, had been produced in the minds of two men, who though widely different, had so many things in common— classical learning, modern literature, wit and humour, and ready repartee—that it would have been much to be regretted if they had been for ever at a distance from each other.

Mr. Burke gave me much credit for this successful *negotiation ;* and pleasantly said, " That there was nothing equal to it in the whole history of the *Corps diplomatique.*"

I attended Dr. Johnson home, and had the satisfaction to hear him tell Mrs. Williams how much he had been pleased with Mr. Wilkes's company, and what an agreeable day he had passed.

§ 123

On the evening of the next day, I took leave of him, being to set out for Scotland. I thanked him with great warmth for all his kindness. "Sir," said he, "you are very welcome. Nobody repays it with more."

How very false is the notion that has gone round the world, of the rough, and passionate, and harsh manners of this great and good man. That he had occasional sallies of heat of temper, and that he was sometimes, perhaps, too "easily provoked" by absurdity and folly, and sometimes too desirous of triumph in colloquial contest, must be allowed. The quickness both of his perception and sensibility disposed him to sudden explosions of satire; to which his extraordinary readiness of wit was a strong and almost irresistible incitement. To adopt one of the finest images in Mr. Home's "Douglas,"

" ————On each glance of thought
Decision followed, as the thunderbolt
Pursues the flash ! "————

I admit that the beadle within him was often so eager to apply the lash that the judge had not time to consider the case with sufficient deliberation.

That he was occasionally remarkable for violence of temper may be granted : but let us ascertain the degree, and not let it be supposed that he was in a perpetual rage, and never without a club in his hand to knock down every one who approached him. On the contrary, the truth is, that by much the greatest part of his time he was civil, obliging, nay, polite in the true sense of the word ; so much so, that many gentlemen who were long acquainted with him never received, or even heard a strong expression from him.

The following letters concerning an epitaph which he wrote for the monument of Dr. Goldsmith, in Westminster Abbey, afford at once a proof of his unaffected modesty, his carelessness as to his own writings, and of the great respect which he entertained for the taste and judgment of the excellent and eminent person to whom they are addressed :

" TO SIR JOSHUA REYNOLDS.

" DEAR SIR,

" I HAVE been kept away from you, I know not well how, and of those vexatious hindrances I know not when there will be an end. I therefore send you the poor dear Doctor's epitaph. Read it first yourself ; and if you then think it right, show it to the Club. I am, you know, willing to be corrected. If you think anything much amiss, keep it to yourself till we come together. I have sent two copies, but prefer the card. The dates must be settled by Dr. Percy. I am, Sir, your most humble servant,

" SAM. JOHNSON.

" May 16, 1776."

" TO THE SAME.

" SIR,

" MISS REYNOLDS has a mind to send the epitaph to Dr. Beattie ; I am very willing, but having no copy, cannot immediately recollect it. She tells me you have lost it. Try to recollect, and put down as much as you retain ; you perhaps may have kept what I have dropped. The lines for which I am at a loss are something of *rerum civilium sive naturalium.* It was a sorry trick to lose it ; help me if you can. I am, Sir, your most humble servant,

" SAM. JOHNSON.

" June 22, 1776.

" The gout grows better, but slowly."

It was, I think, after I had left London in this year, that this epitaph gave occasion to a *remonstrance* to the MONARCH OF LITERATURE, for an account of which I am indebted to Sir William Forbes of Pitsligo.

That my readers may have the subject more fully and clearly before them, I shall first insert the epitaph.

" OLIVARII GOLDSMITH,
Poetæ, Physici, Historici,
Qui nullum fere scribendi genus
Non tetigit,
Nullum quod tetigit non ornavit :
Sive risus essent movendi,
Sive lacrymæ,
Affectuum potens at lenis dominator :
Ingenio sublimis, vividus, versatilis,
Oratione grandis, nitidus, venustus :
Hoc monumento memoriam coluit
Sodalium amor,
Amicorum fides,
Lectorum veneratio.
Natus in Hibernia Forniæ Longfordiensis,
In loco cui nomen Pallas,
Nov. XXIX. MDCCXXXI ;
Eblanæ literis institutus ;
Obiit Londini,
April IV, MDCCLXXIV."

Sir William Forbes writes to me thus :

" I enclose the *Round Robin*. This *jeu d'esprit* took its rise one day at dinner at our friend Sir Joshua Reynolds's. All the company present, except myself, were friends and acquaintances of Dr. Goldsmith. The epitaph written for him by Dr. Johnson became the subject of conversation, and various emendations were suggested, which it was agreed should be submitted to the Doctor's consideration.—But the question was, who should have the courage to propose them to him ? At last it was hinted, that there could be no way so good as that of a *Round Robin*, as the sailors call it, which they make use of when they enter into a conspiracy, so as not to let it be known who puts his name first or last to the paper. This proposition was instantly assented to : and Dr. Barnard, Dean of Derry, now Bishop of Killaloe, drew up an address to Dr. Johnson on the occasion, replete with wit and

ROUND ROBIN, *addressed to* SAMUEL JOHNSON, LL D. *with* FAC SIMILES *of the Signatures.*

We the Circumscribers, having read with great pleasure, an intended Epitaph for the Monument of Dr Goldsmith, which, considered abstractedly appears to be, for elegant Composition and Masterly Style, in every respect worthy of the Pen of its learned Author, are yet of opinion, that the Character of the Deceased as a Writer, particularly as a Poet, is perhaps not delineated with all the exactness which Dr Johnson is capable of giving it. We therefore, with deference to his superior judgement, humbly request, that he would, at least take the trouble of revising it, and of making such additions and alterations as he shall think proper, upon a farther perusal. But if we might venture to express our wishes, they would lead us to request, that he would write the Epitaph in English, rather than in Latin: As we think, that the Memory of so eminent an English Writer ought to be perpetuated in the Language to which his Works are likely to be so lasting an Ornament, Which we also know to have been the opinion of the late Doctor himself

humour, but which it was feared the Doctor might think treated the subject with too much levity. Mr. Burke then proposed the address as it stands in the paper in writing, to which I had the honour to officiate as clerk.

" Sir Joshua agreed to carry it to Dr. Johnson, who received it with much good humour, and desired Sir Joshua to tell the gentlemen, that he would alter the epitaph in any manner they pleased, as to the sense of it ; but *he would never consent to disgrace the walls of Westminster Abbey, with an English inscription.*

" I consider this *Round Robin* as a species of literary curiosity worth preserving, as it marks, in a certain degree, Dr. Johnson's character."

My readers are presented with a faithful transcript of a paper, which I doubt not of their being desirous to see.

Sir William Forbes's observation is very just. The anecdote now related proves, in the strongest manner, the reverence and awe with which Johnson was regarded by some of the most eminent men of his time in various departments, and even by such of them as lived most with him ; while it also confirms what I have again and again inculcated, that he was by no means of that ferocious and irascible character which has been ignorantly imagined.

This hasty composition is also to be remarked, as one of the thousand instances which evince the extraordinary promptitude of Mr. Burke ; who while he is equal to the greatest things, can adorn the least ; can, with equal facility, embrace the vast and complicated speculations of politics, or the ingenious topics of literary investigation.

§ 124

In 1777, it appears from his " Prayers and Meditations," that Johnson suffered much from a state of mind " unsettled and perplexed," and from that constitutional gloom, which, together with his extreme humility and anxiety with regard to his religious state, made him contemplate himself through too dark and unfavourable a medium. It may be said of him, that he " saw GOD in clouds." Certain we may be of his injustice to himself in the following lamentable paragraph, which it is painful to think came from the contrite heart of this great man, to whose labours the world is so much indebted : " When I survey my past life, I discover nothing but a barren waste of time, with some disorders of body, and disturbances of the mind, very near to madness, which I hope He that made me will suffer to extenuate many faults, and excuse many deficiencies." [*Pr. and Med.*, p. 155.] But we find his devotions in this year eminently fervent ; and we are comforted by observing intervals of quiet composure, and gladness.

On Easter Day we find the following emphatic prayer :

" Almighty and most merciful Father, who seest all our miseries, and knowest all our necessities, look down upon me and pity me. Defend me from the violent incursion of evil thoughts, and enable me to form and keep such resolutions as may conduce to the discharge of the duties which thy providence shall appoint me ; and so help me by thy Holy Spirit, that my heart may surely there be fixed, where true joys are to be found, and that I may serve thee with pure affection and a cheerful mind. Have mercy upon me, O GOD, have mercy upon me ; years and infirmities oppress me, terror and anxiety beset me. Have mercy upon me, my Creator and my Judge. In all perplexities relieve and free me ; and so help me by thy Holy Spirit, that I may now so commemorate the death of thy Son our Saviour JESUS CHRIST, as that when this short and painful life shall have an end, I may, for his sake, be received to everlasting happiness. Amen." [*Pr. and Med.*, p. 158.]

While he was at church, the agreeable impressions upon his mind are thus commemorated :

" I was for some time distressed, but at last ob-

tained, I hope from the GOD of Peace, more quiet than
I have enjoyed for a long time. I had made no resolutions, but as my heart grew lighter, my hopes revived,
and my courage increased ; and I wrote with my
pencil in my Common Prayer Book,

> ' Vita ordinanda.
> Biblia legenda.
> Theologiæ opera danda.
> Serviendum et lætandum.' "

§ 125

In the evening the Reverend Mr. Seward, of Lichfield, who was passing through Ashbourne in his way
home, drank tea with us. Johnson described him
thus :—" Sir, his ambition is to be a fine talker ; so
he goes to Buxton, and such places, where he may find
companies to listen to him. And, Sir, he is a valetudinarian, one of those who are always mending
themselves. I do not know a more disagreeable
character than a valetudinarian, who thinks he may
do anything that is for his ease, and indulges himself
in the grossest freedoms : Sir, he brings himself to the
state of a hog in a stye."

Dr. Taylor's nose happening to bleed, he said, it was
because he had omitted to have himself blooded four
days after a quarter of a year's interval. Dr. Johnson,
who was a great dabbler in physic, disapproved much
of periodical bleeding. "For," said he, "you accustom
yourself to an evacuation which Nature cannot per-
form of herself, and therefore she cannot help you,
should you from forgetfulness or any other cause omit
it ; so you may be suddenly suffocated. You may
accustom yourself to other periodical evacuations
because, should you omit them, Nature can supply the
omission ; but Nature cannot open a vein to blood
you."—" I do not like to take an emetic," said Taylor,

" for fear of breaking some small vessels."—" Poh ! " said Johnson, " if you have so many things that will break you had better break your neck at once, and there's an end on't. You will break no small vessels:" (blowing with high derision).

I mentioned to Dr. Johnson, that David Hume's persisting in his infidelity when he was dying shocked me much. JOHNSON : " Why should it shock you, Sir ? Hume owned he had never read the New Testament with attention. Here then was a man who had been at no pains to inquire into the truth of religion, and had continually turned his mind the other way. It was not to be expected that the prospect of death would alter his way of thinking, unless GOD should send an angel to set him right." I said, I had reason to believe that the thought of annihilation gave Hume no pain. JOHNSON : " It was not so, Sir. He had a vanity in being thought easy. It is more probable that he should assume an appearance of ease, than so very improbable a thing should be, as a man not afraid of going (as, in spite of his delusive theory, he cannot be sure but he may go) into an unknown state, and not being uneasy at leaving all he knew. And you are to consider, that upon his own principle of annihilation he had no motive to speak the truth." The horror of death which I had always observed in Dr. Johnson, appeared strong to-night. I ventured to tell him, that I had been, for moments in my life, not afraid of death ; therefore I could suppose another man in that state of mind for a considerable space of time. He said, he " never had a moment in which death was not terrible to him." He added, that it had been observed, that scarce any man dies in public, but with apparent resolution ; from that desire of praise which never quits us. I said, Dr. Dodd seemed to be willing to die, and full of hopes of happiness. " Sir," said he, " Dr. Dodd would have given both his hands and both his legs to have lived. The better a man is, the more afraid is he of death, having a clearer view of infinite purity." He owned, that our being in an unhappy uncertainty as to our salvation, was mysterious; and said, " Ah! we must wait till we are in another state of being, to have many things explained to us."

§ 126

He observed, that a gentleman of eminence in literature had got into a bad style of poetry of late. " He puts," said he, " a very common thing in a strange dress till he does not know it himself, and thinks other people do not know it." BOSWELL : " That is owing to his being so much versant in old English poetry." JOHNSON : " What is that to the purpose, Sir ? If I say a man is drunk, and you tell me it is owing to his taking much drink, the matter is not mended. No, Sir, —— has taken to an odd mode. For example; he'd write thus :

> ' Hermit hoar, in solemn cell,
> Wearing out life's evening gray.'

Gray evening is common enough ; but *evening gray* he'd think fine.—Stay;—we'll make out the stanza :—

> ' Hermit hoar, in solemn cell,
> Wearing out life's evening gray ;
> Smite thy bosom, sage, and tell,
> What is bliss ? and which the way ? "

BOSWELL : " But why smite his bosom, Sir ? " JOHNSON : " Why, to show he was in earnest " (smiling).— He at an after period added the following stanza :

> " Thus I spoke ; and speaking sigh'd ;
> —Scarce repress'd the starting tear ;—
> When the smiling sage reply'd—
> —Come, my lad, and drink some beer."

§ 127

Friday, September 19, after breakfast, Dr. Johnson and I set out in Dr. Taylor's chaise to go to Derby. The day was fine and we resolved to go by Keddlestone, the seat of Lord Scarsdale, that I might see his Lordship's fine house. I was struck with the magnificence of the building ; and the extensive park, with the finest verdure, covered with deer, and cattle, and sheep, delighted me. The number of old oaks, of an immense size, filled me with a sort of respectful admiration : for one of them 60*l*. was offered. The excellent smooth gravel roads ; the large piece of water formed by his Lordship from some small brooks, with a handsome barge upon it ; the venerable Gothic church, now the family chapel, just by the house ; in short, the grand group of objects agitated and distended my mind in a most agreeable manner. " One should think," said I, " that the proprietor of all this *must* be happy."—" Nay, Sir," said Johnson, " all this excludes but one evil—poverty."

Our names were sent up, and a well-dressed elderly housekeeper, a most distinct articulator, showed us the house ; which I need not describe, as there is an account of it published in Adams's " Works in Architecture." Dr. Johnson thought better of it to-day, than when he saw it before ; for he had lately attacked it violently, saying : " It would do excellently for a town-hall. The large room with the pillars," said he, " would do for the judges to sit in at the assizes ; the circular room for a jury-chamber ; and the room above for prisoners." Still he thought the large room ill-lighted, and of no use but for dancing in ; and the bed-chambers but indifferent rooms ; and that the immense sum which it cost was injudiciously laid out. Dr. Taylor had put him in mind of his *appearing* pleased with the house. " But," said he, " that was when Lord Scarsdale was present. Politeness obliges us to appear pleased with a man's works when he is present. No man will be so ill-bred as to question you. You may therefore pay compliments without saying what is not true. I should say to Lord Scarsdale of his large room, ' My Lord, this is the most *costly* room that I ever saw ; ' which is true."

Dr. Manningham, physician in London, who was visiting at Lord Scarsdale's, accompanied us through many of the rooms, and soon afterwards my Lord himself, to whom Dr. Johnson was known, appeared and did the honours of the house. We talked of Mr. Langton. Johnson, with a warm vehemence of affectionate regard, exclaimed, "The earth does not bear a worthier man than Bennet Langton." We saw a good many fine pictures, which I think are described in one of Young's Tours. There is a printed catalogue of them, which the housekeeper put into my hand ; I should like to view them at leisure. I was much struck with Daniel interpreting Nebuchadnezzar's dream, by Rembrandt.—We were shown a pretty large library. In his Lordship's dressing-room lay Johnson's small Dictionary : he showed it to me, with some eagerness, saying, " Look ye ! *Quæ regio in terris nostri non plena laboris.*" He observed, also, Goldsmith's " Animated Nature " ; and said, " Here's our friend ! The poor Doctor would have been happy to hear of this."

In our way, Johnson strongly expressed his love of driving fast in a post-chaise. " If," said he, " I had no duties, and no reference to futurity, I would spend my life in driving briskly in a post-chaise with a pretty woman ; but she should be one who could understand me and would add something to the conversation." I observed, that we were this day to stop just where the Highland army did in 1745. JOHNSON : " It was a noble attempt." BOSWELL : " I wish we could have an authentic history of it." JOHNSON : " If you were not an idle dog you might write it, by collecting from everybody what they can tell, and putting down your authorities." BOSWELL : " But I could not have the advantage of it in my lifetime." JOHNSON : " You might have the satisfaction of its fame, by printing it in Holland : and as to profit, consider how long it was before writing came to be considered in a pecuniary view. Baretti says, he is the first man that ever received copy-money in Italy."

§ 128

Dr. Johnson told us at tea, that when some of Dr. Dodd's pious friends were trying to console him by saying that he was going to leave " a wretched world," he had honesty enough not to join in the cant :—" No, no," said he, " it has been a very agreeable world to me." Johnson added, " I respect Dodd for thus speaking the truth ; for, to be sure, he had for several years enjoyed a life of great voluptuousness."

He told us, that Dodd's city friends stood by him so, that a thousand pounds were ready to be given to the jailer if he would let him escape. He added, that he knew a friend of Dodd's, who walked about Newgate for some time on the evening before the day of his execution, with five hundred pounds in his pocket, ready to be paid to any of the turnkeys who could get him out ; but it was too late ; for he was watched with much circumspection. He said, Dodd's friends had an image of him made of wax, which was to have been left in his place ; and he believed it was carried into the prison.

Johnson disapproved of Dr. Dodd's leaving the world persuaded that " The Convict's Address to his unhappy Brethren " was of his own writing. " But, Sir," said I, " you contributed to the deception ; for when Mr. Seward expressed a doubt to you that it was not Dodd's own, because it had a great deal more force of mind in it than anything known to be his, you answered,—' Why should you think so ? Depend upon it, Sir, when a man knows he is to be hanged in a fortnight, it concentrates his mind wonderfully.' " JOHNSON : " Sir, as Dodd got it from me to pass as his own, while that could do him any good, that was an *implied promise* that I should not own it. To own it, therefore, would have been telling a lie, with the addition of breach of promise, which was worse than simply telling a lie to make it be believed it was Dodd's. Besides, Sir, I did not *directly* tell a lie : I left the matter uncertain. Perhaps I thought that Seward would not believe it the less to be mine for what I said ; but I would not put it in his power to say I had owned it."

§ 129

We entered seriously upon a question of much importance to me, which Johnson was pleased to consider with friendly attention. I had long complained to him that I felt discontented in Scotland, as too narrow a sphere, and that I wished to make my chief residence in London, the great scene of ambition, instruction, and amusement : a scene, which was to me, comparatively speaking, a heaven upon earth. JOHNSON : " Why, Sir, I never knew any one who had such a *gust* for London as you have : and I cannot blame you for your wish to live there : yet, Sir, were I in your father's place, I should not consent to your settling there ; for I have the old feudal notions, and I should be afraid that Auchinleck would be deserted, as you would soon find it more desirable to have a country-seat in a better climate. I own, however, that to consider it as a *duty* to reside on a family estate is a prejudice ; for we must consider, that working-people get employment equally, and the produce of the land is sold equally, whether a great family resides at home or not ; and if the rents of an estate be carried to London, they return again in the circulation of commerce ; nay, Sir, we must perhaps allow, that carrying the rents to a distance is a good, because it contributes to that circulation. We must however, allow, that a well-regulated great family may improve a neighbourhood in civility and elegance, and give an example of good order, virtue, and piety ; and so its residence at home may be of much advantage. But if a great family be disorderly and vicious, its residence at home is very pernicious to a neighbourhood. There is not now the same inducement to live in the country as formerly ; the pleasures of social life are much better enjoyed in town ; and there is no longer in the country that power and influence in proprietors of land which they had in old times, and which made the country so agreeable to them. The Laird of Auchinleck now is not near so great a man as the Laird of Auchinleck was a hundred years ago."

I told him, that one of my ancestors never went from home without being attended by thirty men on horseback. Johnson's shrewdness and spirit of inquiry were exerted upon every occasion. " Pray," said he, " how did your ancestor support his thirty men and thirty horses when he went at a distance from home, in an age when there was hardly any money in circulation?" I suggested the same difficulty to a friend who mentioned Douglas's going to the Holy Land with a numerous train of followers. Douglas could, no doubt, maintain followers enough while living upon his own lands, the produce of which supplied them with food ; but he could not carry that food to the Holy Land ; and as there was no commerce by which he could be supplied with money, how could he maintain them in foreign countries ?

I suggested a doubt, that if I were to reside in London, the exquisite zest with which I relished it in occasional visits might go off, and I might grow tired of it. JOHNSON : " Why, Sir, you find no man, at all intellectual, who is willing to leave London. No, Sir, when a man is tired of London he is tired of life; for there is in London all that life can afford."

To obviate his apprehension, that by settling in London I might desert the seat of my ancestors, I assured him that I had old feudal principles to a degree of enthusiasm; and that I felt all the *dulcedo* of the *natale solum*. I reminded him, that the Laird of Auchinleck had an elegant house, in front of which he could ride ten miles forward upon his own territories, upon which he had upwards of six hundred people attached to him; that the family-seat was rich in natural romantic beauties of rock, wood, and water: and that in my " morn of life " I had appropriated the finest descriptions in the ancient classics, to certain scenes there, which were thus associated in my mind. That when all this was considered I should certainly pass a part of the year at home, and enjoy it the more from variety, and from bringing with me a share of the intellectual stores of the metropolis. He listened to all this, and kindly " hoped it might be as I now supposed."

He said, a country gentleman should bring his lady to visit London as soon as he can, that they may have agreeable topics for conversation when they are by themselves

§ 130

During this interview at Ashbourne, Johnson seemed to be more uniformly social, cheerful, and alert, than I had almost ever seen him. He was prompt on great occasions and on small. Taylor, who praised everything of his own to excess, in short, " whose geese were all swans," as the proverb says, expatiated on the excellence of his bull-dog, which, he told us, was " perfectly well shaped." Johnson, after examining the animal attentively, thus repressed the vain-glory of our host :—" No, Sir, he is *not* well shaped; for there is not the quick transition from the thickness of

the forepart, to the *tenuity*—the thin part—behind,—
which a bull-dog ought to have." This *tenuity* was
the only *hard word* that I heard him use during this
interview, and it will be observed, he instantly put
another expression in its place. Taylor said a small
bull-dog was as good as a large one. JOHNSON : " No,
Sir ; for, in proportion to his size, he has strength :
and your argument would prove, that a good bull-dog
may be as small as a mouse." It was amazing how he
entered with perspicuity and keenness upon everything
that occurred in conversation. Most men, whom I
know, would no more think of discussing a question
about a bull-dog, than of attacking a bull.

I cannot allow any fragment whatever that floats in
my memory concerning the great subject of this work
to be lost. Though a small particular may appear
trifling to some, it will be relished by others ; while
every little spark adds something to the general blaze ;
and to please the true, candid, warm admirers of
Johnson, and in any degree increase the splendour of
his reputation, I bid defiance to the shafts of ridicule,
or even of malignity. Showers of them have been dis-
charged at my " Journal of a Tour to the Hebrides " ;
yet it still sails unhurt along the stream of time, and as
an attendant upon Johnson,

" Pursues the triumph, and partakes the gale."

One morning after breakfast, when the sun shone
bright, we walked out together and " pored " for some
time with placid indolence upon an artificial water-fall,
which Dr. Taylor had made by building a strong dyke
of stone across the river behind the garden. It was
now somewhat obstructed by branches of trees and
other rubbish, which had come down the river, and
settled close to it. Johnson, partly from a desire to
see it play more freely, and partly from that inclination to activity which will animate, at times, the most

inert and sluggish mortal, took a long pole which was lying on a bank, and pushed down several parcels of this wreck with painful assiduity, while I stood quietly by, wondering to behold the sage thus curiously employed, and smiling with a humorous satisfaction each time when he carried his point. He worked till he was quite out of breath ; and having found a large dead cat so heavy that he could not move it after several efforts, " Come," said he (throwing down the pole), " *you* shall take it now ; " which I accordingly did, and being a fresh man, soon made the cat tumble over the cascade. This may be laughed at as too trifling to record ; but it is a small characteristic trait in the Flemish picture which I give of my friend, and in which, therefore, I mark the most minute particulars. And let it be remembered, that " Æsop at play " is one of the instructive apologues of antiquity.

§ 131

In the evening our gentleman-farmer, and two others, entertained themselves and the company with a great number of tunes on the fiddle. Johnson desired to have " Let ambition fire thy mind," played over again, and appeared to give a patient attention to it ; though he owned to me that he was very insensible to the power of music. I told him that it affected me to such a degree, as often to agitate my nerves painfully, producing in my mind alternate sensations of pathetic dejection, so that I was ready to shed tears ; and of daring resolution, so that I was inclined to rush into the thickest part of the battle. " Sir," said he, " I should never hear it, if it made me such a fool."

Much of the effect of music, I am satisfied, is owing to the association of ideas. That air, which instantly and irresistibly excites in the Swiss, when in a foreign land, the *maladie du pays*, has, I am told, no intrinsic power of sound. And I know from my own experience, that Scotch reels, though brisk, make me melancholy, because I used to hear them in my early years, at a time when Mr. Pitt called for soldiers " from the mountains of the north," and numbers of brave Highlanders were going abroad, never to return. Whereas the airs in " The Beggar's Opera," many of which are very soft, never fail to render me gay, because they are associated with the warm sensations and high spirits of London.—This evening, while some of the tunes of ordinary composition were played with no great skill, my frame was agitated, and I was conscious of a generous attachment to Dr. Johnson, as my preceptor and friend, mixed with an affectionate regret that he was an old man, whom I should probably lose in a short time. I thought I could defend him at the point of my sword. My reverence and affection for him were in full glow. I said to him, " My dear Sir, we must meet every year, if you don't quarrel with me." JOHNSON : " Nay, Sir, you are more likely to quarrel with me, than I with you. My regard for you is greater almost than I have words to express ; but I do not choose to be always repeating it ; write it down in the first leaf of your pocket-book, and never doubt of it again."

§ 132

While Johnson and I stood in calm conference by ourselves in Dr. Taylor's garden, at a pretty late hour in a serene autumn night, looking up to the heavens, I directed the discourse to the subject of a future state. My friend was in a placid and most benignant frame of mind. " Sir," said he, " I do not imagine that all things will be made clear to us immediately after death, but that the ways of Providence will be explained to us very gradually." I ventured to ask him whether, although the words of some texts of Scripture seemed strong in support of the dreadful doctrine of an eternity of punishment, we might not hope that the denunciation was figurative, and would not literally be executed. JOHNSON : " Sir, you are to consider the intention of punishment in a future state. We have no reason to be sure that we shall then be no longer liable to offend against GOD. We do not know that even the angels are quite in a state of security ; nay, we know that some of them have fallen. It may therefore, perhaps, be necessary, in order to preserve both men and angels in a state of rectitude, that they should have continually before them the punishment of those who have deviated from it ; but we may hope that by some other means a fall from rectitude may be prevented. Some of the texts of Scripture upon this subject, are, as you observe, indeed strong ; but they may admit of a mitigated interpretation." He talked to me upon this awful and delicate question in a gentle tone, and as if afraid to be decisive.

After supper I accompanied him to his apartment, and at my request he dictated to me an argument in favour of the negro who was then claiming his liberty, in an action in the Court of Session in Scotland. He had always been very zealous against slavery in every form, in which I with all deference thought that he discovered " a zeal without knowledge." Upon one occasion, when in company with some very grave men at Oxford, his toast was, " Here's to the next insurrection of the negroes in the West Indies." His violent prejudice against our West Indian and American settlers appeared whenever there was an opportunity. Towards the conclusion of his " Taxation no Tyranny," he says, " How is it that we hear the loudest *yelps* for liberty among the drivers of negroes ? "

§ 133

When I said now to Johnson, that I was afraid I kept him too late up, " No, Sir," said he, " I don't care though I sit all night with you." This was an animated speech from a man in his sixty-ninth year.

Had I been as attentive not to displease him as I ought to have been, I know not but this vigil might have been fulfilled ; but I unluckily entered upon the controversy concerning the right of Great Britain to tax America, and attempted to argue in favour of our fellow-subjects on the other side of the Atlantic. I insisted that America might be very well governed, and made to yield sufficient revenue by the means of *influence*, as exemplified in Ireland, while the people might be pleased with the imagination of their participating of the British Constitution, by having a body of representatives without whose consent money could not be exacted from them. Johnson could not bear my thus opposing his avowed opinion, which he had exerted himself with an extreme degree of heat to enforce ; and the violent agitation into which he was thrown, while answering, or rather reprimanding me, alarmed me so, that I heartily repented of my having unthinkingly introduced the subject. I myself, however, grew warm, and the change was great from the calm state of philosophical discussion in which we had a little before been pleasingly employed.

I talked of the corruption of the British Parliament, in which I alleged that any question, however unreasonable or unjust, might be carried by a venal majority ; and I spoke with high admiration of the Roman Senate, as if composed of men sincerely desirous to resolve what they should think best for their country. My friend would allow no such character to the Roman Senate : and he maintained that the British Parliament was not corrupt, and that there was no occasion to corrupt its members ; asserting, that there was hardly ever any question of great importance before Parliament, any question in which a man might not very well vote either upon one side or the other. He said there had been none in his time except that respecting America.

We were fatigued by the contest, which was produced by my want of caution ; and he was not then in the humour to slide into easy and cheerful talk. It therefore so happened, that we were after an hour or two very willing to separate and go to bed.

On Wednesday, September 24, I went into Dr. Johnson's room before he got up, and finding that the storm of the preceding night was quite laid, I sat down upon his bed-side, and he talked with as much readiness and good humour as ever. He recommended to me to plant a considerable part of a large moorish farm which I had purchased, and he made several calculations of the expense and profit ; for he delighted in exercising his mind on the science of numbers. He pressed upon me the importance of planting at the first in a very sufficient manner, quoting the saying " *In bello non licet bis errare :* " and adding, " this is equally true in planting."

I spoke with gratitude of Dr. Taylor's hospitality ; and as evidence that it was not on account of his good table alone that Johnson visited him often, I mentioned a little anecdote which had escaped my friend's recollection, and at hearing which repeated, he smiled. One evening, when I was sitting with him, Frank delivered this message : " Sir, Dr. Taylor sends his compliments to you, and begs you will dine with him to-morrow. He has got a hare."—" My compliments," said Johnson, " and I'll dine with him—hare or rabbit."

After breakfast I departed, and pursued my journey northwards. I took my post-chaise from the Green Man, a very good inn at Ashbourne, the mistress of which, a mighty civil gentlewoman, curtseying very low, presented me with an engraving of the sign of her house ; to which she had subjoined, in her own handwriting, an address in such singular simplicity of style that I have preserved it pasted upon one of the boards of my original Journal at this time, and shall here insert it for the amusement of my readers :

" *M. KILLINGLEY'S duty waits upon Mr. Boswell, is exceedingly obliged to him for this favour ; whenever he comes this way, hopes for a continuance of the same. Would Mr. Boswell name the house to his extensive acquaintance, it would be a singular favour conferr'd on one who has it not in her power to make any other return but her most grateful thanks, and sincerest prayers for his happiness in time, and in a blessed eternity.*

" *Tuesday morn.*"

From this meeting at Ashbourne I derived a considerable accession to my Johnsonian store. I communicated my original Journal to Sir William Forbes, in whom I have always placed deserved confidence ; and what he wrote to me concerning it is so much to my credit as the biographer of Johnson, that my readers will, I hope, grant me their indulgence for here inserting it : " It is not once or twice going over it," says Sir William, " that will satisfy me ; for I find in it a high degree of instruction as well as entertainment ; and I derive more benefit from Dr. Johnson's admirable discussions than I should be able to draw from his personal conversation ; for, I suppose there is not a man in the world to whom he discloses his sentiments so freely as to yourself."

I cannot omit a curious circumstance which occurred at Edensor Inn, close by Chatsworth, to survey the magnificence of which I had gone a considerable way out of my road to Scotland. The inn was then kept by a very jolly landlord, whose name, I think, was Malton. He happened to mention that " the celebrated Dr. Johnson had been in his house." I inquired *who* this Dr. Johnson was, that I might hear my host's notion of him. " Sir," said he, " Johnson, the great writer ; *Oddity*, as they call him. He's the greatest writer in England ; he writes for the Ministry ; he has a correspondence abroad, and lets them know what's going on."

§ 134

Talking of ghosts, he said, " It is wonderful that five thousand years have now elapsed since the creation of the world, and still it is undecided whether or not there has ever been an instance of the spirit of any person appearing after death. All argument is against it ; but all belief is for it."

He said, " John Wesley's conversation is good, but he is never at leisure. He is always obliged to go at a certain hour. This is very disagreeable to a man who loves to fold his legs and have out his talk, as I do."

§ 135

On Tuesday, April 7, I breakfasted with him at his house. He said, " Nobody was content." I mentioned to him a respectable person in Scotland whom he knew [Lord Auchinleck] ; and I asserted, that I really believed he was always content. JOHNSON : " No, Sir, he is not content with the present ; he has always some new scheme, some new plantation, something which is future. You know he was not content as a widower ; for he married again." BOSWELL : " But he is not restless." JOHNSON : " Sir, he is only locally at rest. A chemist is locally at rest ; but his mind is hard at work. This gentleman has done with external exertions. It is too late for him to engage in distant projects." BOSWELL : " He seems to amuse himself quite well ; to have his attention fixed, and his tranquillity preserved by very small matters. I have tried this ; but it would not do with me."

JOHNSON (laughing) : " No, Sir ; it must be born with a man to be contented to take up with little things. Women have a great advantage that they may take up with little things, without disgracing themselves; a man cannot, except with fiddling. Had I learnt to fiddle, I should have done nothing else." BOSWELL: "Pray, Sir, did you ever play on any musical instrument?" JOHNSON: "No, Sir. I once bought me a flageolet but I never made out a tune." BOSWELL: "A flageolet, Sir!—so small an instrument? I should have liked to hear you play on the violoncello. *That* should have been *your* instrument." JOHNSON: "Sir, I might as well have played on the violoncello as another; but I should have done nothing else. No, Sir; a man would never undertake great things, could he be amused with small. I once tried knotting. Dempster's sister undertook to teach me; but I could not learn it." BOSWELL: "So, Sir; it will be related in pompous narrative, 'Once for his amusement he tried knotting;' nor did this Hercules disdain the distaff." JOHNSON: "Knitting of stockings is a good amusement. As a freeman of Aberdeen I should be a knitter of stockings." He asked me to go down with him and dine at Mr. Thrale's at Streatham, to which I agreed. I had lent him "An Account of Scotland, in 1702," written by a man of various inquiry, an English chaplain to a regiment stationed there. JOHNSON: "It is sad stuff, Sir, miserably written, as books in general then were. There is now an elegance of style universally diffused. No man now writes so ill as Martin's 'Account of the Hebrides' is written. A man could not write so ill, if he should try. Set a merchant's clerk now to write, and he'll do better."

§ 136

On Thursday, April 9, I dined with him at Sir Joshua Reynolds's, with the Bishop of St. Asaph (Dr. Shipley), Mr. Allan Ramsay, Mr. Gibbon, Mr. Cambridge, and Mr. Langton. Mr. Ramsay had lately returned from Italy, and entertained us with his observations upon Horace's villa, which he had examined with great care. I relished this much, as it brought fresh into my mind what I had viewed with great pleasure thirteen years before. The Bishop, Dr. Johnson, and Mr. Cambridge, joined with Mr. Ramsay, in recollecting the various lines in Horace relating to the subject.

Horace's journey to Brundusium being mentioned, Johnson observed, that the brook which he describes is to be seen now exactly as at that time ; and that he had often wondered how it happened, that small brooks, such as this, kept the same situation for ages, notwithstanding earthquakes, by which even mountains have been changed, and agriculture, which produces such a variation upon the surface of the earth. CAMBRIDGE : " A Spanish writer has this thought in a poetical conceit. After observing that most of the solid structures of Rome are totally perished, while the Tiber remains the same, he adds,

> ' Lo que èra Firme huió solamente,
>   Lo Fugitivo permanece y dura.' "

JOHNSON : " Sir, that is taken from *Janus Vitalis :*

> ' ————————————immota labescunt ;
>   Et quæ perpetuo sunt agitata manent.' "

§ 137

The Bishop said, it appeared from Horace's writings that he was a cheerful, contented man. JOHNSON : " We have no reason to believe that, my Lord. Are we to think Pope was happy, because he says so in his writings ? We see in his writings what he wished the state of his mind to appear. Dr. Young, who pined for preferment, talks with contempt of it in his writings, and affects to despise everything that he did not despise." BISHOP OF ST. ASAPH : " He was like other chaplains, looking for vacancies : but that is not peculiar to the clergy. I remember when I was with the army, after the battle of Lafeldt, the officers seriously grumbled that no general was killed." CAMBRIDGE : " We may believe Horace more, when he says,

> Romæ Tibur amem ventosus, Tibure Roman ; '
> (*Epist.* i. viii. 12.)

than when he boasts of his consistency :

> ' Me constare mihi scis, et discedere tristem,
> Quandocunque trahunt invisa negotia Romam.' "
> (*Epist.* i. xiv. 16.)

BOSWELL : " How hard is it that man can never be at rest." RAMSAY : " It is not in his nature to be at rest. When he is at rest, he is in the worst state that he can be in ; for he has nothing to agitate him. He is then like the man in the Irish song,

> ' There liv'd a young man in Ballinacrazy,
> Who wanted a wife for to make him un*ai*sy.' "

Goldsmith being mentioned, Johnson observed, that it was long before his merit came to be acknowledged : that he once complained to him, in ludicrous terms of distress, " Whenever I write anything, the public *make a point* to know nothing about it : " but that his " Traveller " brought him into high reputation. LANGTON : " There is not one bad line in that poem ; no one of Dryden's careless verses." SIR JOSHUA : " I was glad to hear Charles Fox say, it was one of the finest poems in the English language." LANGTON : " Why were you glad ? You surely had no doubt of this before." JOHNSON : " No ; the merit of ' The Traveller ' is so well established, that Mr. Fox's praise cannot augment it, nor his censure diminish it." SIR JOSHUA : " But his friends may suspect they had too great a partiality for him." JOHNSON : " Nay, Sir, the partiality of his friends was always against him. It was with difficulty we could give him a hearing. Goldsmith had no settled notions upon any subject ; so he talked always at random. It seemed to be his intention to blurt out whatever was in his mind, and see what would become of it. He was angry too, when catched in an absurdity ; but it did not prevent him from falling into another the next minute. I remember Chamier, after talking with him some time, said, ' Well, I do believe he wrote this poem himself : and, let me tell you, that is believing a great deal.' Chamier once asked him, what he meant by *slow*, the last word in the first line of ' The Traveller.'

    ' Remote, unfriended, melancholy, slow,'—

Did he mean tardiness of locomotion ? Goldsmith, who would say something without consideration, answered, ' Yes.' I was sitting by, and said, ' No, Sir ; you do not mean tardiness of locomotion ; you mean, that sluggishness of mind which comes upon a man in solitude.' Chamier believed then that I had written the line, as much as if he had seen me write it. Goldsmith, however, was a man who, whatever he wrote, did it better than any other man could do. He deserved a place in Westminster Abbey ; and every year he lived, would have deserved it better. He had, indeed, been at no pains to fill his mind with knowledge. He transplanted it from one place to another ; and it did not settle in his mind ; so he could not tell what was in his own books."

We talked of living in the country. JOHNSON : " No wise man will go to live in the country, unless he has something to do which can be better done in the country. For instance : if he is to shut himself up for a year to study a science, it is better to look out to the fields, than to an opposite wall. Then if a man walks out in the country, there is nobody to keep him from walking in again ; but if a man walks out in London, he is not sure when he shall walk in again. A great city is, to be sure, the school for studying life ; and ' The proper study of mankind is man,' as Pope observes." BOSWELL : " I fancy London is the best place for society ; though I have heard that the very first society of Paris is still beyond anything that we have here." JOHNSON : " Sir, I question if in Paris such a company as is sitting round this table could be got together in less than half a year. They talk in France of the felicity of men and women living together : the truth is, that there the men are not higher than the women, they know no more than the women do, and they are not held down in their conversation by the presence of women." RAMSAY : " Literature is upon the growth, it is in its spring in France : here it is rather *passée*." JOHNSON : " Literature was in France long before we had it. Paris was the second city for the revival of letters : Italy had it first, to be sure. What have we done for literature, equal to what was done by the Stephani and others in France ? Our literature came to us through France. Caxton printed only two books, Chaucer and Gower, that were not translations from the French ; and Chaucer, we know, took much from the Italians. No, Sir, if literature be in its spring in France, it is a second spring ; it is after a winter. We are now before the French in literature ; but we had it long after them. In England, any man who wears a sword and a powdered wig is ashamed to be illiterate. I believe it is not so in France. Yet there is, probably, a great deal of learning in France, because they have such a number of religious establishments ; so many men who have nothing else to do but to study. I do not know this ; but I take it upon the common principles of chance. Where there are many shooters, some will hit."

We talked of old age. Johnson (now in his seventieth year), said, " It is a man's own fault, it is from want of use, if his mind grows torpid in old age." The Bishop asked, if an old man does not lose faster than he gets. JOHNSON : " I think not, my Lord, if he exerts himself." One of the company rashly observed, that he thought it was happy for an old man that insensibility comes upon him. JOHNSON (with a noble elevation and disdain) : " No, Sir, I should never be happy by being less rational." BISHOP OF ST. ASAPH : " Your wish then, Sir, is, γηράσκειν διδασκόμενος." JOHNSON : " Yes, my Lord." His Lordship mentioned a charitable establishment in Wales where people were maintained, and supplied with everything, upon the condition of their contributing the weekly produce of their labour ; and he said, they grew quite torpid for want of property. JOHNSON : " They have no object for hope. Their condition cannot be better. It is rowing without a port."

One of the company asked him the meaning of the expression in Juvenal, *unius lacertæ*. JOHNSON : " I think it clear enough ; as much ground as one may have a chance to find a lizard upon."

Commentators have differed as to the exact meaning of the expression by which the poet intended to enforce the sentiment contained in the passage where these words occur. It is enough that they mean to denote even a very small possession, provided it be a man's own :

" Est aliquid, quocunque loco, quocunque recessu,
Unius sese dominum fecisse lacertæ."

(Sat. iii. 230.)

This season, there was a whimsical fashion in the newspapers of applying Shakespeare's words to describe living persons well known in the world ; which

was done under the title of " Modern Characters from
Shakespeare"; many of which were admirably
adapted. The fancy took so much, that they were
afterwards collected into a pamphlet. Somebody
said to Johnson, across the table, that he had not been
in those characters. "Yes," said he, "I have. I
should have been sorry to be left out." He then
repeated what had been applied to him,

> " You must borrow me GARGANTUA's mouth."
> (*As You Like It*, iii. 2.)

Miss Reynolds not perceiving at once the meaning of
this, he was obliged to explain it to her, which had
something of an awkward and ludicrous effect. " Why,
Madam, it has a reference to me, as using big words,
which require the mouth of a giant to pronounce
them. Gargantua is the name of a giant in ' Rabe-
lais.' " BOSWELL : " But, Sir, there is another
amongst them for you :

> ' He would not flatter Neptune for his trident,
>   Or Jove for his power to thunder.' "
> (*Coriolanus*, iii. 1.)

JOHNSON : " There is nothing marked in that. No,
Sir, Gargantua is the best." Notwithstanding this
ease and good humour, when I, a little while afterwards, repeated his sarcasm on Kenrick, which was
received with applause, he asked, " *Who* said that ? "
and on my suddenly answering *Gargantua*, he looked
serious, which was a sufficient indication that he did
not wish it to be kept up.

§ 138

On Friday, April 10, I found Johnson at home
in the morning. We resumed the conversation of
yesterday. He put me in mind of some of it which

had escaped my memory, and enabled me to record it more perfectly than I otherwise could have done. He was much pleased with my paying so great attention to his recommendation in 1763, the period when our acquaintance began, that I should keep a journal; and I could perceive he was secretly pleased to find so much of the fruit of his mind preserved; and as he had been used to imagine and say that he always laboured when he said a good thing—it delighted him, on a review, to find that his conversation teemed with point and imagery.

I said to him, " You were yesterday, Sir, in remarkably good humour; but there was nothing to offend you, nothing to produce irritation or violence. There was no bold offender. There was not one capital conviction. It was a maiden assize. You had on your white gloves."

§ 139

We talked of war. JOHNSON: " Every man thinks meanly of himself for not having been a soldier, or not having been at sea." BOSWELL: " Lord Mansfield does not." JOHNSON: " Sir, if Lord Mansfield were in a company of general officers and admirals who have been in service, he would shrink; he'd wish to creep under the table." BOSWELL: " No; he'd think he could *try* them all." JOHNSON: " Yes, if he could catch them; but they'd try him much sooner. No, Sir; were Socrates and Charles the Twelfth of Sweden both present in any company, and Socrates to say, ' Follow me, and hear a lecture in philosophy;' and Charles, laying his hand on his sword, to say, ' Follow me, and dethrone the Czar;' a man would be ashamed to follow Socrates. Sir, the impression is universal: yet it is strange. As to the sailor, when you look down from the quarter-deck to the space below, you see the utmost extremity of human misery; such crowding, such filth, such

stench!" BOSWELL: "Yet sailors are happy."
JOHNSON: "They are happy as brutes are happy, with
a piece of fresh meat,—with the grossest sensuality.
But, Sir, the profession of soldiers and sailors has
the dignity of danger. Mankind reverence those who
have got over fear, which is so general a weakness."
SCOTT: "But is not courage mechanical, and to be
acquired?" JOHNSON: "Why yes, Sir, in a collec-
tive sense. Soldiers consider themselves only as part
of a great machine." SCOTT: "We find people fond
of being sailors." JOHNSON: "I cannot account
for that, any more than I can account for other
strange perversions of imagination."

His abhorrence of the profession of a sailor was
uniformly violent; but in conversation he always
exalted the profession of a soldier. And yet I have, in
my large and various collection of his writings, a letter
to an eminent friend, in which he expresses himself
thus: "My godson called on me lately. He is
weary, and rationally weary of a military life. If you
can place him in some other state, I think you may
increase his happiness, and secure his virtue. A
soldier's time is passed in distress and danger, or in
idleness and corruption." Such was his cool reflection in his study; but whenever he was warmed and
animated by the presence of company, he, like other
philosophers, whose minds are impregnated with
poetical fancy, caught the common enthusiasm for
splendid renown.

§ 140

Mrs. Knowles affected to complain that men had
much more liberty allowed them than women.
JOHNSON: "Why, Madam, women have all the
liberty they should wish to have. We have all the
labour and the danger, and the women all the advantage. We go to sea, we build houses, we do everything, in short, to pay our court to the women."

MRS. KNOWLES: "The Doctor reasons very wittily, but not convincingly. Now, take the instance of building; the mason's wife, if she is ever seen in liquor, is ruined; the mason may get himself drunk as often as he pleases, with little loss of character; nay, may let his wife and children starve." JOHNSON: "Madam, you must consider, if the mason does get himself drunk, and let his wife and children starve, the parish will oblige him to find security for their maintenance. We have different modes of restraining evil. Stocks for the men, a ducking-stool for women, and a pound for beasts. If we require more perfection from women than from ourselves, it is doing them honour. And women have not the same temptations that we have; they may always live in virtuous company; men must mix in the world indiscriminately. If a woman has no inclination to do what is wrong, being secured from it is no restraint to her. I am at liberty to walk into the Thames; but if I were to try it, my friends would restrain me in Bedlam, and I should be obliged to them." MRS. KNOWLES: "Still, Doctor, I cannot help thinking it a hardship that more indulgence is allowed to men than to women. It gives a superiority to men, to which I do not see how they are entitled." JOHNSON: "It is plain, Madam, one or other must have the superiority. As Shakespeare says, 'If two men ride on a horse, one must ride behind.'" DILLY: "I suppose, Sir, Mrs. Knowles would have them ride in panniers, one on each side." JOHNSON: "Then, Sir, the horse would throw them both." MRS. KNOWLES: "Well, I hope that in another world the sexes will be equal." BOSWELL: "That is being too ambitious, Madam. *We* might as well desire to be equal with the angels. We shall all, I hope, be happy in a future state, but we must not expect to be all happy in the same degree. It is enough, if we be happy according to our several capacities. A worthy carman will get to heaven as well as Sir Isaac Newton. Yet, though equally good, they will not have the same degrees of happiness." JOHNSON : " Probably not."

§ 141

From this pleasing subject, he, I know not how or why, made a sudden transition to one upon which he was a violent aggressor ; for he said, " I am willing to love all mankind, *except an American :* " and his inflammable corruption bursting into horrid fire, he " breathed out threatenings and slaughter " ; calling them, " rascals—robbers—pirates " ; and exclaiming, he'd " burn and destroy them." Miss Seward, looking to him with mild but steady astonishment, said, " Sir, this is an instance, that we are always most violent against those whom we have injured."—He was irritated still more by this delicate and keen reproach ; and roared out another tremendous volley, which one might fancy could be heard across the Atlantic. During this tempest I sat in great uneasiness, lamenting his heat of temper ; till, by degrees, I diverted his attention to other topics.

DR. MAYO (to Dr. Johnson) : " Pray, Sir, have you read Edwards, of New England, on Grace ? " JOHNSON : " No, Sir." BOSWELL : " It puzzled me so much as to the freedom of the human will, by stating, with wonderful acute ingenuity, our being actuated by a series of motives which we cannot resist, that the only relief I had was to forget it." MAYO : " But he makes the proper distinction between moral and physical necessity." BOSWELL : " Alas, Sir, they come both to the same thing. You may be bound as hard by chains when covered by leather, as when the iron appears. The argument for the moral necessity of human actions is always, I observe, fortified by supposing universal prescience to be one of the attributes of the Deity." JOHNSON : " You are surer that you are free, than you are of prescience ; you are surer that you can lift up your finger or not as you please, than you are of any conclusion from a deduction of reasoning. But let us consider a little the objection from prescience. It is certain I am either to go home to-night or not ; that does not prevent my freedom." BOSWELL : "That it is certain you are *either* to go home or not, does not prevent your freedom ; because the liberty of choice between the two is compatible with that certainty. But if *one* of these events be certain *now*, you have no *future* power of volition. If it be certain you are to go home to-night, you *must* go home." JOHNSON : "If I am well acquainted with a man, I can judge with great probability how he will act in any case, without his being restrained by my judging. God may have this probability increased to certainty." BOSWELL : "When it is increased to *certainty*, freedom ceases, because that cannot be certainly foreknown, which is not certain at the time, but if it be certain at the time, it is a contradiction in terms to maintain that there can be afterwards any *contingency* dependent upon the exercise of will or anything else." JOHNSON : "All theory is against the freedom of the will ; all experience for it."—I did not push the subject any farther. I was glad to find him so mild in discussing a question of the most abstract nature, involved with theological tenets which he generally would not suffer to be in any degree opposed.

§ 142

Of John Wesley, he said, "He can talk well on any subject." BOSWELL : "Pray, Sir, what has he made of his story of the ghost ?" JOHNSON : "Why, Sir, he believes it ; but not on sufficient authority. He did not take time enough to examine the girl. It was at Newcastle, where the ghost was said to have appeared to a young woman several times, mentioning something about the right to an old house, advising application to be made to an attorney, which was done ; and, at the same time, saying the attorney would do nothing, which proved to be the fact. ' This,' says John, ' is a proof that a ghost knows our thoughts.' Now (laughing) it is not necessary to know our thoughts, to tell that an attorney will sometimes do nothing. Charles Wesley, who is a more stationary man, does not believe the story. I am sorry that John did not take more pains to inquire into the evidence for it." MISS SEWARD (with an incredulous smile) : "What, Sir! about a ghost ? " JOHNSON (with solemn vehemence) : " Yes, Madam ; this is a question which, after five thousand years, is yet undecided ; a question, whether in theology or philosophy, one of the most important that can come before the human understanding."

Mrs. Knowles mentioned as a proselyte to Quakerism, Miss ——, a young lady well known to Dr. Johnson, for whom he had shown much affection ; while she ever had, and still retained, a great respect for him. Mrs. Knowles at the same time took an opportunity of letting him know, " that the amiable young creature was sorry at finding that he was offended at her leaving the Church of England and embracing a simpler faith ; " and, in the gentlest and most persuasive manner, solicited his kind indulgence for what was sincerely a matter of conscience. JOHNSON (frowning very angrily) : " Madam, she is an odious wench. She could not have any proper conviction that it was her duty to change her religion, which is the most important of all subjects, and should be studied with all care, and with all the helps we can get. She knew no more of the Church which she left, and that which she embraced, than she did of the difference between the Copernican and Ptolemaic systems." MRS. KNOWLES : " She had the New Testament before her." JOHNSON: "Madam, she could not understand the New Testament, the most difficult book in the world, for which the study of a life is required." MRS. KNOWLES: "It is clear as to essentials." JOHNSON: "But not as to controversial points. The heathens were easily converted, because they had nothing to give up ; but we ought not, without very strong conviction indeed, to desert the religion in which we have been educated. That is the religion given you, the religion in which it may be said Providence has placed you. If you live conscientiously in that religion, you may be safe. But error is dangerous indeed, if you err when you choose a religion for yourself." MRS. KNOWLES: "Must we then go by implicit faith ?" JOHNSON: "Why, Madam, the greatest part of our knowledge is implicit faith ; and as to religion, have we heard all that a disciple of Confucius, all that a Mahometan, can say for himself ?" He then rose again into passion and attacked the young proselyte in the severest terms of reproach, so that both the ladies seemed to be much shocked.

We remained together till it was pretty late. Notwithstanding occasional explosions of violence, we were all delighted upon the whole with Johnson. I compared him at this time to a warm West Indian climate, where you have a bright sun, quick vegetation, luxuriant foliage, luscious fruits ; but where the same heat sometimes produces thunder, lightning, earthquakes, in a terrible degree.

§ 143

And now I am to give a pretty full account of one of the most curious incidents in Johnson's life, of which he himself has made the following minute on this day : "In my return from church, I was accosted by Edwards, an old fellow-collegian, who had not seen me since 1729. He knew me, and asked if I remembered one Edwards ; I did not at first recollect the name, but gradually as we walked along recovered it, and told him a conversation that had passed at an alehouse between us. My purpose is to continue our acquaintance." (*Prayers and Meditations*, 164.)

It was in Butcher Row that this meeting happened. Mr. Edwards, who was a decent-looking elderly man in gray clothes and a wig of many curls, accosted Johnson with familiar confidence, knowing who he was, while Johnson returned his salutation with a courteous formality, as to a stranger. But as soon as Edwards had brought to his recollection their having been at Pembroke College together nine-and-forty years ago, he seemed much pleased, asked where he lived, and said he should be glad to see him at Bolt Court. EDWARDS : "Ah, Sir ! we are old men now." JOHNSON (who never liked to think of being old) : " Don't let us discourage one another." EDWARDS : " Why, Doctor, you look stout and hearty. I am happy to see you so ; for the newspapers told us you were very ill." JOHNSON : " Ay, Sir, they are always telling lies of *us old fellows*."

Wishing to be present at more of so singular a conversation as that between two fellow-collegians, who had lived forty years in London without ever having chanced to meet, I whispered to Mr. Edwards that Dr. Johnson was going home, and that he had better accompany him now. So Edwards walked along with us, I eagerly assisting to keep up the conversation. Mr. Edwards informed Dr. Johnson that he had practised long as a solicitor in Chancery, but that he now lived in the country upon a little farm, about sixty acres, just by Stevenage in Hertfordshire, and that he came to London (to Barnard's Inn, No. 6) generally twice a week. Johnson appearing to me in a reverie, Mr. Edwards addressed himself to me, and expatiated on the pleasure of living in the country. BOSWELL :

" I have no notion of this, Sir. What you have to entertain you, is, I think, exhausted in half an hour."
EDWARDS : " What ! don't you love to have hope realized ? I see my grass, and my corn, and my trees growing. Now, for instance, I am curious to see if this frost has not nipped my fruit-trees." JOHNSON (who we did not imagine was attending) : " You find, Sir, you have fears as well as hopes."—So well did he see the whole, when another saw but the half of a subject.

When we got to Dr. Johnson's house and were seated in his library, the dialogue went on admirably. EDWARDS : " Sir, I remember you would not let us say *prodigious* at college. For even then, Sir (turning to me), he was delicate in language, and we all feared him." JOHNSON (to Edwards) : " From your having practised the law long, Sir, I presume you must be rich." EDWARDS : " No, Sir ; I got a good deal of money ; but I had a number of poor relations to whom I gave great part of it." JOHNSON : " Sir, you have been rich in the most valuable sense of the word." EDWARDS : " But I shall not die rich." JOHNSON : " Nay, sure, Sir, it is better to *live* rich, than to *die* rich." EDWARDS : " I wish I had continued at college." JOHNSON : " Why do you wish that, Sir ? " EDWARDS : " Because I think I should have had a much easier life than mine has been. I should have been a parson, and had a good living, like Bloxham and several others, and lived comfortably." JOHNSON : " Sir, the life of a parson, of a conscientious clergyman, is not easy. I have always considered a clergyman as the father of a larger family than he is able to maintain. I would rather have Chancery suits upon my hands than the cure of souls. No, sir, I do not envy a clergyman's life as an easy life, nor do I envy the clergyman who makes it an easy life."—Here taking himself up all of a sudden, he exclaimed, " O ! Mr. Edwards ! I'll convince you that I recollect you. Do you remember our drinking together at an alehouse near Pembroke Gate? At that time, you told me of the Eton boy, who, when verses on our SAVIOUR'S turning water into wine were prescribed as an exercise, brought up a single line, which was highly admired:

'Vidit et erubuit lympha pudica DEUM.'

And I told you of another fine line in 'Camden's Remains,' a eulogy upon one of our Kings, who was succeeded by his son, a prince of equal merit:

'Mira cano, Sol occubuit, nox nulla secuta est.'"

EDWARDS: "You are a philosopher, Dr. Johnson. I have tried too in my time to be a philosopher; but, I don't know how, cheerfulness was always breaking in."—Mr. Burke, Sir Joshua Reynolds, Mr. Courtenay, Mr. Malone, and, indeed, all the eminent men to whom I have mentioned this, have thought it an exquisite trait of character. The truth is, that philosophy, like religion, is too generally supposed to be hard and severe, at least so grave as to exclude all gaiety.

EDWARDS: "I have been twice married, Doctor. You, I suppose, have never known what it was to have a wife." JOHNSON: "Sir, I have known what it was to have a wife, and (in a solemn, tender, faltering tone) I have known what it was to *lose a wife.*—It had almost broke my heart."

EDWARDS: "How do you live, Sir? For my part, I must have my regular meals, and a glass of good wine. I find I require it." JOHNSON: "I now drink no wine, Sir. Early in life I drank wine: for many years I drank none, I then for some years drank a great deal." EDWARDS: "Some hogsheads, I warrant you." JOHNSON: "I then had a severe illness, and left it off, and I have never began it again. I never felt any difference upon myself from eating one thing rather than another, nor from one kind of weather rather than another. There are people, I believe, who feel a difference ; but I am not one of them. And as to regular meals, I have fasted from the Sunday's dinner to the Tuesday's dinner without any inconvenience. I believe it is best to eat just as one is hungry : but a man who is in business, or a man who has a family, must have stated meals. I am a straggler. I may leave this town and go to Grand Cairo, without being missed here or observed there." EDWARDS : "Don't you eat supper, Sir ? " JOHNSON : " No, Sir." ED-WARDS : " For my part, now, I consider supper as a turnpike through which one must pass in order to get to bed."

JOHNSON : " You are a lawyer, Mr. Edwards. Lawyers know life practically. A bookish man should always have them to converse with. They have what he wants." EDWARDS : " I am grown old : I am sixty-five." JOHNSON : " I shall be sixty-eight next birthday. Come, Sir, drink water, and put in for a hundred."

Mr. Edwards mentioned a gentleman who had left his whole fortune to Pembroke College. JOHNSON : " Whether to leave one's whole fortune to a college be right, must depend upon circumstances. I would leave the interest of a fortune I bequeathed to a college to my relations or my friends, for their lives. It is the same thing to a college, which is a permanent society, whether it gets the money now or twenty years hence ; and I would wish to make my relations or friends feel the benefit of it."

This interview confirmed my opinion of Johnson's most humane and benevolent heart. His cordial and placid behaviour to an old fellow-collegian, a man so different from himself ; and his telling him that he would go down to his farm and visit him, showed a

kindness of disposition very rare at an advanced age.
He observed, "How wonderful it was that they
had both been in London forty years, without having
ever once met, and both walkers in the street too ! "
Mr. Edwards, when going away, again recurred to his
consciousness of senility, and looking full in Johnson's
face, said to him, " You'll find in Dr. Young,

    ' O my coevals ! remnants of yourselves.' "

Johnson did not relish this at all ; but shook his head
with impatience.   Edwards walked off seemingly
highly pleased with the honour of having been thus
noticed by Dr. Johnson.   When he was gone, I said to
Johnson, I thought him but a weak man. JOHNSON.
" Why yes, Sir. Here is a man who has passed through
life without experience : yet I would rather have him
with me than a more sensible man who will not talk
readily. This man is always willing to say what he
has to say." Yet Dr. Johnson had himself by no
means that willingness which he praised so much, and
I think so justly ; for who has not felt the painful
effect of the dreary void, when there is a total silence
in a company for any length of time ; or, which is as
bad, or perhaps worse, when the conversation is with
difficulty kept up by a perpetual effort ?

    Johnson once observed to me, " Tom Tyers de-
scribed me the best : ' Sir,' said he, ' you are like a
ghost : you never speak till you are spoken to.' "

§ 144

Goldsmith, in his diverting simplicity, complained
one day, in a mixed company, of Lord Camden.   " I
met him," said he, " at Lord Clare's house in the
country, and he took no more notice of me than if I
had been an ordinary man." The company having
laughed heartily, Johnson stood forth in defence of

his friend. " Nay, gentlemen," said he, " Dr. Goldsmith is in the right. A nobleman ought to have made
up to such a man as Goldsmith ; and I think it is
much against Lord Camden that he neglected him."

Nor could he patiently endure to hear that such
respect as he thought due only to higher intellectual
qualities, should be bestowed on men of slighter,
though perhaps more amusing, talents. I told him,
that one morning, when I went to breakfast with Garrick, who was very vain of his intimacy with Lord
Camden, he accosted me thus :—" Pray now, did you
—did you meet a little lawyer turning the corner, eh?"
—" No, Sir," said I. " Pray what do you mean by
the question ? "—" Why " (replied Garrick, with an
affected indifference, yet as if standing on tip-toe),
" Lord Camden has this moment left me. We have
had a long walk together." JOHNSON : " Well, Sir,
Garrick talked very properly. Lord Camden *was a
little lawyer* to be associating so familiarly with a
player."

Sir Joshua Reynolds observed, with great truth,
that Johnson considered Garrick to be as it were his
property. He would allow no man either to blame or
to praise Garrick in his presence, without contradict-
ing him.

§ 145

On Tuesday, April 28, he was engaged to dine at
General Paoli's, where, as I have already observed, I
was still entertained in elegant hospitality, and with
all the ease and comfort of a home. I called on him,
and accompanied him in a hackney coach. We stopped
first at the bottom of Hedge Lane, into which he went
to leave a letter " with good news for a poor man in
distress," as he told me. I did not question him particularly as to this. He himself often resembled Lady
Bolingbroke's lively description of Pope : that " he
was *un politique aux choux et aux raves*." He would

say, " I dine to-day in Grosvenor Square ; " this might
be with a duke ; or, perhaps, " I dine to-day at the
other end of the town ; " or, " A gentleman of great
eminence called on me yesterday."—He loved thus to
keep things floating in conjecture : *Omne ignotum pro
magnifico est.* I believe I ventured to dissipate the
cloud, to unveil the mystery, more freely and frequently than any of his friends. We stopped again
at Wirgman's, the well-known *toy-shop*, in St. James's
Street, at the corner of St. James's Place, to which he
had been directed, but not clearly, for he searched
about some time, and could not find it at first ; and
said, " To direct one only to a corner shop is *toying*
with one." I supposed he meant this as a play upon
the word *toy ;* it was the first time that I knew him
stoop to such sport. After he had been some time in
the shop, he sent for me to come out of the coach, and
help him to choose a pair of silver buckles, as those he
had were too small. Probably this alteration in dress
had been suggested by Mrs. Thrale, by associating
with whom, his external appearance was much improved. He got better clothes ; and the dark colour,
from which he never deviated, was enlivened by metal
buttons. His wigs, too, were much better ; and during their travels in France, he was furnished with
a Paris-made wig, of handsome construction. This
choosing of silver buckles was a negotiation : " Sir,"
said he, " I will not have the ridiculous large ones now
in fashion ; and I will give no more than a guinea for
a pair." Such were the *principles* of the business ;
and, after some examination, he was fitted. As we
drove along, I found him in a talking humour, of which
I availed myself. BOSWELL : " I was this morning in
Ridley's shop, Sir ; and was told, that the collection
called ' Johnsoniana ' has sold very much." JOHNSON :
" Yet the ' Journey to the Hebrides ' has not had a
great sale." BOSWELL : " That is strange." JOHN-
SON : " Yes, Sir ; for in that book I have told

the world a great deal that they did not know before."

BOSWELL : " I drank chocolate, Sir, this morning with Mr. Eld : and, to my no small surprise, found him to be a *Staffordshire Whig*, a being which I did not believe had existed." JOHNSON : " Sir, there are rascals in all countries." BOSWELL : " Eld said, a Tory was a creature generated between a non-juring parson and one's grandmother." JOHNSON : " And I have always said, the first Whig was the Devil." BOSWELL : " He certainly was, Sir. The Devil was impatient of subordination ; he was the first who resisted power :

' Better to reign in Hell, than serve in Heaven.' "

§ 146

On Wednesday, April 29, I dined with him at Mr. Allan Ramsay's, where were Lord Binning, Dr. Robertson the historian, Sir Joshua Reynolds, and the Honourable Mrs. Boscawen, widow of the Admiral, and mother of the present Viscount Falmouth ; of whom, if it be not presumptuous in me to praise her, I would say, that her manners are the most agreeable, and her conversation the best of any lady with whom I ever had the happiness to be acquainted. Before Johnson came we talked a good deal of him ; Ramsay said, he had always found him a very polite man, and that he treated him with great respect, which he did very sincerely. I said, I worshipped him. ROBERT-SON : " But some of you spoil him : you should not worship him ; you should worship no man." BOS-WELL : " I cannot help worshipping him, he is so much superior to other men." ROBERTSON : " In criticism, and in wit and conversation, he is no doubt very excellent ; but in other respects he is not above other men ; he will believe anything, and will strenuously defend the most minute circumstances connected with the Church of England." BOSWELL : " Believe me, Doctor, you are much mistaken as to this ; for when you talk with him calmly in private he is very liberal in his way of thinking." ROBERTSON : " He and I have been always very gracious ; the first time I met him was one evening at Strahan's, when he had just had an unlucky altercation with Adam Smith, to whom he had been so rough, that Strahan, after Smith was gone, had remonstrated with him, and told him that I was coming soon, and that he was uneasy to think that he might behave in the same manner to me. ' No, no, Sir,' said Johnson, ' I warrant you Robertson and I shall do very well.' Accordingly he was gentle and good-humoured and courteous with me, the whole evening ; and he has been so upon every occasion that we have met since. I have often said (laughing), that I have been in a great measure indebted to Smith for my good reception." BOSWELL : " His power of reasoning is very strong, and he has a peculiar art of drawing characters, which is as rare as good portrait painting." SIR JOSHUA REYNOLDS : " He is undoubtedly admirable in this ; but, in order to mark the characters which he draws, he overcharges them, and gives people more than they really have, whether of good or bad."

No sooner did he, of whom we had been thus talking so easily, arrive, than we were all as quiet as a school upon the entrance of the head-master ; and were very soon sat down to a table covered with such variety of good things, as contributed not a little to dispose him to be pleased.

§ 147

On Saturday, May 2, I dined with him at Sir Joshua Reynolds's, where there was a very large company, and a great deal of conversation ; but owing to some circumstances which I cannot now recollect, I have no

record of any part of it, except that there were several
people there by no means of the Johnsonian school ;
so that less attention was paid to him than usual, which
put him out of humour ; and upon some imaginary
offence from me, he attacked me with such rudeness,
that I was vexed and angry, because it gave those
persons an opportunity of enlarging upon his supposed ferocity, and ill treatment of his best friends.
I was so much hurt, and had my pride so much roused,
that I kept away from him for a week ; and, perhaps,
might have kept away much longer, nay, gone to
Scotland without seeing him again, had not we fortunately met and been reconciled. To such unhappy
chances are human friendships liable.

On Friday, May 8, I dined with him at Mr. Langton's. I was reserved and silent, which I suppose he
perceived, and might recollect the cause. After dinner,
when Mr. Langton was called out of the room, and we
were by ourselves, he drew his chair near to mine, and
said, in a tone of conciliating courtesy, "Well, how
have you done ? " BOSWELL : "Sir, you have made
me very uneasy by your behaviour to me when we
were last at Sir Joshua Reynolds's. You know, my
dear Sir, no man has a greater respect and affection
for you, or would sooner go to the end of the world to
serve you. Now to treat me so—" He insisted that
I had interrupted him, which I assured him was not
the case ; and proceeded—"But why treat me so
before people who neither love you nor me ? " JOHN-
SON : "Well, I am sorry for it. I'll make it up to you
twenty different ways, as you please." BOSWELL :
"I said to-day to Sir Joshua, when he observed that
you *tossed* me sometimes—I don't care how often, or
how high he tosses me, when only friends are present, for
then I fall upon soft ground : but I do not like falling on
stones, which is the case when enemies are present.—
I think this is a pretty good image, Sir." JOHNSON :
"Sir, it is one of the happiest I have ever heard."

The truth is, there was no venom in the wounds which he inflicted at any time, unless they were irritated by some malignant infusion by other hands. We were instantly as cordial again as ever, and joined in hearty laugh at some ludicrous but innocent peculiarities of one of our friends. BOSWELL : " Do you think, Sir, it is always culpable to laugh at a man to his face ? " JOHNSON : " Why, Sir, that depends upon the man and the thing. If it is a slight man, and a slight thing, you may ; for you take nothing valuable from him."

§ 148

This year Johnson gave the world a luminous proof that the vigour of his mind in all its faculties, whether memory, judgment, or imagination, was not in the least abated ; for this year came out the first four volumes of his " Prefaces, Biographical and Critical, to the most Eminent of the English Poets," published by the booksellers of London. The remaining volumes came out in the year 1780. The Poets were selected by the several booksellers who had the honorary copyright, which is still preserved among them by mutual compact, notwithstanding the decision of the House of Lords against the perpetuity of literary property. We have his own authority [*Life of Watts*], that by his recommendation the poems of Blackmore, Watts, Pomfret, and Yalden, were added to the collection. Of this work I shall speak more particularly hereafter.

§ 149

On Wednesday, April 7, I dined with him at Sir Joshua Reynolds's. I have not marked what company was there. Johnson harangued upon the qualities of different liquors ; and spoke with great contempt of claret, as so weak, that " a man would be drowned by it before it made him drunk." He was

persuaded to drink one glass of it, that he might judge,
not from recollection, which might be dim, but from
immediate sensation. He shook his head, and said:
" Poor stuff ! No, Sir, claret is the liquor for boys ;
port for men ; but he who aspires to be a hero (smiling) must drink brandy. In the first place, the flavour
of brandy is most grateful to the palate ; and then
brandy will do soonest for a man what drinking *can* do
for him. There are, indeed, few who are able to drink
brandy. That is a power rather to be wished for than
attained. And yet (proceeded he), as in all pleasure
hope is a considerable part, I know not but fruition
comes too quick by brandy. Florence wine I think the
worst ; it is wine only to the eye ; it is wine neither
while you are drinking it, nor after you have drunk it ;
it neither pleases the taste, nor exhilarates the spirits."
I reminded him how heartily he and I used to drink
wine together, when we were first acquainted ; and
how I used to have a headache after sitting up with
him. He did not like to have this recalled, or, perhaps,
thinking that I boasted improperly, resolved to have
a witty stroke at me ; " Nay, Sir, it was not the *wine*
that made your head ache, but the *sense* that I put
into it." Boswell : " What, Sir, will sense make the
head ache ? " Johnson : " Yes, Sir (with a smile),
when it is not used to it."—No man who has a true
relish of pleasantry could be offended at this ; especially if Johnson in a long intimacy had given him
repeated proofs of his regard and good estimation. I
used to say, that as he had given me 1,000*l*. in praise,
he had a good right now and then to take a guinea
from me.

§ 150

In talking of Hackman, Johnson argued, as Judge
Blackstone had done, that his being furnished with
two pistols was a proof that he meant to shoot two
persons. Mr. Beauclerk said : " No ; for that every

wise man who intended to shoot himself, took two pistols, that he might be sure of doing it at once. Lord ——'s cook shot himself with one pistol, and lived ten days in great agony. Mr. ——, who loved buttered muffins, but durst not eat them because they disagreed with his stomach, resolved to shoot himself; and then he ate three buttered muffins for breakfast, before shooting himself, knowing that he should not be troubled with indigestion: *he* had two charged pistols; one was found lying charged upon the table by him, after he had shot himself with the other."—" Well," said Johnson, with an air of triumph, " you see here one pistol was sufficient." Beauclerk replied smartly, " Because it happened to kill him." And either then or very little afterwards, being piqued at Johnson's triumphant remark, added, " This is what you don't know, and I do." There was then a cessation of the dispute ; and some minutes intervened, during which dinner and the glass went on cheerfully ; when Johnson suddenly and abruptly exclaimed : " Mr. Beauclerk, how came you to talk so petulantly to me, as ' This is what you don't know, but what I know ? ' One thing *I* know, which *you* don't seem to know, that you are very uncivil." BEAUCLERK : " Because *you* began by being uncivil (which you always are)." The words in parentheses were, I believe, not heard by Dr. Johnson. Here again there was a cessation of arms. Johnson told me, that the reason why he waited at first some time without taking any notice of what Mr. Beauclerk said, was because he was thinking whether he should resent it. But when he considered that there were present a young Lord and an eminent traveller, two men of the world with whom he had never dined before, he was apprehensive that they might think they had a right to take such liberties with him as Beauclerk did, and therefore resolved he would not let it pass ; adding, " that he would not appear a coward." A little while after this, the conversation

turned on the violence of Hackman's temper. Johnson then said : " It was his business to *command* his
temper, as my friend, Mr. Beauclerk, should have
done some time ago." BEAUCLERK : " I should learn
of *you*, Sir." JOHNSON : " Sir, you have given *me*
opportunities enough of learning, when I have been in
your company. No man loves to be treated with contempt." BEAUCLERK (with a polite inclination towards
Johnson) : " Sir, you have known me twenty years,
and however I may have treated others, you may be
sure I could never treat you with contempt." JOHN-
SON : " Sir, you have said more than was necessary."
Thus it ended ; and Beauclerk's coach not having
come for him till very late, Dr. Johnson and another
gentleman sat with him a long time after the rest of
the company were gone ; and he and I dined at Beauclerk's on the Saturday se'nnight following.

After this tempest had subsided, I recollect the
following particulars of his conversation :

" I am always for getting a boy forward in his learning ; for that is a sure good. I would let him at first
read *any* English book which happens to engage his
attention ; because you have done a great deal, when
you have brought him to have entertainment from a
book. He'll get better books afterwards."

§ 151

On Saturday, April 24, I dined with him at Mr.
Beauclerk's, with Sir Joshua Reynolds, Mr. Jones
(afterwards Sir William), Mr. Langton, Mr. Steevens,
Mr. Paradise, and Dr. Higgins. I mentioned that Mr.
Wilkes had attacked Garrick to me, as a man who had
no friend. JOHNSON : " I believe he is right, Sir. Οἱ
φίλοι, οὐ φίλος—He had friends but no friend. Garrick was so diffused, he had no man to whom he wished
to unbosom himself. He found people always ready to
applaud him, and that always for the same thing ; so

he saw life with great uniformity." I took upon me, for once, to fight with Goliah's weapons, and play the sophist.—" Garrick did not need a friend, as he got from everybody all that he wanted. What is a friend? One who supports you and comforts you, while others do not. Friendship, you know, Sir, is the cordial drop, ' to make the nauseous draught of life go down : ' but if the draught be not nauseous, if it be all sweet, there is no occasion for that drop." JOHNSON : " Many men would not be content to live so. I hope I should not. They would wish to have an intimate friend, with whom they might compare minds, and cherish private virtues." One of the company mentioned Lord Chesterfield, as a man who had no friend. JOHNSON : " There were more materials to make friendship in Garrick, had he not been so diffused." BOSWELL : " Garrick was pure gold, but beat out to thin leaf. Lord Chesterfield was tinsel." JOHNSON : " Garrick was a very good man, the cheerfulest man of his age ; a decent liver in a profession which is supposed to give indulgence to licentiousness ; and a man who gave away, freely, money acquired by himself. He began the world with a great hunger for money ; the son of a half-pay officer, bred in a family whose study was to make fourpence do as much as others made fourpence-halfpenny do. But when he had got money, he was very liberal." I presumed to animadvert on his eulogy on Garrick, in his "Lives of the Poets." "You say, Sir, his death eclipsed the gaiety of nations." JOHNSON : " I could not have said more nor less. It is the truth ; *eclipsed* not *extinguished ;* and his death *did* eclipse ; it was like a storm." BOSWELL : " But why nations ? Did his gaiety extend farther than his own nation ? " JOHNSON : " Why, Sir, some exaggeration must be allowed. Besides, nations may be said—if we allow the Scotch to be a nation, and to have gaiety,—which they have not. *You* are an exception, though. Come, gentlemen, let us candidly

admit that there is one Scotchman who is cheerful."
BEAUCLERK: "But he is a very unnatural Scotchman." I, however, continued to think the compliment to Garrick hyperbolically untrue. His acting
had ceased some time before his death; at any rate
he had acted in Ireland but a short time, at an early
period of his life, and never in Scotland. I objected
also to what appears an anticlimax of praise, when
contrasted with the preceding panegyric,—" and
diminished the public stock of harmless pleasure!"—
" Is not *harmless pleasure* very tame?" JOHNSON:
" Nay, Sir, harmless pleasure is the highest praise.
Pleasure is a word of dubious import; pleasure is in
general dangerous and pernicious to virtue; to be able
therefore to furnish pleasure that is harmless, pleasure
pure and unalloyed, is as great a power as man can
possess." This was, perhaps, as ingenious a defence
as could be made; still, however, I was not satisfied.

§ 152

" As Johnson always allowed the extraordinary
talents of Mr. Burke, so Mr. Burke was fully sensible
of the wonderful powers of Johnson. Mr. Langton
recollects having passed an evening with both of them,
when Mr. Burke repeatedly entered upon topics which
it was evident he would have illustrated with extensive
knowledge and richness of expression; but Johnson
always seized upon the conversation, in which, however, he acquitted himself in a most masterly manner.
As Mr. Burke and Mr. Langton were walking home,
Mr. Burke observed that Johnson had been very great
that night; Mr. Langton joined in this, but added, he
could have wished to hear more from another person
(plainly intimating that he meant Mr. Burke); ' Oh,
no,' said Mr. Burke, ' it is enough for me to have rung
the bell to him.' "

" Beauclerk having observed to him of one of their

friends, that he was awkward at counting money, 'Why, Sir,' said Johnson, 'I am likewise awkward at counting money. But then, Sir, the reason is plain; I have had very little money to count.'"

"He had an abhorrence of affectation. Talking of old Mr. Langton, of whom he said, 'Sir, you will seldom see such a gentleman, such are his stores of literature, such his knowledge in divinity, and such his exemplary life;' he added, 'And, Sir, he has no grimace, no gesticulation, no bursts of admiration on trivial occasions; he never embraces you with an overacted cordiality.'"

"Being in company with a gentleman who thought fit to maintain Dr. Berkeley's ingenious philosophy, that nothing exists but as perceived by some mind; when the gentleman was going away, Johnson said to him, 'Pray, Sir, don't leave us; for we may perhaps forget to think of you, and then you will cease to exist.'"

§ 153

In 1781, Johnson at last completed his "Lives of the Poets," of which he gives this account: "Some time in March I finished the 'Lives of the Poets,' which I wrote in my usual way, dilatorily and hastily, unwilling to work, and working with vigour and haste." (*Prayers and Meditations*, p. 190.) In a memorandum previous to this, he says of them: "Written, I hope, in such a manner as may tend to the promotion of piety." (*Prayers and Meditations*, p. 174.)

This is the work, which of all Dr. Johnson's writings will perhaps be read most generally, and with most pleasure. Philology and biography were his favourite pursuits, and those who lived most in intimacy with him, heard him upon all occasions, when there was a proper opportunity, take delight in expatiating upon the various merits of the English Poets: upon the niceties of their characters, and the events of their progress through the world which they contribute to illuminate. His mind was so full of that kind of information, and it was so well arranged in his memory, that in performing what he had undertaken in this way, he had little more to do than to put his thoughts upon paper ; exhibiting first each poet's life, and then subjoining a critical examination of his genius and works. But when he began to write, the subject swelled in such a manner, that instead of prefaces to each poet, of no more than a few pages, as he had originally intended, he produced an ample, rich, and most entertaining view of them in every respect. In this he resembled Quintilian, who tells us, that in the composition of his Institutions of Oratory, " *Latius se tamen aperiente materia, plus quam imponebatur oneris sponte suscepi.*" The booksellers, justly sensible of the great additional value of the copyright, presented him with another hundred pounds, over and above two hundred, for which his agreement was to furnish such prefaces as he thought fit.

§ 154

The Life of Pope was written by Johnson *con amore*, both from the early possession which that writer had taken of his mind, and from the pleasure which he must have felt, in for ever silencing all attempts to lessen his poetical fame, by demonstrating his excellence, and pronouncing the following triumphant eulogium :—

" After all this, it is surely superfluous to answer the question that has once been asked, whether Pope was a poet ? otherwise than by asking in return, if Pope be not a poet, where is poetry to be found ? To circumscribe poetry by a definition, will only show the narrowness of the definer ; though a definition which shall exclude Pope, will not easily be made. Let us look round upon the present time, and back upon the past ; let us inquire to whom the voice of mankind has decreed the wreath of poetry ; let their productions be examined, and their claims stated, and the pretensions of Pope will be no more disputed."

I remember once to have heard Johnson say, " Sir, a thousand years may elapse before there shall appear another man with a power of versification equal to that of Pope." That power must undoubtedly be allowed its due share in enhancing the value of his captivating composition.

§ 155

On Monday, March 19, I arrived in London, and on Tuesday the 20th met him in Fleet Street, walking, or rather indeed moving, along ; for his peculiar march is thus described in a very just and picturesque manner in a short Life of him published very soon after his death :—" When he walked the streets, what with the constant roll of his head, and the concomitant motion of his body, he appeared to make his way by that motion, independent of his feet." That he was often much stared at while he advanced in this manner, may easily be believed ; but it was not safe to make sport of one so robust as he was. Mr. Langton saw him one day, in a fit of absence, by a sudden start, drive the load off a porter's back, and walk forward briskly without being conscious of what he had done. The porter was very angry but stood still, and eyed the huge figure with much earnestness, till he was satisfied that his wisest course was to be quiet and take up his burden again.

Our accidental meeting in the street after a long separation, was a pleasing surprise to us both. He stepped aside with me into Falcon Court, and made kind inquiries about my family, and as we were in a hurry going different ways, I promised to call on him next day; he said he was engaged to go out in the morning. "Early, Sir?" said I. JOHNSON: "Why, Sir, a London morning does not go with the sun."

I waited on him next evening, and he gave me a great portion of his original manuscript of his "Lives of the Poets," which he had preserved for me.

I found on visiting his friend, Mr. Thrale, that he was now very ill, and had removed, I suppose by the solicitation of Mrs. Thrale, to a house in Grosvenor Square. I was sorry to see him sadly changed in his appearance.

He told me I might now have the pleasure to see Dr. Johnson drink wine again, for he had lately returned to it. When I mentioned this to Johnson, he said, "I drink it now sometimes, but not socially." The first evening that I was with him at Thrale's I observed he poured a large quantity of it into a glass, and swallowed it greedily. Everything about his character and manners was forcible and violent; there never was any moderation; many a day did he fast, many a year did he refrain from wine; but when he did eat, it was voraciously; when he did drink wine, it was copiously. He could practise abstinence, but not temperance.

§ 156

Mr. Thrale appeared very lethargic to-day. I saw him again on Monday evening, at which time he was not thought to be in immediate danger; but early in the morning of Wednesday the 4th, he expired. Johnson was in the house, and thus mentions the event: "I felt almost the last flutter of his pulse, and looked for the last time upon the face that for fifteen years had never been turned upon me but with respect and benignity." (*Prayers and Meditations*, p. 191.) Upon that day there was a *call* of the LITERARY CLUB; but

Johnson apologized for his absence by the following note :—

"MR. JOHNSON knows that Sir Joshua Reynolds and the other gentlemen will excuse his incompliance with the call, when they are told that Mr. Thrale died this morning.

"Wednesday."

Mr Thrale's death was a very essential loss to Johnson, who, although he did not foresee all that afterwards happened, was sufficiently convinced that the comforts which Mr. Thrale's family afforded him would now in a great measure cease. He, however, continued to show a kind attention to his widow and children as long as it was acceptable : and he took upon him, with a very earnest concern, the office of one of his executors, the importance of which seemed greater than usual to him, from his circumstances having been always such, that he had scarcely any share in the real business of life. His friends of the CLUB were in hopes that Mr. Thrale might have made a liberal provision for him for his life, which, as Mr. Thrale left no son and a very large fortune, it would have been highly to his honour to have done ; and, considering Dr. Johnson's age, could not have been of long duration ; but he bequeathed him only two hundred pounds, which was the legacy given to each of his executors. I could not but be somewhat diverted by hearing Johnson talk in a pompous manner of his new office, and particularly of the concerns of the brewery, which it was at last resolved should be sold. Lord Lucan tells a very good story, which, if not precisely exact, is certainly characteristical : that when the sale of Thrale's brewery was going forward, Johnson appeared bustling about, with an inkhorn and pen in his buttonhole, like an exciseman ; and on being asked what he really considered to be the value of the property which was to be disposed of, answered, " We are not here to sell a parcel of boilers and vats, but the potentiality of growing rich beyond the dreams of avarice."

§ 157

On Saturday, April 7, I dined with him at Mr. Hoole's with Governor Bouchier and Captain Orme, both of whom had been long in the East Indies ; and being men of good sense and observation, were very entertaining. Johnson defended the oriental regulation of different *castes* of men, which was objected to as totally destructive of the hopes of rising in society by personal merit. He showed that there was a *principle* in it sufficiently plausible by analogy. " We see," said he, " in metals that there are different species ; and so likewise in animals, though one species may not differ very widely from another, as in the species of dogs,—the cur, the spaniel, and the mastiff. The Brahmins are the mastiffs of mankind."

On Thursday, April 12, I dined with him at a bishop's, where were Sir Joshua Reynolds, Mr. Berenger, and some more company. He had dined the day before at another bishop's. I have unfortunately recorded none of his conversation at the bishop's where we dined together : but I have preserved his ingenious defence of his dining twice abroad in Passion Week ; a laxity, in which I am convinced he would not have indulged himself at the time when he wrote his solemn paper in " The Rambler," upon that awful season. It appeared to me, that by being much more in company, and enjoying more luxurious living, he had contracted a keener relish for pleasure, and was consequently less rigorous in his religious rites. This he would not acknowledge ; but he reasoned with admirable sophistry, as follows : " Why, Sir, a bishop's calling company together in this week, is, to use the vulgar phrase, not *the thing*. But you must consider laxity is a bad thing; but preciseness is also a bad thing; and your general character may be more hurt by preciseness than by dining with a bishop in Passion Week. There might be a handle for reflection. It might be said, ' He refuses to dine with a bishop in Passion Week, but was three Sundays absent from church.' " BOSWELL: "Very true, Sir. But suppose a man to be uniformly of good conduct, would it not be better that he should refuse to dine with a bishop in this week, and so not encourage a bad practice by his example ? " JOHNSON: "Why, Sir, you are to consider whether you might not do more harm by lessening the influence of a bishop's character by your disapprobation in refusing him, than by going to him."

§ 158

On Friday, April 13, being Good Friday, I went to St. Clement's Church with him as usual. There I saw again his old fellow-collegian, Edwards, to whom I said, " I think, Sir, Dr. Johnson and you meet only at church."—" Sir," said he, " it is the best place we can meet in, except heaven, and I hope we shall meet there too." Dr. Johnson told me that there was very little communication between Edwards and him, after their unexpected renewal of acquaintance. " But," said he, smiling, " he met me once, and said, ' I am told you have written a very pretty book called " The Rambler." ' I was unwilling that he should leave the world in total darkness, and sent him a set."

§ 159

Some time after this, upon his making a remark which escaped my attention, Mrs. Williams and Mrs. Hall were both together striving to answer him. He grew angry, and called out loudly, " Nay, when you both speak at once, it is intolerable." But checking himself, and softening, he said, " This one may say, though you *are* ladies." Then he brightened into gay humour, and addressed them in the words of one of the songs in " The Beggar's Opera " :

" But two at a time there's no mortal can bear."

" What, Sir," said I, " are you going to turn Captain Macheath ? " There was something as pleasantly ludicrous in this scene as can be imagined. The contrast between Macheath, Polly and Lucy—and Dr. Samuel Johnson ; blind, peevish Mrs. Williams ; and lean, lank, preaching Mrs. Hall, was exquisite.

§ 160

On Friday, April 20, I spent with him one of the happiest days that I remember to have enjoyed in the whole course of my life. Mrs. Garrick, whose grief for the loss of her husband was, I believe, as sincere as wounded affection and admiration could produce, had this day, for the first time since his death, a select party of his friends to dine with her. The company was Miss Hannah More, who lived with her and whom she called her chaplain, Mrs. Boscawen, Mrs. Elizabeth Carter, Sir Joshua Reynolds, Dr. Burney, Dr. Johnson, and myself. We found ourselves very elegantly entertained at her house in the Adelphi, where I have passed many a pleasing hour with him "who gladdened life." She looked well, talked of her husband with complacency, and, while she cast her eyes on his portrait which hung over the chimney-piece, said, that " death was now the most agreeable object to her." The very semblance of David Garrick was cheering. Mr. Beauclerk, with happy propriety, inscribed under that fine portrait of him, which by Lady Diana's kindness is now the property of my friend Mr. Langton, the following passage from his beloved Shakespeare :

"   ————A merrier man,
    Within the limit of becoming mirth,
    I never spent an hour's talk withal :
    His eye begets occasion for his wit ;
    For every object that the one doth catch
    The other turns to a mirth-moving jest ;
    Which his fair tongue, conceit's expositor,
    Delivers in such apt and gracious words,
    That aged years play truant at his tales
    And younger hearings are quite ravished ;
    So sweet and voluble is his discourse."
                        LOVE'S LABOUR'S LOST, ii. 1.

We were all in fine spirits ; and I whispered to Mrs. Boscawen, " I believe this is as much as can be made of life." In addition to a splendid entertainment, we were regaled with Lichfield ale, which had a peculiar appropriate value. Sir Joshua, and Dr. Burney, and I, drank cordially of it to Dr. Johnson's health ; and though he would not join us, he as cordially answered, " Gentlemen, I wish you all as well as you do me."

The general effect of this day dwells upon my mind in fond remembrance ; but I do not find much conversation recorded. What I have preserved shall be faithfully given.

One of the company mentioned Mr. Thomas Hollis, the strenuous Whig, who used to send over Europe presents of democratical books with their boards stamped with daggers and caps of Liberty. Mrs. Carter said, " He was a bad man : he used to talk uncharitably." JOHNSON : " Poh ! poh ! Madam ; who is the worse for being talked of uncharitably ? Besides, he was a dull poor creature as ever lived : and I believe he would not have done harm to a man whom he knew to be of very opposite principles to his own. I remember once at the Society of Arts, when an advertisement was to be drawn up, he pointed me out as the man who could do it best. This, you will observe, was kindness to me. I however slipped away and escaped it."

§ 161

In the evening we had a large company in the drawing-room ; several ladies, the Bishop of Killaloe, Dr. Percy, Mr. Chamberlayne of the Treasury, &c. &c. Somebody said, the life of a mere literary man could not be very entertaining. JOHNSON : " But it certainly may. This is a remark which has been made, and repeated, without justice ; why should the life of a literary man be less entertaining than the life of any other man ? Are there not as interesting varieties in such a life ? As *a literary life* it may be very entertaining." BOSWELL : " But it must be better, surely, when it is diversified with a little active variety—such as his having gone to Jamaica ;—or— his having gone to the Hebrides." Johnson was not displeased at this.

Talking of a very respectable author, he told us a curious circumstance in his life, which was, that he had married a printer's devil. REYNOLDS : " A printer's devil, Sir ! Why, I thought a printer's devil was a creature with a black face and in rags." JOHNSON : " Yes, Sir. But I suppose he had her face washed, and put clean clothes on her." (Then looking very serious, and very earnest) " And she did not disgrace him ;—the woman had a bottom of good sense." The word *bottom* thus introduced was so ludicrous when contrasted with his gravity, that most of us could not forbear tittering and laughing ; though I recollect that the Bishop of Killaloe kept his countenance with perfect steadiness, while Miss Hannah More slily hid her face behind a lady's back who sat on the same settee with her. His pride could not bear that any expression of his should excite ridicule, when he did not intend it ; he therefore resolved to assume and exercise despotic power, glanced sternly around, and called out in a strong tone, " Where's the merriment ? " Then collecting himself, and looking awful, to make us feel how he could impose restraint, and as it were searching his mind for a still more ludicrous word, he slowly pronounced, " I say the *woman* was *fundamentally* sensible ; " as if he had said, hear this now, and laugh if you dare. We all sat composed as at a funeral.

He and I walked away together ; we stopped a little while by the rails of the Adelphi, looking on the Thames, and I said to him with some emotion, that I was now thinking of two friends we had lost, who once lived in the buildings behind us, Beauclerk and Garrick. " Ay, Sir," said he, tenderly, " and two such friends as cannot be supplied."

§ 162

On Tuesday, May 8, I had the pleasure of again dining with him and Mr. Wilkes, at Mr. Dilly's. No *negotiation* was now required to bring them together ; for Johnson was so well satisfied with the former interview, that he was very glad to meet Wilkes again, who was this day seated between Dr. Beattie and Dr. Johnson (between *Truth* and *Reason*, as General Paoli said, when I told him of it). WILKES : " I have been thinking, Dr. Johnson, that there should be a bill brought into Parliament that the controverted elections for Scotland should be tried in that country, at their own abbey of Holyrood House, and not here ; for the consequence of trying them here is, that we have an inundation of Scotchmen who come up and never go back again. Now here is Boswell, who is come upon the election for his own county, which will not last a fortnight." JOHNSON : " Nay, Sir, I see no reason why they should be tried at all ; for, you know, one Scotchman is as good as another." WILKES :

" Pray, Boswell, how much may be got in a year by an advocate at the Scotch bar?" BOSWELL: "I believe two thousand pounds." WILKES: "How can it be possible to spend that money in Scotland?" JOHNSON: "Why, Sir, the money may be spent in England; but there is a harder question. If one man in Scotland gets possession of two thousand pounds, what remains for all the rest of the nation?" WILKES: "You know, in the last war, the immense booty which Thurot carried off by the complete plunder of seven Scotch isles; he re-embarked with *three and sixpence.*" Here again Johnson and Wilkes joined in extravagant sportive raillery upon the supposed poverty of Scotland, which Dr. Beattie and I did not think it worth our while to dispute.

The subject of quotation being introduced, Mr. Wilkes censured it as pedantry. JOHNSON: "No, Sir, it is a good thing; there is a community of mind in it. Classical quotation is the *parole* of literary men all over the world." WILKES: "Upon the Continent they all quote the Vulgate Bible. Shakespeare is chiefly quoted here; and we quote also Pope, Prior, Butler, Waller, and sometimes Cowley."

We talked of letter-writing. JOHNSON: "It is now become so much the fashion to publish letters, that in order to avoid it, I put as little into mine as I can." BOSWELL: "Do what you will, Sir, you cannot avoid it. Should you even write as ill as you can, your letters would be published as curiosities:

' Behold a miracle! instead of wit,
    See two dull lines with Stanhope's pencil writ.' "

He gave us an entertaining account of *Bet Flint*, a woman of the town, who, with some eccentric talents and much effrontery, forced herself upon his acquaintance. " Bet," said he, " wrote her own Life in verse, which she brought to me, wishing that I would furnish her with a preface to it. (Laughing.) I used to say of her, that she was generally slut and drunkard ;—occasionally whore and thief. She had, however, genteel lodgings, a spinnet on which she played, and a boy that walked before her chair. Poor Bet was taken up on a charge of stealing a counterpane, and tried at the Old Bailey. Chief Justice [Willes], who loved a wench, summed up favourably, and she was acquitted. After which, Bet said, with a gay and satisfied air, ' Now that the counterpane is *my own*, I shall make a petticoat of it.' "

Talking of oratory, Mr. Wilkes described it as accompanied with all the charms of poetical expression. JOHNSON : " No, Sir ; oratory is the power of beating down your adversary's arguments, and putting better in their place." WILKES : " But this does not move the passions." JOHNSON : " He must be a weak man who is to be so moved." WILKES (naming a celebrated orator) : " Amidst all the brilliancy of [Burke's] imagination, and the exuberance of his wit, there is a strange want of *taste*. It was observed of Apelles's Venus, that her flesh seemed as if she had been nourished by roses : his oratory would sometimes make one suspect that he eats potatoes and drinks whisky."

Mr. Wilkes observed, how tenacious we are of forms in this country ; and gave as an instance, the vote of the House of Commons for remitting money to pay the army in America *in Portugal pieces*, when, in reality, the remittance is made not in Portugal money, but in our specie. JOHNSON : " Is there not a law, Sir, against exporting the current coin of the realm ? " WILKES : " Yes, Sir ; but might not the House of Commons, in case of real evident necessity, order our own current coin to be sent into our own colonies ? " —Here Johnson, with that quickness of recollection which distinguished him so eminently, gave the *Middlesex Patriot* an admirable retort upon his own ground.

" Sure, Sir, *you* don't think a *resolution of the House of Commons* equal to *the law of the land*." WILKES (at once perceiving the application) : " GOD forbid, Sir." —To hear what had been treated with such violence in " The False Alarm," now turned into pleasant repartee, was extremely agreeable. Johnson went on :—" Locke observes well, that a prohibition to export the current coin is impolitic ; for when the balance of trade happens to be against a state, the current coin *must* be exported."

Mr. Beauclerk's great library was this season sold in London by auction. Mr. Wilkes said, he wondered to find in it such a numerous collection of sermons : seeming to think it strange that a gentleman of Mr. Beauclerk's character in the gay world, should have chosen to have many compositions of that kind. JOHNSON : " Why, Sir, you are to consider, that sermons make a considerable branch of English literature ; so that a library must be very imperfect if it has not a numerous collection of sermons : and in all collections, Sir, the desire of augmenting them grows stronger in proportion to the advance in acquisition ; as motion is accelerated by the continuance of the *impetus*. Besides, Sir (looking at Mr. Wilkes with a placid but significant smile), a man may collect sermons with intention of making himself better by them. I hope Mr. Beauclerk intended, that some time or other that should be the case with him."

Mr. Wilkes said to me, loud enough for Dr. Johnson to hear, " Dr. Johnson should make me a present of his ' Lives of the Poets ' as I am a poor patriot, who cannot afford to buy them." Johnson seemed to take no notice of this hint ; but in a little while, he called to Mr. Dilly, " Pray, Sir, be so good as to send a set of my ' Lives ' to Mr. Wilkes, with my compliments." This was accordingly done ; and Mr. Wilkes paid Dr. Johnson a visit, was courteously received, and sat with him a long time.

The company gradually dropped away. Mr. Dilly himself was called downstairs upon business ; I left the room for some time ; when I returned, I was struck with observing Dr. Samuel Johnson and John Wilkes, Esq., literally *tête-à-tête ;* for they were reclined upon their chairs, with their heads leaning almost close to each other, and talking earnestly, in a kind of confidential whisper, of the personal quarrel between George the Second and the King of Prussia. Such a scene of perfectly easy sociality between two such opponents in the war of political controversy, as that which I now beheld, would have been an excellent subject for a picture. It presented to my mind the happy days which are foretold in Scripture, when the lion shall lie down with the kid.

§ 163

He disliked much all speculative desponding considerations, which tended to discourage men from diligence and exertion. He was in this like Dr. Shaw, the great traveller, who, Mr. Daines Barrington told me, used to say, " I hate a *cui bono* man." Upon being asked by a friend what he should think of a man who was apt to say *non est tanti ;*—" That he's a stupid fellow, Sir," answered Johnson : " What would these *tanti* men be doing the while ? " When I, in a low-spirited fit, was talking to him with indifference of the pursuits which generally engage us in a course of action, and inquiring a *reason* for taking so much trouble : " Sir," said he, in an animated tone, " it is driving on the system of life."

§ 164

I asked him, if he was not dissatisfied with having so small a share of wealth, and none of those dis-

tinctions in the state which are the objects of ambition. He had only a pension of three hundred a year.
Why was he not in such circumstances as to keep his
coach ? Why had he not some considerable office ?
JOHNSON : " Sir, I have never complained of the
world ; nor do I think that I have reason to complain.
It is rather to be wondered at that I have so much.
My pension is more out of the usual course of things
than any instance that I have known. Here, Sir, was
a man avowedly no friend to Government at the time,
who got a pension without asking for it. I never
courted the great ; they sent for me ; but I think
they now give me up. They are satisfied : they have
seen enough of me." Upon my observing that I could
not believe this, for they must certainly be highly
pleased by his conversation : conscious of his own
superiority, he answered, " No, Sir ; great lords and
great ladies don't love to have their mouths stopped."
This was very expressive of the effect which the force
of his understanding and brilliancy of his fancy could
not but produce ; and, to be sure, they must have
found themselves strangely diminished in his company. When I warmly declared how happy I was at
all times to hear him :—" Yes, Sir," said he ; " but
if you were Lord Chancellor, it would not be so : you
would then consider your own dignity."

§ 165

Johnson's charity to the poor was uniform and
extensive, both from inclination and principle. He
not only bestowed liberally out of his own purse, but
what is more difficult as well as rare, would beg from
others, when he had proper objects in view. This he
did judiciously as well as humanely. Mr. Philip Metcalfe tells me, that when he has asked him for some
money for persons in distress, and Mr. Metcalfe
has offered what Johnson thought too much, he

insisted on taking less, saying, " No, no, Sir : we must not *pamper* them."

§ 166

At a time when he was less able than he had once been to sustain a shock, he was suddenly deprived of Mr. Levett, which event he thus communicated to Dr. Lawrence :

" SIR,

" OUR old friend, Mr. Levett, who was last night eminently cheerful, died this morning. The man who lay in the same room, hearing an uncommon noise, got up and tried to make him speak, but without effect. He then called Mr. Holder, the apothecary, who, though when he came he thought him dead, opened a vein, but could draw no blood. So has ended the long life of a very useful and very blameless man. I am, Sir, your most humble servant,

" January 17, 1782."   " SAM. JOHNSON.

In one of his memorandum-books in my possession, is the following entry :—

" January 20, Sunday. Robert Levett was buried in the churchyard of Bridewell, between one and two in the afternoon. He died on Thursday 17, about seven in the morning, by an instantaneous death. He was an old and faithful friend ; I have known him from about 46. *Commendavi.* May GOD have mercy on him. May he have mercy on me."

Such was Johnson's affectionate regard for Levett, that he honoured his memory with the following pathetic verses :—

" CONDEMN'D to Hope's delusive mine,
    As on we toil from day to day,
By sudden blast or slow decline
    Our social comforts drop away.

Well try'd through many a varying year,
　　See LEVETT to the grave descend ;
Officious, innocent, sincere,
　　Of every friendless name the friend.

Yet still he fills affection's eye,
　　Obscurely wise, and coarsely kind,
Nor, letter'd Arrogance, deny
　　Thy praise to merit unrefin'd.

When fainting Nature call'd for aid,
　　And hov'ring Death prepar'd the blow,
His vigorous remedy display'd
　　The power of art without the show.

In Misery's darkest caverns known,
　　His ready help was ever nigh,
Where hopeless Anguish pour'd his groan,
　　And lonely Want retir'd to die.

No summons mock'd by chill delay,
　　No petty gains disdain'd by pride ;
The modest wants of every day
　　The toil of every day supply'd.

His virtues walk'd their narrow round,
　　Nor made a pause, nor left a void ;
And sure the eternal Master found
　　His single talent well employ'd.

The busy day, the peaceful night,
　　Unfelt, uncounted, glided by ;
His frame was firm, his powers were bright,
　　Though now his eightieth year was nigh.

Then, with no throbs of fiery pain,
　　No cold gradations of decay,
Death broke at once the vital chain,
　　And freed his soul the nearest way."

§ 167

The death of Mr. Thrale had made a very material
alteration with respect to Johnson's reception in that

family. The manly authority of the husband no longer curbed the lively exuberance of the lady; and as her vanity had been fully gratified, by having the Colossus of Literature attached to her for many years, she gradually became less assiduous to please him. Whether her attachment to him was already divided by another object, I am unable to ascertain: but it is plain that Johnson's penetration was alive to her neglect or forced attention; for on the 6th of October this year, we find him making a " parting use of the library " at Streatham, and pronouncing a prayer which he composed on leaving Mr. Thrale's family.

" Almighty GOD, Father of all mercy, help me by thy grace, that I may, with humble and sincere thankfulness, remember the comforts and conveniences which I have enjoyed at this place; and that I may resign them with holy submission, equally trusting in thy protection when thou givest, and when thou takest away. Have mercy upon me, O LORD, have mercy upon me.

" To thy fatherly protection, O LORD, I commend this family. Bless, guide, and defend them, that they may so pass through this world, as finally to enjoy in thy presence everlasting happiness, for JESUS CHRIST's sake. Amen." (*Prayers and Meditations,* 214.)

One cannot read this prayer, without some emotions not very favourable to the lady whose conduct occasioned it.

In one of his memorandum-books I find " Sunday, went to church at Streatham. *Templo valedixi cum osculo.*"

§ 168

Johnson thought the poems published as translations from Ossian had so little merit, that he said,

" Sir, a man might write such stuff for ever, if he would *abandon* his mind to it."

He said, " A man should pass a part of his time with *the laughers*, by which means anything ridiculous or particular about him might be presented to his view, and corrected." I observed, he must have been a bold laugher who would have ventured to tell Dr. Johnson of any of his particularities.

Having observed the vain ostentatious importance of many people in quoting the authority of dukes and lords, as having been in their company, he said, he went to the other extreme, and did not mention his authority when he should have done it, had it not been that of a duke or a lord.

Dr. Goldsmith said once to Dr. Johnson, that he wished for some additional members to the LITERARY CLUB, to give it an agreeable variety ; " for " said he, " there can now be nothing new among us ; we have travelled over one another's minds." Johnson seemed a little angry and said, " Sir, you have not travelled over *my* mind, I promise you."

§ 169

Johnson's dexterity in retort, when he seemed to be driven to an extremity by his adversary, was very remarkable. Of his power in this respect, our common friend, Mr. Windham of Norfolk, has been pleased to furnish me with an eminent instance. However unfavourable to Scotland, he uniformly gave liberal praise to George Buchanan, as a writer. In a conversation concerning the literary merits of the two countries, in which Buchanan was introduced, a Scotchman, imagining that on this ground he should have an undoubted triumph over him, exclaimed, " Ah, Dr. Johnson, what would you have said of Buchanan, had he been an Englishman ? "—" Why, Sir," said Johnson after a little pause, " I should *not* have said of Buchanan, had he been an *Englishman*, what I will now say of him as a *Scotchman*,—that he was the only man of genius his country ever produced."

And this brings to my recollection another instance of the same nature. I once reminded him that when Dr. Adam Smith was expatiating on the beauty of Glasgow, he had cut him short by saying, " Pray, Sir, have you ever seen Brentford ? " and I took the liberty to add, " My dear Sir, surely that was *shocking*." —" Why, then, Sir," he replied, " you have never seen Brentford."

Though his usual phrase for conversation was *talk*, yet he made a distinction ; for when he once told me that he dined the day before at a friend's house, with " a very pretty company," and I asked him if there was good conversation, he answered, " No, Sir ; we had *talk* enough, but no *conversation* ; there was nothing *discussed*."

§ 170

The heterogeneous composition of human nature was remarkably exemplified in Johnson. His liberality in giving his money to persons in distress was extraordinary. Yet there lurked about him a propensity to paltry saving. One day I owned to him that " I was occasionally troubled with a fit of *narrowness*." " Why, Sir," said he, " so am I. *But I do not tell it*." He has now and then borrowed a shilling of me ; and when I asked him for it again, seemed to be rather out of humour. A droll little circumstance once occurred : as if he meant to reprimand my minute exactness as a creditor, he thus addressed me ; —" Boswell, *lend* me sixpence—*not to be repaid*."

This great man's attention to small things was very remarkable. As an instance of it, he one day said to me : " Sir, when you get silver in change for a guinea, look carefully at it ; you may find some curious piece of coin."

Though a stern, *true-born Englishman*, and fully prejudiced against all other nations, he had discernment enough to see, and candour enough to censure, the cold reserve too common among Englishmen towards strangers : " Sir," said he, " two men of any other nation who are shown into a room together, at a house where they are both visitors, will immediately find some conversation. But two Englishmen will probably go each to a different window, and remain in obstinate silence. Sir, we as yet do not enough understand the common rights of humanity."

Johnson was at a certain period of his life a good deal with the Earl of Shelburne, now Marquis of Lansdowne, as he doubtless could not but have a due value for that nobleman's activity of mind and uncommon acquisitions of important knowledge, however much he might disapprove of other parts of his Lordship's character, which were widely different from his own.

Morice Morgann, Esq., author of the very ingenious " Essay on the Character of Falstaff," being a particular friend of his Lordship, had once an opportunity of entertaining Johnson for a day or two at Wycombe, when this Lord was absent, and by him I have been favoured with two anecdotes.

One is not a little to the credit of Johnson's candour. Mr. Morgann and he had a dispute pretty late at night, in which Johnson would not give up, though he had the wrong side, and in short, both kept the field. Next morning, when they met in the breakfast-room, Dr. Johnson accosted Mr. Morgann thus : " Sir, I have been thinking on our dispute last night—*You were in the right*."

The other was as follows : Johnson, for sport perhaps, or from the spirit of contradiction, eagerly maintained that Derrick had merit as a writer. Mr. Morgann argued with him directly in vain. At length he had recourse to this device. " Pray, Sir," said he, " whether do you reckon Derrick or Smart the best poet ? " Johnson at once felt himself roused ; and answered, " Sir, there is no settling the point of precedency between a louse and a flea."

Once, when checking my boasting too frequently of myself in company, he said to me : " Boswell, you often vaunt so much as to provoke ridicule. You put me in mind of a man who was standing in the kitchen of an inn with his back to the fire, and thus accosted the person next him, ' Do you know, Sir, who I am ? ' ' No, Sir,' said the other, ' I have not that advantage.' ' Sir,' said he, ' I am the *great* TWALMLEY, who invented the New Floodgate Iron." The Bishop of Killaloe, on my repeating the story to him, defended TWALMLEY by observing that he was entitled to the epithet of *great ;* for Virgil in his group of worthies in the Elysian fields—

Hic manus, ob patriam pugnando vulnera passi, &c.

mentions

Inventas aut qui vitam excoluere per artes. (*Æn.* vi.)

He was pleased to say to me one morning when we were left alone in his study, " Boswell, I think I am easier with you than with almost anybody."

He would not allow Mr. David Hume any credit for his political principles, though similar to his own ; saying of him, " Sir, he was a Tory by chance."

His acute observation of human life made him remark, " Sir, there is nothing by which a man exasperates most people more, than by displaying a superior ability of brilliancy in conversation. They seem pleased at the time ; but their envy makes them curse him at their hearts."

§ 171

Johnson's love of little children, which he discovered upon all occasions, calling them "pretty dears," and giving them sweetmeats, was an undoubted proof of the real humanity and gentleness of his disposition.

His uncommon kindness to his servants, and serious concern, not only for their comfort in this world, but their happiness in the next, was another unquestionable evidence of what all, who were intimately acquainted with him, knew to be true.

Nor would it be just, under this head, to omit the fondness which he showed for animals which he had taken under his protection. I never shall forget the indulgence with which he treated Hodge, his cat ; for whom he himself used to go out and buy oysters, lest the servants having that trouble should take a dislike to the poor creature. I am, unluckily, one of those who have an antipathy to a cat, so that I am uneasy when in the room with one ; and I own, I frequently suffered a good deal from the presence of the same Hodge. I recollect him one day scrambling up Dr. Johnson's breast apparently with much satisfaction, while my friend, smiling and half-whistling, rubbed down his back, and pulled him by the tail ; and when I observed he was a fine cat, saying, " Why, yes, Sir, but I have had cats whom I liked better than this ; " and then, as if perceiving Hodge to be out of countenance, adding, " but he is a very fine cat, a very fine cat indeed."

This reminds me of the ludicrous account which he gave Mr. Langton, of the despicable state of a young gentleman of good family. " Sir, when I heard of him last he was running about town shooting cats." And then in a sort of kindly reverie, he bethought himself of his own favourite cat, and said, " But Hodge shan't be shot : no, no, Hodge shall not be shot."

§ 172

On Saturday, April 12, I visited him, in company with Mr. Windham of Norfolk, whom, though a Whig, he highly valued. One of the best things he ever said was to this gentleman ; who before he set out for Ireland as Secretary to Lord Northington, when Lord Lieutenant, expressed to the sage some modest and virtuous doubts, whether he could bring himself to practise those arts which it is supposed a person in that situation has occasion to employ. "Don't be afraid, Sir," said Johnson, with a pleasant smile, "you will soon make a very pretty rascal."

§ 173

On Thursday, May 1, I visited him in the evening along with young Mr. Burke. He said : "It is strange that there should be so little reading in the world, and so much writing. People in general do not willingly read, if they can have anything else to amuse them. There must be an external impulse ; emulation, or vanity, or avarice. The progress which the understanding makes through a book has more pain than pleasure in it. Language is scanty, and inadequate to express the nice gradations and mixtures of our feelings. No man reads a book of science from pure inclination. The books that we do read with pleasure are light compositions, which contain a quick succession of events. However, I have this year read all Virgil through. I read a book of the ' Æneid ' every night ; so it was done in twelve nights, and I had a great delight in it. The ' Georgics ' did not give me so much pleasure, except the fourth book. The ' Eclogues ' I have almost all by heart. I do not think the story of the ' Æneid ' interesting. I like the story of the ' Odyssey ' much better ; and this not on account of the wonderful things which it contains ; for there

are wonderful things enough in the ' Æneid ';—the
ships of the Trojans turned to sea-nymphs,—the tree
at Polydorus's tomb dropping blood. The story of the
' Odyssey ' is interesting, as a great part of it is
domestic.—It has been said there is pleasure in writing, particularly in writing verses. I allow, you may
have pleasure from writing, after it is over, if you have
written well ; but you don't go willingly to it again.
I know when I have been writing verses, I have run
my finger down the margin, to see how many I had
made and how few I had to make."

§ 174

I have no minute of any interview with Johnson
till Thursday, May 15th, when I find what follows :
BOSWELL : " I wish much to be in Parliament, Sir."
JOHNSON : " Why, Sir, unless you come resolved to
support any administration, you would be the worse
for being in Parliament, because you would be obliged
to live more expensively."—BOSWELL : " Perhaps,
Sir, I should be the less happy for being in Parliament.
I never would sell my vote, and I should be vexed if
things went wrong." JOHNSON : " That's cant, Sir.
It would not vex you more in the House, than in the
gallery : public affairs vex no man." BOSWELL :
" Have not they vexed yourself a little, Sir ? Have
not you been vexed by all the turbulence of this reign,
and by that absurd vote of the House of Commons,
' That the influence of the Crown has increased, is
increasing, and ought to be diminished ' ? " JOHN-
SON : " Sir, I have never slept an hour less, nor ate
an ounce less meat. I would have knocked the factious
dogs on the head, to be sure ; but I was not vexed."
BOSWELL : " I declare, Sir, upon my honour, I did
imagine I was vexed and took a pride in it ; but it
was, perhaps, cant ; for I own I neither ate less, nor
slept less." JOHNSON : " My dear friend, clear your

mind of cant. You may *talk* as other people do : you may say to a man, ' Sir, I am your most humble servant.' You are *not* his most humble servant. You may say, ' These are bad times ; it is a melancholy thing to be reserved to such times.' You don't mind the times. You tell a man, ' I am sorry you had such bad weather the last day of your journey, and were so much wet.' You don't care sixpence whether he is wet or dry. You may *talk* in this manner ; it is a mode of talking in society : but don't *think* foolishly."

§ 175

I assured him that, in the extensive and various range of his acquaintance, there never had been any one who had a more sincere respect and affection for him than I had. He said : " I believe it, Sir. Were I in distress, there is no man to whom I should sooner come than to you. I should like to come and have a cottage in your park, toddle about, live mostly on milk, and be taken care of by Mrs. Boswell. She and I are good friends now : are we not ?."

Talking of devotion, he said : " Though it be true that ' GOD dwelleth not in temples made with hands,' yet in this state of being, our minds are more piously affected in places appropriated to divine worship, than in others. Some people have a particular room in their houses, where they say their prayers ; of which I do not disapprove, as it may animate their devotion."

He embraced me and gave me his blessing, as usual when I was leaving him for any length of time. I walked from his door to-day, with a fearful apprehension of what might happen before I returned.

§ 176

My anxious apprehensions at parting with him this year, proved to be but too well founded ; for not long afterwards he had a dreadful stroke of the palsy, of which there are very full and accurate accounts in letters written by himself, to show with what composure of mind, and resignation to the Divine Will, his steady piety enabled him to behave.

" TO MR. EDMUND ALLEN.

" DEAR SIR,

" IT has pleased GOD this morning, to deprive me of the powers of speech : and as I do not know but that it may be his farther good pleasure to deprive me soon of my senses, I request you will on the receipt of this note, come to me, and act for me, as the exigencies of my case may require.

" I am, sincerely yours,
" SAM. JOHNSON.

" June 17, 1783."

§ 177

Such was the general vigour of his constitution, that he recovered from this alarming and severe attack with wonderful quickness ; so that in July he was able to make a visit to Mr. Langton at Rochester, where he passed about a fortnight, and made little excursions as easily as at any time of his life.

§ 178

He this autumn received a visit from the celebrated Mrs. Siddons. He gives this account of it in one of his letters to Mrs. Thrale [October 27] :—

" Mrs. Siddons, in her visit to me, behaved with great modesty and propriety, and left nothing behind her to be censured or despised. Neither praise nor money, the two powerful corrupters of mankind, seem to have depraved her. I shall be glad to see her again.

Her brother Kemble calls on me, and pleases me very well. Mrs. Siddons and I talked of plays; and she told me her intention of exhibiting this winter the characters of Constance, Catharine, and Isabella, in Shakespeare."

Mr. Kemble has favoured me with the following minute of what passed at this visit:

" When Mrs. Siddons came into the room, there happened to be no chair ready for her, which he observing, said with a smile, ' Madam, you who so often occasion a want of seats to other people, will the more easily excuse the want of one yourself.'"

§ 179

In the end of this year he was seized with a spasmodic asthma of such violence, that he was confined to the house in great pain, being sometimes obliged to sit all night in his chair, a recumbent posture being so hurtful to his respiration, that he could not endure lying in bed; and there came upon him at the same time that oppressive and fatal disease, a dropsy. It was a very severe winter, which probably aggravated his complaints; and the solitude in which Mr. Levett and Mrs. Williams had left him, rendered his life very gloomy. Mrs. Desmoulins, who still lived, was herself so very ill, that she could contribute very little to his relief. He, however, had none of that unsocial shyness which we commonly see in people afflicted with sickness. He did not hide his head from the world, in solitary abstraction; he did not deny himself to the visits of his friends and acquaintances; but at all times, when he was not overcome by sleep, was ready for conversation as in his best days.

§ 180

On the evening of Saturday, May 15, he was in fine spirits, at our Essex Head Club. He told us: " I dined yesterday at Mrs. Garrick's with Mrs. Carter, Miss Hannah More, and Miss Fanny Burney. Three such women are not to be found : I know not where I could find a fourth, except Mrs. Lennox, who is superior to them all." BOSWELL : " What ! had you them all to yourself, Sir ? " JOHNSON : " I had them all as much as they were had ; but it might have been better had there been more company there." BOSWELL : " Might not Mrs. Montague have been a fourth ? " JOHNSON : " Sir, Mrs. Montague does not make a trade of her wit ; but Mrs. Montague is a very extraordinary woman ; she has a constant stream of conversation, and it is always impregnated ; it has always meaning." BOSWELL : " Mr. Burke has a constant stream of conversation." JOHNSON : " Yes, Sir ; if a man were to go by chance at the same time with Burke under a shed, to shun a shower, he would say—' This is an extraordinary man.' If Burke should go into a stable to see his horse dressed, the ostler would say—' We have had an extraordinary man here.' " BOSWELL : " Foote was a man who never failed in conversation. If he had gone into a stable—" JOHNSON : " Sir, if he had gone into the stable, the ostler would have said, ' Here has been a comical fellow ; ' but he would not have respected him." BOSWELL : " And, Sir, the ostler would have answered him, would have given him as good as he brought, as the common saying is." JOHNSON : " Yes, Sir ; and Foote would have answered the ostler.— When Burke does not descend to be merry, his conversation is very superior indeed. There is no proportion between the powers which he shows in serious talk and in jocularity. When he lets himself down to that, he is in the kennel." I have in another place opposed, and I hope with success, Dr. Johnson's very singular and erroneous notion as to Mr. Burke's pleasantry. Mr. Windham now said low to me, that he differed from our great friend in this observation; for that Mr. Burke was often very happy in his merriment. It would not have been right for either of us to have contradicted Johnson at this time, in a society all of whom did not know and value Mr. Burke as much as we did. It might have occasioned something more rough, and at any rate would probably have checked the flow of Johnson's good humour. He called to us with a sudden air of exultation, as the thought started into his mind: "O gentlemen, I must tell you a very great thing. The Empress of Russia has ordered the 'Rambler' to be translated into the Russian language; so I shall be read on the banks of the Wolga. Horace boasts that his fame would extend as far as the banks of the Rhone; now the Wolga is farther from me than the Rhone is from Horace." BOSWELL: "You must certainly be pleased with this, Sir." JOHNSON: "I am pleased, Sir, to be sure. A man is pleased to find he has succeeded in that which he has endeavoured to do."

One of the company mentioned his having seen a noble person driving in his carriage, and looking exceedingly well, notwithstanding his great age. JOHNSON: "Ah, Sir; that is nothing. Bacon observes, that a stout healthy old man is like a tower undermined."

On Sunday, May 16, I found him alone; he talked of Mrs. Thrale with much concern, saying, "Sir, she has done everything wrong, since Thrale's bridle was off her neck;" and was proceeding to mention some circumstances which have since been the subject of public discussion, when he was interrupted by the arrival of Dr. Douglas, now Bishop of Salisbury.

§ 181

We talked of our worthy friend Mr. Langton. He said, " I know not who will go to Heaven if Langton does not. Sir, I could almost say, *Sit anima mea cum Langtono*."

He however charged Mr. Langton with what he thought want of judgment upon an interesting occasion. " When I was ill," said he, " I desired he would tell me sincerely in what he thought my life was faulty. Sir, he brought me a sheet of paper, on which he had written down several texts of Scripture, recommending Christian charity. And when I questioned him what occasion I had given for such an animadversion, all that he could say amounted to this,—that I sometimes contradicted people in conversation. Now what harm does it do to any man to be contradicted?" BOSWELL : " I suppose he meant the *manner* of doing it ; roughly, and harshly." JOHNSON : " And who is the worse for that ? " BOSWELL : " It hurts people of weaker nerves." JOHNSON : " I know no such weak-nerved people." Mr. Burke, to whom I related this conference, said, " It is well, if when a man comes to die, he has nothing heavier upon his conscience than having been a little rough in conversation."

Johnson, at the time when the paper was presented to him, though at first pleased with the attention of his friend, whom he thanked in an earnest manner, soon exclaimed in a loud and angry tone, " What is your drift, Sir ? " Sir Joshua Reynolds pleasantly observed, that it was a scene for a comedy, to see a penitent get into a violent passion and belabour his confessor.

§ 182

He had now a great desire to go to Oxford, as his first jaunt after his illness ; we talked of it for some

days, and I had promised to accompany him. He was
impatient and fretful to-night, because I did not at
once agree to go with him on Thursday. When I considered how ill he had been, and what allowance should
be made for the influence of sickness upon his temper,
I resolved to indulge him, though with some inconvenience to myself, as I wished to attend the musical
meeting in honour of Handel, in Westminster Abbey,
on the following Saturday.

In the midst of his own diseases and pains, he was
ever compassionate to the distresses of others, and
actively earnest in procuring them aid, as appears
from a note to Sir Joshua Reynolds, of June, in these
words : " I am ashamed to ask for some relief for a
poor man, to whom, I hope, I have given what I can
be expected to spare. The man importunes me, and
the blow goes round. I am going to try another air on
Thursday."

On Thursday, June 3, the Oxford post-coach took
us up in the morning at Bolt Court. The other two
passengers were Mrs. Beresford and her daughter, two
very agreeable ladies from America ; they were going
to Worcestershire, where they then resided. Frank
had been sent by his master the day before to take
places for us ; and I found from the way-bill that Dr.
Johnson had made our names be put down. Mrs.
Beresford, who had read it, whispered me, " Is this
the great Dr. Johnson ? " I told her it was ; so she
was then prepared to listen. As she soon happened to
mention, in a voice so low that Johnson did not hear it,
that her husband had been a member of the American
Congress, I cautioned her to beware of introducing that
subject, as she must know how very violent Johnson
was against the people of that country. He talked a
great deal. But I am sorry I have preserved little
of the conversation. Miss Beresford was so much
charmed, that she said to me aside, " How he does
talk ! Every sentence is an essay." She amused

herself in the coach with knotting ; he would scarcely allow this species of employment any merit. " Next to mere idleness," said he, " I think knotting is to be reckoned in the scale of insignificance ; though I once attempted to learn knotting. Dempster's sister (looking to me) endeavoured to teach me it ; but I made no progress."

I was surprised at his talking without reserve in the public post-coach of the state of his affairs : " I have," said he, " about the world, I think, above a thousand pounds, which I intend shall afford Frank an annuity of seventy pounds a year." Indeed his openness with people at a first interview was remarkable. He said once to Mr. Langton, " I think I am like Squire Richard in ' The Journey to London,' *I'm never strange in a strange place.*" He was truly *social.* He strongly censured what is much too common in England among persons of condition—maintaining an absolute silence, when unknown to each other ; as for instance, when occasionally brought together in a room before the master or mistress of the house has appeared. " Sir, that is being so uncivilized as not to understand the common rights of humanity."

At the inn where we stopped he was exceedingly dissatisfied with some roast mutton which he had for dinner. The ladies, I saw, wondered to see the great philosopher, whose wisdom and wit they had been admiring all the way, get into ill-humour from such a cause. He scolded the waiter, saying, " It is as bad as bad can be : it is ill-fed, ill-killed, ill-kept, and ill-dressed."

He bore the journey very well, and seemed to feel himself elevated as he approached Oxford, that magnificent and venerable seat of Learning, Orthodoxy, and Toryism. Frank came in the heavy coach, in readiness to attend him ; and we were received with the most polite hospitality at the house of his old friend Dr. Adams, Master of Pembroke College, who had given us a kind invitation. Before we were set down, I communicated to Johnson, my having engaged to return to London directly, for the reason I have mentioned, but that I would hasten back to him again. He was pleased that I had made this journey merely to keep him company. He was easy and placid with Dr. Adams, Mrs. and Miss Adams, and Mrs. Kennicot, widow of the learned Hebræan, who was here on a visit. He soon dispatched the inquiries which were made about his illness and recovery, by a short and distinct narrative; and then assuming a gay air, repeated from Swift,

> " Nor think on our approaching ills,
> And talk of spectacles and pills."

Dr. Newton, the Bishop of Bristol, having been mentioned, Johnson recollecting the manner in which he had been censured by that prelate, thus retaliated: " Tom knew he should be dead before what he has said of me would appear. He durst not have printed it while he was alive." Dr. Adams : " I believe his ' Dissertations on the Prophecies ' is his great work." Johnson : " Why, Sir, it is *Tom's* great work ; but how far it is great, or how much of it is Tom's are other questions. I fancy a considerable part of it was borrowed." Dr. Adams : " He was a very successful man." Johnson : " I don't think so, Sir.—He did not get very high. He was late in getting what he did get ; and he did not get it by the best means. I believe he was a gross flatterer."

I fulfilled my intention by going to London, and returned to Oxford on Wednesday the 9th of June, when I was happy to find myself again in the same agreeable circle at Pembroke College, with the comfortable prospect of making some stay. Johnson welcomed my return with more than ordinary glee.

§ 183

Dr. Johnson and I went in Dr. Adams's coach to dine with Dr. Nowell, Principal of St. Mary Hall, at his beautiful villa at Iffley, on the banks of the Isis, about two miles from Oxford. While we were upon the road, I had the resolution to ask Johnson whether he thought that the roughness of his manner had been an advantage or not, and if he would not have done more good if he had been more gentle. I proceeded to answer myself thus : " Perhaps it has been of advantage, as it has given weight to what you said : you could not, perhaps, have talked with such authority without it." JOHNSON : " No, Sir ; I have done more good as I am. Obscenity and impiety have always been repressed in my company." BOSWELL : " True, Sir ; and that is more than can be said of every bishop. Greater liberties have been taken in the presence of a bishop, though a very good man, from his being milder, and therefore not commanding such awe. Yet, Sir, many people who might have been benefited by your conversation, have been frightened away. A worthy friend of ours has told me, that he has often been afraid to talk to you." JOHNSON : " Sir, he need not have been afraid, if he had anything rational to say. If he had not, it was better he did not talk."

Dr. Nowell is celebrated for having preached a sermon before the House of Commons, on the 30th of January, 1772, full of high Tory sentiments, for which he was thanked as usual, and printed it at their request ; but, in the midst of that turbulence and faction which disgraced a part of the present reign, the thanks were afterwards ordered to be expunged. This strange conduct sufficiently exposes itself ; and Dr. Nowell will ever have the honour which is due to a lofty friend of our monarchical constitution. Dr. Johnson said to me, " Sir, the Court will be very much to blame, if he is not promoted." I told this to Dr.

Nowell ; and asserting my humbler, though not less
zealous exertions in the same cause, I suggested, that
whatever return we might receive, we should still have
the consolation of being like Butler's steady and generous Royalist,—

> " True as the dial to the sun,
> Although it be not shone upon."

We were well entertained and very happy at Dr.
Nowell's, where was a very agreeable company ; and
we drank " Church and King " after dinner, with true
Tory cordiality.

§ 184

Johnson having argued for some time with a perti-
nacious gentleman : his opponent, who had talked in
a very puzzling manner, happened to say, " I don't
understand you, Sir ; " upon which Johnson observed,
" Sir, I have found you an argument ; but I am not
obliged to find you an understanding."

§ 185

His generous humanity to the miserable was almost
beyond example. The following instance is well
attested : Coming home late one night, he found a
poor woman lying in the street, so much exhausted
that she could not walk ; he took her upon his back,
and carried her to his house, where he discovered that
she was one of those wretched females who had fallen
into the lowest state of vice, poverty, and disease.
Instead of harshly upbraiding her, he had her taken
care of with all tenderness for a long time, at a considerable expense, till she was restored to health,
and endeavoured to put her into a virtuous way
of living.

§ 186

Mr. Steevens adds this testimony :

" It is unfortunate, however, for Johnson, that his particularities and frailties can be more distinctly traced than his good and amiable exertions. Could the many bounties he studiously concealed, the many acts of humanity he performed in private, be displayed with equal circumstantiality, his defects would be so far lost in the blaze of his virtues, that the latter only would be regarded."

Though from my very high admiration of Johnson, I have wondered that he was not courted by all the great and all the eminent persons of his time, it ought fairly to be considered that no man of humble birth, who lived entirely by literature, in short no author by profession, ever rose in this country into that personal notice which he did. In the course of this work a numerous variety of names has been mentioned, to which many might be added. I cannot omit Lord and Lady Lucan, at whose house he often enjoyed all that an elegant table and the best company can contribute to happiness ; he found hospitality united with extraordinary accomplishments, and embellished with charms of which no man could be insensible.

On Tuesday, June 22, I dined with him at THE LITERARY CLUB, the last time of his being in that respectable society. The other members present were the Bishop of St. Asaph, Lord Eliot, Lord Palmerston, Dr. Fordyce, and Mr. Malone. He looked ill ; but had such a manly fortitude, that he did not trouble the company with melancholy complaints. They all showed evident marks of kind concern about him, with which he was much pleased, and he exerted himself to be as entertaining as his indisposition allowed him.

The anxiety of his friends to preserve so estimable a life as long as human means might be supposed to have influence, made them plan for him a retreat from the severity of a British winter to the mild climate of Italy. This scheme was at last brought to a serious resolution at General Paoli's, where I had often talked of it. One essential matter, however, I understood was necessary to be previously settled, which was obtaining such an addition to his income as would be sufficient to enable him to defray the expense in a manner becoming the first literary character of a great nation, and, independent of all his other merits, the author of THE DICTIONARY OF THE ENGLISH LANGUAGE. The person to whom I above all others thought I should apply to negotiate this business, was the Lord Chancellor, because I knew that he highly valued Johnson, and that Johnson highly valued his Lordship ; so that it was no degradation of my illustrious friend to solicit for him the favour of such a man. I have mentioned what Johnson said of him to me when he was at the bar ; and after his Lordship was advanced to the seals, he said of him, " I would prepare myself for no man in England but Lord Thurlow. When I am to meet with him, I should wish to know a day before." How he would have prepared himself, I cannot conjecture. Would he have selected certain topics, and considered them in every view, so as to be in readiness to argue them at all points ? and what may we suppose those topics to have been ? I once started the curious inquiry to the great man who was the subject of this compliment : he smiled, but did not pursue it.

I first consulted with Sir Joshua Reynolds, who perfectly coincided in opinion with me ; and I therefore, though personally very little known to his Lordship, wrote to him, stating the case, and requesting his good offices for Dr. Johnson. I mentioned that I was obliged to set out for Scotland early in the following week, so that if his Lordship should have any commands for me as to this pious negotiation, he would be pleased to send them before that time ; otherwise Sir Joshua Reynolds would give all attention to it.

This application was made not only without any suggestion on the part of Johnson himself, but was utterly unknown to him, nor had he the smallest suspicion of it. Any insinuations, therefore, which since his death have been thrown out, as if he had stooped to ask what was superfluous, are without any foundation. But, had he asked it, it would not have been superfluous ; for though the money he had saved proved to be more than his friends imagined, or than I believe he himself, in his carelessness concerning worldly matters knew it to be, had he travelled upon the Continent an augmentation of his income would by no means have been unnecessary.

§ 187

We now behold Johnson for the last time in his native city, for which he ever retained a warm affection, and which, by a sudden apostrophe, under the word *Lich*, he introduces with reverence, into his immortal Work, THE ENGLISH DICTIONARY :—" *Salve magna parens !* " While here, he felt a revival of all the tenderness of filial affection, an instance of which appeared in his ordering the grave-stone and inscription over Elizabeth Blaney to be substantially and carefully renewed.

To Mr. Henry White, a young clergyman, with whom he now formed an intimacy, so as to talk to him with great freedom, he mentioned that he could not in general accuse himself of having been an undutiful son. " Once, indeed," said he, " I was disobedient ; I refused to attend my father to Uttoxeter market. Pride was the source of that refusal, and the remembrance of it was painful. A few years ago I desired to atone for this fault ; I went to Uttoxeter in very bad weather, and stood for a considerable time bare-

headed in the rain, on the spot where my father's
stall used to stand. In contrition I stood, and I hope
the penance was expiatory."

§ 188

As Johnson had now very faint hopes of recovery,
and as Mrs. Thrale was no longer devoted to him, it
might have been supposed that he would naturally
have chosen to remain in the comfortable house of his
beloved wife's daughter, and end his life where he
began it. But there was in him an animated and lofty
spirit, and however complicated diseases might depress
ordinary mortals, all who saw him beheld and acknowledged the *invictum animum Catonis*. Such was
his intellectual ardour even at this time, that he said
to one friend, " Sir, I look upon every day to be lost,
in which I do not make a new acquaintance ; " and to
another, when talking of his illness, " I will be conquered ; I will not capitulate." And such was his
love of London, so high a relish had he of its magnificent
extent, and variety of intellectual entertainment, that
he languished when absent from it, his mind having
become quite luxurious from the long habit of enjoying the metropolis ; and, therefore, although at Lichfield, surrounded with friends who loved and revered
him, and for whom he had a very sincere affection, he
still found that such conversation as London affords,
could be found nowhere else. These feelings, joined,
probably, to some flattering hopes of aid from the
eminent physicians and surgeons in London, who
kindly and generously attended him without accepting fees, made him resolve to return to the capital.

From Lichfield he came to Birmingham, where he
passed a few days with his worthy old schoolfellow,
Mr. Hector, who thus writes to me : " He was very
solicitous with me to recollect some of our most early
transactions, and transmit them to him, for I per-

ceived nothing gave him greater pleasure than calling
to mind those days of our innocence. I complied with
his request, and he only received them a few days
before his death. I have transcribed for your inspection exactly the minutes I wrote to him." This paper
having been found in his repositories after his death,
Sir John Hawkins has inserted it entire, and I have
made occasional use of it and other communications
from Mr. Hector, in the course of this work. I have
both visited and corresponded with him since Dr.
Johnson's death, and by my inquiries concerning a
great variety of particulars have obtained additional
information. I followed the same mode with the
Reverend Dr. Taylor, in whose presence I wrote down
a good deal of what he could tell ; and he, at my
request, signed his name, to give it authenticity. It is
very rare to find any person who is able to give a
distinct account of the life even of one whom he has
known intimately, without questions being put to
them. My friend Dr. Kippis has told me, that on this
account it is a practice with him to draw out a biographical catechism.

Johnson then proceeded to Oxford, where he was
again kindly received by Dr. Adams, who was pleased
to give me the following account in one of his letters
(Feb. 17th, 1785) :

" His last visit was, I believe, to my house, which
he left after a stay of four or five days. We had much
serious talk together, for which I ought to be the
better as long as I live. You will remember some discourse which we had in the summer upon the subject
of prayer, and the difficulty of this sort of composition. He reminded me of this, and of my having
wished him to try his hand, and to give us a specimen
of the style and manner that he approved. He added,
that he was now in a right frame of mind, and as he
could not possibly employ his time better, he would in

earnest set about it. But I find upon inquiry, that no papers of this sort were left behind him, except a few short ejaculatory forms suitable to his present situation."

Dr. Adams had not then received accurate information on this subject ; for it has since appeared that various prayers had been composed by him at different periods, which, intermingled with pious resolutions, and some short notes of his life, were entitled by him " Prayers and Meditations," and have, in pursuance of his earnest requisition, in the hopes of doing good, been published, with a judicious well-written preface, by the Reverend Mr. Strahan, to whom he delivered them. This admirable collection, to which I have frequently referred in the course of this work, evinces, beyond all his compositions for the public, and all the eulogies of his friends and admirers, the sincere virtue and piety of Johnson. It proves with unquestionable authenticity, that amidst all his constitutional infirmities, his earnestness to conform his practice to the precepts of Christianity was unceasing, and that he habitually endeavoured to refer every transaction of his life to the will of the Supreme Being.

He arrived in London on the 16th of November, and next day sent to Dr. Burney the following note, which I insert as the last token of his remembrance of that ingenious and amiable man, and as another of the many proofs of the tenderness and benignity of his heart :

" MR. JOHNSON, who came home last night, sends his respects to dear Dr. Burney, and all the dear Burneys, little and great."

§ 189

My readers are now, at last, to behold SAMUEL JOHNSON preparing himself for that doom, from which the most exalted powers afford no exemption to man. Death had always been to him an object of terror ; so that, though by no means happy, he still clung to life with an eagerness at which many have wondered. At any time when he was ill, he was very much pleased to be told that he looked better. An ingenious member of the *Eumelian Club* informs me, that upon one occasion, when he said to him that he saw health returning to his cheek, Johnson seized him by the hand and exclaimed, " Sir, you are one of the kindest friends I ever had."

§ 190

It is not my intention to give a very minute detail of the particulars of Johnson's remaining days, of whom it was now evident, that the crisis was fast approaching, when he must " *die like men, and fall like one of the princes.*" Yet it will be instructive, as well as gratifying to the curiosity of my readers, to record a few circumstances, on the authenticity of which they may perfectly rely, as I have been at the utmost pains to obtain an accurate account of his last illness from the best authority.

Dr. Heberden, Dr. Brocklesby, Dr. Warren, and Dr. Butter, physicians, generously attended him without accepting any fees, as did Mr. Cruickshank, surgeon ; and all that could be done from professional skill and ability was tried, to prolong a life so truly valuable. He himself, indeed, having, on account of his very bad constitution, been perpetually applying himself to medical inquiries, united his own efforts with those of the gentlemen who attended him ; and imagining that the dropsical collection of water which oppressed him might be drawn off by making incisions in his body, he, with his usual resolute defiance of pain, cut deep, when he thought that his surgeon had done it too tenderly.

About eight or ten days before his death, when Dr.

Brocklesby paid him his morning visit, he seemed very low and desponding, and said, " I have been as a dying man all night." He then emphatically broke out in the words of Shakespeare,—

> " Canst thou not minister to a mind diseas'd ;
> Pluck from the memory a rooted sorrow ;
> Raze out the written troubles of the brain ;
> And, with some sweet oblivious antidote,
> Cleanse the stuff'd bosom of that perilous stuff
> Which weighs upon the heart ? "

To which Dr. Brocklesby readily answered, from the same great poet :

> " —————————therein the patient
> Must minister to himself."

Johnson expressed himself much satisfied with the application.

On another day, after this, when talking on the subject of prayer, Dr. Brocklesby repeated from Juvenal,

> " Orandum est, ut sit mens sana in corpore sano,"

and so on to the end of the tenth Satire ; but in running it quickly over, he happened, in the line,

> " Qui spatium vitæ extremum inter munera ponat,"

to pronounce *supremum* for *extremum ;* at which Johnson's critical ear instantly took offence, and discoursing vehemently on the unmetrical effect of such a lapse, he showed himself as full as ever of the spirit of the grammarian.

Having no other relations, it had been for some time Johnson's intention to make a liberal provision for his faithful servant Mr. Francis Barber, whom he looked upon as particularly under his protection, and whom he had all along treated truly as an humble friend. Having asked Dr. Brocklesby what would be a proper annuity to a favourite servant, and being answered that it must depend on the circumstances of the master; and that, in the case of a nobleman, fifty pounds a year was considered as an adequate reward for many years' faithful service;—" Then," said Johnson, " shall I be *nobilissimus*, for I mean to leave Frank seventy pounds a year, and I desire you to tell him so." It is strange, however, to think, that Johnson was not free from that general weakness of being averse to execute a will, so that he delayed it from time to time ; and had it not been for Sir John Hawkins's repeatedly urging it, I think it is probable that his kind resolution would not have been fulfilled.

§ 191

During his last illness, Johnson experienced the steady and kind attachment of his numerous friends. Mr. Hoole has drawn up a narrative of what passed in the visits which he paid him during that time from the 10th of November to the 13th of December, the day of his death, inclusive, and has favoured me with a perusal of it, with permission to make extracts, which I have done. Nobody was more attentive to him than Mr. Langton, to whom he tenderly said, *Te teneam moriens deficiente manu.* And I think it highly to the honour of Mr. Windham, that his important occupations as an active statesman did not prevent him from paying assiduous respect to the dying Sage whom he revered. Mr. Langton informs me that : " One day he found Mr. Burke and four or five more friends sitting with Johnson. Mr. Burke said to him, ' I am afraid, Sir, such a number of us may be oppressive to you.'—' No, Sir,' said Johnson, ' it is not so ; and I must be in a wretched state, indeed, when your company would not be a delight to me.' Mr. Burke, in a tremulous voice, expressive of being very tenderly affected, replied, ' My dear Sir, you have always been too good to me.' Immediately afterwards he went away. This was the last circumstance in the acquaintance of these two eminent men."

§ 192

When Dr. Warren, in the usual style, hoped that he was better; his answer was, "No, Sir; you cannot conceive with what acceleration I advance towards death."

A man whom he had never seen before was employed one night to sit up with him. Being asked next morning how he liked his attendant, his answer was, "Not at all, Sir: the fellow's an idiot; he is as awkward as a turnspit when first put into the wheel, and as sleepy as a dormouse."

Mr. Windham having placed a pillow conveniently to support him, he thanked him for his kindness, and said, "That will do,—all that a pillow can do."

§ 193

Johnson, with that native fortitude, which, amidst all his bodily distress and mental sufferings, never forsook him, asked Dr. Brocklesby, as a man in whom he had confidence, to tell him plainly whether he could recover. "Give me," said he, "a direct answer." The Doctor having first asked him if he could bear the whole truth, which way soever it might lead, and being answered that he could, declared that, in his opinion, he could not recover without a miracle. "Then," said Johnson, "I will take no more physic, not even my opiates; for I have prayed that I may render up my soul to GOD unclouded." In this resolution he persevered, and, at the same time, used only the weakest kinds of sustenance. Being pressed by Mr. Windham to take somewhat more generous nourishment, lest too low a diet should have the very effect which he dreaded, by debilitating his mind, he said, " I will take anything but inebriating sustenance."

§ 194

Johnson having thus in his mind the true Christian scheme, at once rational and consolatory, uniting justice and mercy in the DIVINITY, with the improvement of human nature, previous to his receiving the Holy Sacrament in his apartment, composed and fervently uttered this prayer :

" Almighty and most merciful Father, I am now, as to human eyes it seems, about to commemorate, for the last time, the death of thy SON JESUS CHRIST, our Saviour and Redeemer. Grant, O Lord, that my whole hope and confidence may be in his merits, and thy mercy ; enforce and accept my imperfect repentance ; make this commemoration available to the confirmation of my faith, the establishment of my hope, and the enlargement of my charity ; and make the death of thy SON JESUS CHRIST effectual to my redemption. Have mercy upon me, and pardon the multitude of my offences. Bless my friends : have mercy upon all men. Support me by thy Holy Spirit, in the days of weakness, and at the hour of death ; and receive me, at my death, to everlasting happiness, for the sake of JESUS CHRIST. Amen."

Having, as has been already mentioned, made his will on the 8th and 9th of December, and settled all his worldly affairs, he languished till Monday, the 13th of that month, when he expired, about seven o'clock in the evening, with so little apparent pain that his attendants hardly perceived when his dissolution took place.

Of his last moments, my brother, Thomas David, has furnished me with the following particulars :

"The Doctor, from the time that he was certain his death was near, appeared to be perfectly resigned, was seldom or never fretful or out of temper, and often said to his faithful servant, who gave me this account, 'Attend, Francis, to the salvation of your soul, which is the object of greatest importance :' he also explained to him passages in the Scripture, and seemed to have pleasure in talking upon religious subjects.

"On Monday, the 13th of December, the day on which he died, a Miss Morris, daughter to a particular friend of his, called, and said to Francis, that she begged to be permitted to see the Doctor, that she might earnestly request him to give her his blessing. Francis went into his room followed by the young lady, and delivered the message. The Doctor turned himself in the bed, and said, 'God bless you, my dear !' These were the last words he spoke.—His difficulty of breathing increased till about seven o'clock in the evening, when Mr. Barber and Mrs. Desmoulins, who were sitting in the room, observing that the noise he made in breathing had ceased, went to the bed, and found he was dead."

§ 195

A few days before his death, he had asked Sir John Hawkins, as one of his executors, where he should be buried ; and on being answered, "Doubtless in Westminster Abbey," seemed to feel a satisfaction very natural to a poet ; and indeed in my opinion very natural to every man of any imagination, who has no family sepulchre in which he can be laid with his fathers. Accordingly, upon Monday, December 20, his remains were deposited in that noble and renowned edifice ; and over his grave was placed a large blue flag-stone, with this inscription :

" SAMUEL JOHNSON, LL.D.
Obiit XIII *die Decembris*
Anno Domini
M. DCC. LXXXIV.
Ætatis suæ LXXV."

His funeral was attended by a respectable number of his friends, particularly such of the members of THE LITERARY CLUB as were then in town; and was also honoured with the presence of several of the Reverend Chapter of Westminster. Mr. Burke, Sir Joseph Banks, Mr. Windham, Mr. Langton, Sir Charles Bunbury, and Mr. Colman, bore his pall. His school-fellow, Dr. Taylor, performed the mournful office of reading the burial service.

I trust I shall not be accused of affectation, when I declare, that I find myself unable to express all that I felt upon the loss of such a " Guide, Philosopher, and Friend." I shall, therefore, not say one word of my own, but adopt those of an eminent friend, which he uttered with an abrupt felicity, superior to all studied compositions :—" He has made a chasm, which not only nothing can fill up, but which nothing has a tendency to fill up.—Johnson is dead.—Let us go to the next best :—there is nobody ; no man can be said to put you in mind of Johnson."

THE END

BIBL.
LONDIN.
UNIV.

PRINTED IN GREAT BRITAIN AT
THE PRESS OF THE PUBLISHERS